Commonly known as the 'Queen of Common Sense', Maggie Dent has become one of Australia's favourite parenting authors and educators.

Maggie is the author of eight major books, including the best-selling 2018 release *Mothering Our Boys* and her 2020 release *From Boys to Men*. She hosts the ABC podcast *Parental As Anything* and in July 2021 released a book of the same name.

Maggie is a dedicated advocate for quietly changing lives in our families and communities. She is an ambassador for Telethon in WA and a champion of the Telethon Kids Institute. Maggie is also a proud ambassador for mindfulness app Smiling Mind and The Sanctuary, a crisis shelter in the Sydney Hills District, for women and their children who are fleeing domestic violence.

Maggie is the mother of four sons and a very grateful grandmother to a growing tribe of precious little boys and girls. She lives in the South Coast region of NSW with her good bloke Steve Mountain and their dear little dog, Mr Hugo Walter Dent.

T0246043

Also by Maggie Dent

From Boys to Men

MAGGIE DENT

girlhood

MACMILLAN
Pan Macmillan Australia

Pan Macmillan acknowledges the Traditional Custodians of country throughout Australia and their connections to lands, waters and communities. We pay our respect to Elders past and present and extend that respect to all Aboriginal and Torres Strait Islander peoples today. We honour more than sixty thousand years of storytelling, art and culture.

Some of the people in this book have had their names changed to protect their identities.

First published 2022 in Macmillan by Pan Macmillan Australia Pty Ltd
1 Market Street, Sydney, New South Wales, Australia, 2000

Reprinted 2022 (twice)

Copyright © Maggie Dent 2022

A catalogue record for this book is available from the National Library of Australia

NATIONAL LIBRARY OF AUSTRALIA

Typeset in 10.5/16 pt Sabon by Midland Typesetters, Australia
Printed by IVE

Extracts from *Parental As Anything* © 2021 Maggie Dent and the Australian Broadcasting Corporation. Reprinted by permission of HarperCollins Publishers.
Permission for *The 5 Love Languages of Children* by Gary Chapman and Ross Campbell granted courtesy of Moody Publishers.
Extracts from *The Four Agreements* © 1997 by Don Miguel Ruiz and Janet Mills. Reprinted by permission of Amber-Allen Publishing, San Rafael, California. All rights reserved. www.thefouragreements.com
Extracts from *Raising Girls Who Like Themselves* © Kasey Edwards and Christopher Scanlon 2021. First published by Penguin Life, 2021. Reprinted by permission of Penguin Random House Australia Pty Ltd
Extracts from *Catalyst* © 2011 ABC. Reproduced by permission of the Australian Broadcasting Corporation – Library Sales.

MIX
Paper from responsible sources
FSC
www.fsc.org
FSC® C018183

The paper in this book is FSC® certified. FSC® promotes environmentally responsible, socially beneficial and economically viable management of the world's forests.

I was born and raised on the lands of the Noongar peoples of Western Australia, and I wish to acknowledge and pay my respects to elders, past, present and emerging.
I thank you for being the custodians of my homeland, the country of my childhood which I carry within my heart every day of my life.

I have written this book on the lands of the Dharawal peoples of the South Coast of New South Wales.
I also acknowledge and pay my respects to elders, past, present and emerging.

The ancient knowledge and wisdom that our First Nations people – who are the longest surviving culture in the world – have known and shared for thousands of years still has value for our modern world.

May we all find ways to walk gently and compassionately on these ancient lands and come to a place where every child ever born is respected, valued and has a strong sense of belonging.

I dedicate this book to my precious granddaughters Elliya, Milla, Esmé and Mabel. You bring so much sunshine and light into my world, and I am the luckiest and proudest grandmother ever.

I look forward to many fun adventures together, and many hours of sharing stories, crazy dancing, singing badly and laughing loudly.

We will walk together, garden together, swim together and cook together.

I promise to always see you, hear you and hold you unconditionally in my heart. These are the greatest gifts I can give to you.

All my love, always
Nanny

Praise for *Girlhood*

Maggie Dent's brilliant new masterpiece is a symphony of thoughtful, practical ideas about raising girls to be strong, resilient women.

Girlhood is a research-based, relationally-grounded book that provides sage wisdom for parenting and supporting girls.

It provides essential insights that bring awareness to the invisible shackles still placed on girls in our society. Maggie Dent shows us how to use our relationships to nurture their inner strength and wisdom, guiding future generations towards a world that will be safer and healthier for all humans across gender identifications.

Mona Delahooke, PhD, author of *Beyond Behaviors* and *Brain-Body Parenting*

In this timely book, Maggie shares practical advice on friendships, technology, education and wellbeing, while encouraging parents to nurture confidence, spirit, and a sense of adventure in our girls. An invaluable guide!

Susan Stiffelman, MFT, author of *Parenting Without Power Struggles* and *Parenting With Presence*

Maggie does it again! Amid the confusing and often contradictory advice available to parents these days, Maggie Dent stands out as a voice of wisdom and compassion. She has a magical way of communicating her insights that not only enlightens but instills a sense of calm. This book is a must-read for parents who want to understand the myriad of issues our young daughters face and help them to flourish as confident, secure adults.

Janet Lansbury, bestselling author of *No Bad Kids*, host of *Unruffled*

I have long been a fan of Maggie Dent's work and was excited that her latest book *Girlhood* is focused on girls 8 and under, an under-researched group.

It is a timely response to parents' concerns that their young daughters are pressured to be nice or good girls, or people pleasers who focus on how they look rather than who they are. She suggests that we raise girls to be happy, healthy and heard. It is a wondrous idea, the antithesis of my generation where girls were to be seen and not heard. The future is already looking better.

Wendy McCarthy AO, Life Fellow FAICD, mentor, speaker, writer, social activist, company advisor, patron, Sydney Women's Fund, The Parenthood Director, FPIP

This book magically weaves together the heart, the science, and the soul of who it is that girls are, and what it is to raise them. It is a must read for anyone who has a girl, was ever a girl, or is seeking to understand what it means for a girl to 'become' who she is meant to be. Maggie Dent is not only the Queen of Common Sense – she is the queen of heart-centred, data driven, soulular wisdom. This book will change the world.

Dr Vanessa Lapointe, registered psychologist, parenting educator and mom

Contents

Breakout Key

Keep an eye out for the following breakout boxes throughout this book. They each mean something different:

> **PARENTS AND EDUCATORS' SURVEY**
>
> This box contains a quote from a survey of parents and educators reflecting on their experiences with girls, conducted online in 2021.

> **MAGGIE'S MAIN IDEA**
>
> This box contains important takeaway points from the Queen of Common Sense.

Foreword

Maggie Dent is a national treasure.

For as long as I can remember, Maggie has been advocating for raising well-rounded children by building strong foundations.

As the mother of two teenagers – 16-year-old Grace and 17-year-old Taj – I've found her books, speeches and interviews full of priceless advice, particularly around resilience and self-esteem.

Maggie uses a compelling blend of research, common sense and humour to explain complex concepts in easy-to-understand language.

Girlhood: Raising our little girls to be healthy, happy and heard is a masterclass in nurturing 0–8s during these formative years.

Within these pages, you'll find plenty of practical tools to teach girls to harness their imaginations, use nature play as a way of healing, and find the stillness within – whether they're a 'dandelion' or an 'orchid'!

You'll learn about the 'hyperaroused' state triggered by overuse of small screens, and why banning technology isn't necessarily the answer.

Bravely, Maggie tackles some contentious areas – like the nature/nurture debate – with her trademark combination of academic and personal insights.

She acknowledges that the word 'girl' can be quite limiting, digging deep into gender identity, which is 'being influenced from the moment we are born'.

One example is the 'subtle conditioning' around the notion that 'girls need to be less physically active and spend more time playing passively than boys'.

My husband and I have always found our girl to be far more physically active than her brother, which is something we encouraged from a very young age.

As a society, we don't often discuss girls who are neurodivergent. By way of example, for too long the focus was predominantly on boys with autism spectrum disorders. Maggie suggests that parents of daughters with ADHD reframe their way of thinking, because 'it can be a pathway to a superpower or a significant gift'.

A life-long feminist, she celebrates the expanding role of fathers in children's lives, the importance of the 'sisterhood', and the thorny topic of 'mean girls'.

The latter concept has always flummoxed me. To be honest, I've found it hard to discuss this with our feminist daughter when she asks for guidance. Maggie provides a real-world framework for contextualising these interactions, giving girls a gift for life in building supportive female friendships.

Much of this book focuses on tips for managing anxiety in young girls. Maggie writes magnificently about meditation, mindfulness and gratitude, detailing how to create a regular practice. She urges us to nurture our girls' 'sacred spirit'.

Now, you might be thinking, 'I'm a busy parent. How will I ever find time to read this book!'

Well, I have good news for you. Maggie chunks pertinent information into clearly labelled boxes, so you can snack in and out depending on the challenges you're currently facing.

Perhaps my favourite parts of the book are Maggie's hard-won wisdoms from a life well lived. She doesn't shy away from difficult experiences, or sugar-coat the truth. Her upbringing made her who she is today: forged by fire.

You will love this book. Please, share it with family and friends. Let's work with Maggie to create a robust platform for girls to be happy, healthy and – crucially – heard!

Tracey Spicer AM, April 2022
NSW Premier's Woman of the Year
Agenda Setter of the Year 2018, Women's Agenda
Recipient Sydney Peace Prize for the Me Too Movement
Winner Social Enterprise category, 100 Women of Influence

Introduction

I have been called an undisputed 'boy champion', largely because I am a mum of only sons (four in total) and have advocated for a better understanding of our boys in order to reverse some pretty shoddy statistics. So it might be asked, what is a boy champion doing writing a book about little girls?

Well, to begin with, of the eight major books I have written, only two have been exclusively about boys. The rest of my work has been about all children.

My initial motivation for writing this book is simple: I have four precious granddaughters. Research clearly reveals that our girls are swimming in opportunity yet floundering in unprecedented levels of confusion, self-doubt, self-harm, anxiety and stress.

My most unsettling sense about tween and teen girls living in our consumer-driven, digital world is that the sacredness of femininity has been lost, or significantly diminished. The overt pressure to be perfect, to never fail and to be in constant competition with other girls and women is contributing to the increasing unwellness of our girls, especially in the tween and teen years. Some argue that our girls' confidence drops by 30 per cent between the ages of eight and 14 – that is enormous and extremely concerning. We must discover how we can nurture our girls before they turn eight so that they are able to step onto the pathway to womanhood with the mindset, life skills, resilience, courage and necessary human connectedness and relational safety they need to grow into healthy, happy women who feel accepted, valued, respected and heard.

There are many books written by passionate wise girl champions for our girls from 10 years old upwards. However, there is very little written about the years from pre-birth to age eight. The first stage of childhood is incredibly vital, so my focus is on that window. A whole body of research shows us that the first six years of an individual's life is when:

- sense of self or identity is shaped
- the creation of the human mind occurs
- self-regulating systems are formed
- belief systems and mindsets are created
- social norms are conditioned and embedded in the mind
- 90 per cent of the brain is shaped and formed
- physical strengths and coordination can develop
- emotional and social competence can develop
- the senses of feeling safe and loved are formed
- childlike spirituality is shaped.

I wanted to explore what we can do in the early years of our young girls' lives to build the strong connectedness that every child needs: healthy mindset, vital protective factors and inspiration and hope for everyone raising daughters today. If you are a parent of a little girl and you want her to avoid struggling with poor confidence, low self-esteem, crippling anxiety, self-loathing and a lack of courage, especially in her adolescent years, then this book is exactly what you need.

I have again turned to parents and educators via an online survey to see what would be most valuable to explore in a book about young girls. I also sought to capture the voices of little girls through anecdotes and by getting their parents and early educators to ask them some simple questions (such as 'when are you happiest?'). It was by far my biggest survey, with almost 5,000 responses, and the results helped me enormously to shape my research and writing. Thank you if you were a concerned grown-up who responded. The voices of little girls are all through the book. I had to make sure their voices were heard in a book about them!

Even though I have raised four sons, I have plenty of experience with girls – I was a girl myself! Not only that, I have two sisters and I am a very proud auntie to many beautiful nieces. I am also a non-biological auntie to many more young women, and I have seen them grow from girls to women.

In my teaching career, I always taught in co-ed schools. In my counselling years, I would have seen 75 per cent more girls than boys. While I was living in Western Australia, I ran retreats for women for over 15 years, and I saw that it is so often the experiences of the early years that become stories we tell ourselves, stories that come back to haunt us in womanhood. This is why my focus is on how we can positively shape the early years of our girls' lives rather than try and 'fix' problems later in life. Prevention is always much better than cure.

Background

As a mum of all boys, I often got the message that people thought girls were much easier to raise than boys and that one day you would have someone to take care of you when you became elderly. This implied that boys were harder work to raise and incapable of being caring or sensitive, especially towards their mothers. Both of these are only part truths based on social constructs.

Girls think they are cleverer, more successful and more hard-working than boys from as young as four, according to a recent study. In Australia, statistics that come from the Australian Early Development Census and the Longitudinal Study of Australian Children show that a statistically significant number of our young boys struggle with transition to big school. Experienced early years educators have been telling me for years that there is a noticeable difference between young boys and girls regardless of the reasons why. Neil Farmer, an experienced early years educator and author in the UK, suggests that this appears to be the result of inappropriate learning and teaching strategies allied to lower expectations which results in a self-fulfilling prophecy.

The messages in this book are also important for extended family, educators, community members and coaches and coordinators of extracurricular activities. In the survey of almost 5,000 parents that I conducted for this book, it was clear what worries parents. In response to what societal pressures worry parents the most for our girls under eight, they selected, in order of concern:

1. Focus on how they look rather than who they are
2. Pressure to be people-pleasers
3. Girls being conditioned to be 'nice' or a 'good girl'
4. Gendered clothes, toys and expectations
5. Pressure to rely on boys/men to help with things requiring strength and bravery.

Given that the top concern was about appearance – the pressure to focus on how they look rather than who they are, followed by girls being conditioned to be 'nice' or a good girl – there is much to be done in shifting some of these conscious and unconscious pressures. Other key areas of concern were around her emotional world, especially meltdowns and tantrums, anxiety and irrational fears, moods and sensitivities.

The survey also showed clearly the things that challenged parents of young girls up to age four:

1. Meltdowns/tantrums
2. Resistance to things
3. Anxiety and irrational fears
4. Her moods
5. Sensitivities
6. 'Mean' behaviours

For those with older girls, up to eight, the top concerns were similar:

1. Friendship dramas
2. Anxiety and irrational fears
3. Meltdowns/tantrums
4. Resistance to things
5. Her moods

There was lots of good news in the survey too, as it showed overwhelmingly the things that fascinate and amaze parents about little girls. When presented with the question 'What has amazed you about the girls in your life?' and a list of suggestions, these are the ones parents selected in order:

1. Use of imagination
2. Verbal maturity (use of big words, etc.)
3. Memory
4. Caring capacity (i.e. for people, animals, dead bugs even)
5. Tuning into other kids' feelings
6. Problem-solving capacity
7. Fine-motor skills
8. Physical ability (i.e. gross motor skills)
9. Bravery

As a grandmother I, too, have been absolutely fascinated with some of the deep conversations I've had with my granddaughters. I've been impressed with their memory capabilities, organisational skills, their ability to communicate, their tendency to be feisty and stubborn, full of energy, adventuresome and brave, as well as creative. And their imaginations have astounded me, often.

> Your child is not a blank slate or an empty vessel who needs to be filled up with copious amounts of excellent information. Your child comes to you with a nascent intellect that is consolidating energy and waiting to unfold in good time like a flower in the bud. You would never pry open a rosebud to somehow optimise or improve upon it. Instead you would make sure it has the best soil and nourishing fertiliser to support its optimal unfolding.
>
> – Marcy Axness, *Parenting for Peace* (2012)

This book is for anyone who is on this journey of raising girls to be happy, healthy and heard. This book is for everyone who lives or works with little girls; however, it is especially for parents, grandparents and key caregivers. In the formative years, this circle of influence moulds a girl's mind, body and heart more than anything else in the world, and those formative years shape everything in our little one's lives. We all want the best for our girls, especially given the extra pressures and challenges presented by living in a digital age. We want our girls to grow up to accept and embrace themselves and to create their own place in the world where they can find genuine meaning and purpose. We want them to find their strengths and passions and to connect deeply with their heart and their spirit.

Every single child is born with a unique blend of ancestral influences, biological drivers and a mix of masculine and feminine in a body that has never been on earth before, which means that discovering who your daughter is begins at the moment of birth. A major part of this book is designed to help you discover your daughter's unique strengths, attributes and the possible challenges that will shape who she can become and will become. Hopefully you will find some of the missing clues that will help you to better understand your daughter, and to help you as a parent to make choices that will allow her to shine in her own unique way. You may also help your daughter come to understand herself better so that she can genuinely accept, embrace and love herself as authentically and honestly as she can.

Let's give our girls the best possible start in life by surrounding them with environments full of caring humans in supportive communities who value an unrushed childhood. Please let our girls be little girls for as long as possible. Let's focus on strengthening our little girls' minds, bodies, hearts and spirits by creating a strong, fertile soil for them to grow in, while protecting them from unhelpful cultural messaging. Collectively, we can help not only our daughters, granddaughters and nieces; we can help all little girls in our neighbourhoods and communities to have a healthier, happier life.

Before we continue, I need to give a disclaimer, which is one that I offer with all my work. Gender is more fluid than fixed, and while respecting biological, neurological and hormonal differences, there is not an 'all boys' or 'all girls' reality. On top of that, there is social conditioning that is deeply embedded in culture and ancestry. So when I use the term 'girls', I will be referring to a statistically significant number of girls; however, much of what we will be sharing may also be relevant to boys and people of all other gender identities. I encourage you to take from this what feels right for you. All genders need to be seen as equally fabulous, including our gender-fluid children. Every child ever born is born a unique miracle with their own individuality.

1

Mothering your daughter

I secretly wished to only be the mother of boys. The main reason I didn't want to have a daughter was because of the struggles I had had as a little girl and as a teenager. I had always found boys much less complicated, not only as siblings, but also as friends. In a way, I may have created a belief that the scars from my childhood would mean I would struggle to mother a daughter.

Writing this book took me down the rabbit hole of exploring my own childhood and life, so there are many parts in this book where I mention mothering daughters rather than fathering daughters.

I did some research with the mothers of daughters, particularly ones who have only just stepped into the tween years, to see what are their main concerns, worries and joys about mothering a daughter today. The mother–daughter relationship that each mother experienced as a child was very much in the backs of their minds as they began their journey with their daughter. Some had really loving, wonderful mothers and hoped to repeat the same patterns and behaviours. Others had had mothers who were harsher, more distant, and definitely less communicative and wanted to be a very different mother to their own daughters. Mothering a daughter can be triggering or healing to your own experience as a daughter – in fact, it can be either or both of those things. It certainly was both for me, when thinking about the girls in my life and being reminded of my own girlhood.

Some mums have shared with me that they really wanted their daughters 'to end up better than them'. For some, this meant completing their education because they had not, or excelling at something that they perceived they had failed at. For others it was that they yearned to have a close, loving relationship with their daughter for their whole life, different from what they had with their own mothers. If any of these apply to you, consider that this wish is actually an unfair burden to place on your little girl. She has come onto this earth to be her own unique self, not to fulfil any of your unfinished dreams or life plans.

Given that most mothers today have experienced the conditioning of the patriarchal system, many were very clear that they wanted their daughters to realise that they can be both brave and gentle, courageous and tender, and they deserved to be loved and respected exactly as they are. Many of these mothers had been conditioned to be nice, to be quiet, to put others before themselves. They also acknowledged how difficult it can be to parent your daughter with these shifting social norms and that they don't always get it right.

PARENTS AND EDUCATORS' SURVEY

My daughter is a real character. She is energetic, funny and sensitive to others. She loves being silly with me and we often sing together, make funny songs, characters and voices. She is a joy to have around. She forever repeats my parenting remarks to my son, like she knows what to do better than him, and is seven years younger than him. She is eight.

One of the most important things I learned in personal growth work was that there is only one person who sees the world as you see it, *and that is you.* There is only one person who has created stories from their childhood, which influence them consciously and unconsciously, and many of those stories may not be true. I have worked with a lot of mothers who have an unhealthy attitude to tidiness that often bordered on obsession. They shared how they would be triggered to become the shouting, angry mother by a toddler's messy toys, an unmade bed or a dishwasher that was not packed according to her standards.

A psychologist once shared with me that this pattern of behaviour can be a way of having control in the outer world, because there is little order in the inner, emotional world. He also suggested that for many girls, their worth and value was determined through external efforts like tidiness, dressing neatly, having their hair done well and speaking quietly. This is not saying that having a tidy home is a bad thing. It is suggesting that if you can feel anxious and stressed when your house is not perfect, then you may be unconsciously telling yourself a story that is not true, and could be healed.

Rachel Macy Stafford, a bestselling American author, discovered that her expectations for her daughters and her husband were not only unrealistic, they were creating misery for everyone. Rather than nurturing her family, she was 'controlling and managing them according to her unhealthy reality'. She identified that she was a control freak and began a journey of self-healing.

> There was a time in my life when I barked orders more often than I spoke words of love . . . When I reacted to small everyday inconveniences as if they were major catastrophes . . . When normal human habits and quirks raised my blood pressure to dangerous levels.
> – Rachel Macy Stafford, positiveparentingsolutions.com

The mental fatigue and overwhelm of many mothers may be a sign that expectations may be out of step with reality. Having babies, toddlers and young children is exhausting without working full-time and maintaining a schedule of household chores, regular exercise, self-care, personal appearance and personal relationships. Juggling a career and motherhood can be done, however, some things may need to be more relaxed. For example, I created a lucky dip bed where I would put all the clean washing because I was not prepared to spend an hour a day folding clothes and putting them in the boys' bedrooms. I did not have that spare time, and I noticed it made me really frustrated and resentful when I tried to do it.

One thing that came up often in counselling, in retreats and in the conversations I have had with mums is just how hard mothers are on themselves. Women tend to constantly compare themselves to others, or beat themselves up unnecessarily by reviewing their day and looking at ways they could do better. One of the toughest things to learn when you have a new baby, then a free-spirited toddler, is that *you can't control them or their lives, and it's not your job to try*. Your job is to work out how to meet their unique needs as best you can.

Judging ourselves harshly is something we learn in the early years of our lives. This is why one of my key mantras around parenting is that there is no perfect, and that good-enough parents who succeed often and fail sometimes can still raise healthy, happy children. So please put down the stick that you are beating yourself with and give yourself some kindness and compassion.

Practising genuine self-care is another challenge for many of today's mothers. It can easily trigger guilt because they have been conditioned to care for everyone else ahead of themselves. This took me quite some time to tame and I burned out twice, and my body became so exhausted and depleted I suffered two life-threatening illnesses. It was these illnesses that were the wake-up call that I needed and deserved, telling me to take the time to look after myself and do things that restored me and gave me joy.

Many of the mothers expressed that they had learned that the things that triggered them most about their daughters were more about *them* than their daughters. This is one of the things you learn quite early in therapy, that an experience that challenges you, that your daughter may unintentionally trigger, is not about her, but about *you*. It is the mirror effect.

It can be really hard to accept that your unconscious mind is working hard to shine a light on the unhealed parts of you, but it is important to do so, so that you can become a better human being. Most of our emotional scars are fairly insignificant, however, some can impact us later in life in so many ways.

I was the fifth of six children and my mother was not an emotionally warm parent. I created a story that she didn't love me, which also created another story that I was unlovable. These stories created beliefs that in turn influenced the choices I made not only as a child, but also as a teenage girl and a young mum, and I spent a number of years working in therapy and doing personal growth workshops to be able to make peace with my inner child, learning to accept and love myself exactly as I am.

There are many family therapists and life coaches who can help you change the stories of your childhood if they are negatively impacting how you are raising your daughter. Imagine that you have a small child within yourself, the same age as the daughter who is triggering you. This can help to navigate where the truth really lies – if your pain is really about your daughter, or yourself.

> Nothing about natural, normal, healthy child development is triggering or upsetting. Bear that in mind if you are feeling fired up by what you observe in your child. This is a call for you to explore why you are reacting the way you are.
> – Dr Vanessa Lapointe, *Parenting Right From the Start* (2019)

There were many times when I was working with a rebellious teenage girl who was escaping out the bedroom window, drinking and smoking and not going to school that I found that this had been the mother's experience as well. Unhealed patterns can be unconsciously passed on to our children, no matter how hard we try to prevent it. The only way to ensure a trauma does not resurface in your daughter's life is to shine a light onto your own experience.

PARENTS AND EDUCATORS' SURVEY

When she was 4.5 asking me, 'Mum, do you like being a mum?' I responded with the cliché, 'Of course, I love you and being your mum is wonderful' etc., and she responds with, 'Yes, but do you LIKE it?' Such awareness blows my mind.

Much has changed in the last 20 to 30 years in the research around what matters most in the healthy raising of children. Behaviourism was the flavour of the last century, where parents were told that children's behaviour was something they chose and that using rewards when the children behaved how we wanted them to, and punishments when they behaved in ways we didn't want them to, was the best way to raise 'good' children. The pressure was to control children, often with fear, and sadly, this often came at the cost of emotional connection and relational safety.

Not only are we influenced by the way we were parented, we can also be influenced by our family's history. There is significant research that shows we are likely to replicate the programs of our parents even if we consciously have chosen not to. Early childhood is unpredictable, messy, often noisy and most parents will struggle with sleep deprivation and confusion about how they can be the parent they really want to be. This is completely normal.

There is no way that parents can be perfect and meet every need of their precious little ones – it is impossible. We all carry scars of disappointment from our childhood, and it is the big scars that really shape the programming and the patterns that we unconsciously follow when we become parents. Trauma of any kind increases our chances of struggling with mental health, addictions and deep and profound self-loathing that tends to surface in the adolescent years. Adverse childhood experiences – ACEs – can occur around experiences of significant accidents or illnesses, death and loss, natural disasters, family violence, abandonment, deprivation or abuse. Our bodies and our unconscious minds remember these experiences and often bury emotional pain deep, especially when we have experienced shame. We all have secrets from our childhood that we consciously or unconsciously keep buried. Our amazing minds and bodies do anything they can so that we can survive, because survival is the number one biological drive of every human. But this survival comes at a cost. One therapist suggested that we have a life force that pulses through us, and when we have buried a painful secret or a wound, it takes much of that life force to keep it hidden. When it is exposed to the light and is no longer a secret, we have a stronger life force to keep us healthier and happier.

PARENTS AND EDUCATORS' SURVEY

I worry about meltdowns/tantrums, I would call these big feelings, and while we actually didn't struggle much with these because of wonderful, respectful parenting books, the most challenging moments and times, when I had to take a long hard look at myself and my approach, were all around big feelings or resistance to sleep.

As the stigma around mental health is gradually being challenged and hopefully dissolved, more and more people are seeking help to understand themselves and to heal unhealthy beliefs and patterns of behaviour. I began my self-healing journey when I was around 30 and already the mother of three little boys. Every time I peeled away another layer of my wounded inner child, my life improved, especially my capacity to be the loving mother I wanted to be. It helped me to deconstruct the stories I had created from my childhood that were simply not true. Most importantly, it allowed me to come to a place of unconditional acceptance and love of myself – warts and all. If you have never done any work on your inner child, a good place to begin is the work of Brené Brown.

The mothers I spoke to all agreed that when they began to work on themselves, their relationships improved with not only their daughters, but with their life partners as well.

Therapy comes in all shapes and sizes, from programs that last a year, to weekly ones, weekend ones, online ones and one-on-one therapy. It is important to find what works for you. The retreats for women that I ran were often attended by women who had no concept of how the wounded child within them influences who they are today. Indeed, one retreat happened over a Mother's Day weekend, and it was interesting to note that every woman there had had a difficult or toxic relationship with their mother!

PARENTS AND EDUCATORS' SURVEY

Six years old – she has a 12-year-old brother and loves to tell him off. We have to remind her that we have the parenting covered.

Mothering daughters can definitely be really tricky and yet it can be the most amazing journey you may ever experience. Your daughter has come to be a mirror for you, to allow you to grow and to transform into the higher expression of yourself. There will be times that you will struggle with overprotecting her instead of letting her stretch and grow in her own courage. There will be times she will share her tender secrets that will make your heart melt. There will be times that she will stand with her hands on her hips and confront you to face your own truth like no other person could. Embrace it all, Mummy, with curiosity, compassion and as much patience as you can. It will be worth it.

2

First 1,000 days

Technically, the first thousand days of a child's life are from the moment of conception until their second birthday. Research over the past 20 years has shown that by focusing on this window – especially by meeting the unique needs of pregnant women, babies and toddlers – we can significantly improve the trajectory of a child's life. A strong, healthy start is not just about safety, good nutrition and receiving support. While all of that is incredibly important, creating a robust and secure start in life goes even deeper.

Humans are a social species, which means we are meant to live in relationships in systems such as families and communities. This sense of belonging and safety can impact babies even before birth. The research is quite strong that intergenerational trauma, or trauma experienced during pregnancy, can significantly impact the developing baby. At a conference I attended in Vancouver in Canada in 2012, American paediatrician Professor W Thomas Boyce gave a lecture titled, 'What the Genes Remember: The New Epigenetics of the Early Years'. In groundbreaking longitudinal research, it was shown that childhood adversity, particularly poor attachment (by age three-and-a-half), can change the genes, especially the serotonin transporter gene. This in turn will increase the chances of school failure, chronic illness such as diabetes and cancer, and heart disease and cardiac death.

I have to be honest – I was pretty stunned at that moment. To think that the genomes in our DNA can change after birth due to environmental influences challenged everything about the nurture vs nature debate. Essentially, this means that no matter what DNA a child is born with, the influences of nurture, that is the environment they are in, *can change that coding*. And it works both ways – safe, loving environments can change the DNA positively, while environments where babies and toddlers feel threatened or unsafe can set them on a trajectory towards ill-health. As girls often have better memories and can be more emotionally responsive, their environment is a particularly important influence.

PARENTS AND EDUCATORS' SURVEY

When our daughter, Greta, was 18 months old, we used to hold the four corners of a sheet with our best friends and gently swing her in it! Her laugh and absolute joy at both the movement and the four loving faces smiling down at her is one of my best memories of her early years.

The first fundamental need for all babies is to have strong, safe and warm connectedness with their key caregivers, hopefully their biological parents or with other adults who are present significantly in their lives. This is called 'attachment' and it is the superglue that holds a child in close proximity to a parent/caregiver. A child is meant to seek or pursue proximity, which means being close to their 'big' person, so they feel safe and so they are safe. Attachment is as important to healthy child development as eating or sleeping. Much of the research indicates that strong attachment and bondedness can be among the most significant influences on emotional wellbeing, mental health and physical health for life. The research that our little ones need to be completely dependent on us in order to grow into their own independence in the future is also quite compelling. One of the key features of healthy attachment is that the grown-ups caring for a baby are sensitive to and respond to the infant's unique cues and needs with warmth and tenderness. Ensure your little girl knows you will always be her safe base.

If your daughter needs to find her way into your bed sometimes for a night or two, or sometimes for a few weeks or longer, it can be a sign that the outside world has become a little more uncertain for her. Every new experience, like starting to eat solids, too much sensory stimulation, changes in key caregivers or change of bed, is a potential stress trigger that can overwhelm the nervous system. Given that poor sleep impacts every level of a child's life, please prioritise getting good sleep. Meet her fears and anxiety with comfort and soothing. As she gets older, she will be able to better manage her nervous system, and one day, you will miss the fact that she no longer wants to curl beside you at night.

In my book *9 Things: A Back-to-Basics Guide to Calm, Commonsense, Connected Parenting Birth–8*, the first of the nine things is called connected mothering. What really matters is that our little ones are mothered well, which means they come to experience a strong sense of healthy connectedness and attachment. Fathers can mother, grandparents can mother, foster parents can mother and stepparents can mother. Connected mothering takes enormous amounts of time and energy in the first thousand days of life, but it needs to be a priority for anyone who becomes a parent.

In traditional cultures, women were surrounded by many other women having babies and raising little ones. There was always a warm lap and a tender heart close by, and all children were seen as the responsibility of everyone in the kinship village. As civilisation has progressed, the reality of having a supportive and caring village around a new parent has become more difficult to achieve. However, living through a global pandemic has emphasised to us how incredibly important our long-distance village still remains for our emotional and mental wellbeing, especially in the absence of face-to-face communication and safe intimate touch.

When your firstborn is born, so too are you born as a parent. Biological parents can experience a significant identity shift in the first thousand days of their newborn's life, and it can be a confusing time, no matter how much you love your new baby.

Dr Vanessa Lapointe conveys it well:

Then your child arrives. You feel the earth move beneath you. Your axis tilts. You're in the midst of one of the most incredible psychological and emotional shifts a human being can experience; you are now a parent responsible for another life in this world.

– Dr Vanessa Lapointe, *Parenting Right From the Start* (2019).

It is important to remember that parenting is one of the hardest things you will ever do, and ensuring you have access to support, guidance and respite really does help. All parents can benefit from the formal and informal supports of positive people who care and who they can rely on when some of those tricky, challenging experiences arrive, often unexpectedly.

PARENTS AND EDUCATORS' SURVEY

Between the age of 18 months and three, our eldest daughter would play tea parties with us. As she didn't have any liquid to put in her cup, she would recycle water from her drink bottle and then to the cup. She would then offer it to her family and friends to drink. And she insisted very heavily on drinking it as well. We always tried to have a towel on our laps to help us.

Our world of screens and technology is definitely displacing some of the wonderful, authentic and meaningful connectedness that little ones need with safe grown-ups. Nothing works better than humans interacting with humans in the same room.

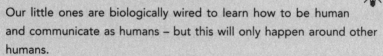

MAGGIE'S MAIN IDEA

Our little ones are biologically wired to learn how to be human and communicate as humans – but this will only happen around other humans.

John Medina in his book *Brain Rules for Baby* wrote about research that showed that babies and toddlers under three years of age do not tend to take in sound from external sources like TVs and iPads. They are biologically wired to process sounds from humans because they are learning how communication, including non-verbal communication, takes place. Facial expressions are being wired into your little ones at the same time. The first thousand days is a fantastic window within which to marinate little girls in as much human sound as possible, preferably out of the mouths of humans. Reading to them, singing to them and talking to them not only helps to build that relationship, it is forming the foundations in their brain so they can understand fundamental sounds that will help them communicate and learn to read in the future. A study by Hart and Rissley (1995) shows that the greater the amount of language a child hears in the early years, the better they will be able to read. The study found that families in higher socioeconomic situations tend to speak more to their children, and the difference was estimated to be 30 million words over the first five years of life. Children from a higher income family were exposed to nearly twice as many words as working-class children, and close to four times as many words as children from families on welfare.

There is no question that smartphones are stealing precious moments of communication between little ones and their key grown-ups, and this can lead to a form of digital abandonment. If you have forgotten the words to nursery rhymes or songs that children like, by all means use your technology to find the words. But the secret is to sing along with the child, not just allow the remote sound to take place. As a grandparent, I have been quite annoying for my sons and daughters-in-law with my endless singing of 'The Wheels On The Bus', 'This Old Man', 'Five Little Ducks' and 'Twinkle Twinkle Little Star'. Thankfully, my grandchildren do not care that I really can't sing in tune! My favourite site for wonderful audio resources in Australia is the ABC Kids Listen app.

PARENTS AND EDUCATORS' SURVEY

When she was about 16–18 months old she was obsessed with the *In The Night Garden* show. She got a washing basket and hopped in with Iggle Piggle toy on her own, displaying her ability of recalling stories/shows.

The wonderfully wise Sally Goddard Blythe, director of The Institute for Neuro-Physiological Psychology in the UK, has concerns about parenting today. She has observed that our modern world is making it more difficult for babies and toddlers to spend significant time with their parents, which is where she believes the healthiest mothering can occur. On reading Goddard Blythe's book, *What Babies and Children Really Need* (2008), it turns out that what they really need – time – is what many 21st-century parents simply cannot provide because we live in a society that does not allow for it. Many countries prioritise potential economic wellbeing over the real, genuine wellbeing of little ones. If society acknowledged and promoted the importance of the first thousand days to the future growth and wellbeing of their children, parents might be able to make different choices when navigating the journey of raising their young ones. This does not mean they are unable to work, or that being a working mum is a negative thing; it simply suggests that choices around who cares for their baby would be made much more consciously.

The importance of secondary attachment

Many countries in the world have recognised the importance of primary attachment and they provide paid parental leave to either or both parents. Secondary attachment is not only possible, it is seriously valuable. This occurs when a baby or toddler has a sense of strong connectedness to a grown-up who is not a biological parent. This can include grandparents, nannies or early childhood educators.

PARENTS AND EDUCATORS' SURVEY

My dad looked after my girl before she went to day care/school. At around 18 months old, I came home and they were both giggling like crazy. Dad was pretending to drop balls and she was in nonstop giggle mode. They were both red and breathless from laughing! Such a simple thing that brought so much joy.

I once worked with an early childhood centre in Sydney, and I was curious about the age of the youngest child they had ever cared for. The director remembered instantly a little girl who was born on the Friday and brought to them one week later. This girl's mother was a project manager for a large corporation and was needed back at work much earlier than she had hoped. The director explained that staff were tearful on that first day. They cried because they were being gifted such an important, tiny baby to take care of, and they cried with sadness for the mother–child relationship. Two of the educators were assigned to be significant secondary attachment figures, and the little girl attended the centre until she began school. After she had begun primary school, she would often drop by on her way home from school to catch up with her special grown-ups. The director had tears in her eyes as she explained that these same two educators had been invited to her high school graduation, such was the loving bond the girl still felt.

For working parents who have other significant adult carers for their sensitive children, especially working mums who may have guilt around this issue, the key advice is to:

1. If possible, delay having your child cared for outside of your home, especially full-time, for as long as possible in the first 1,000 days
2. Transition gradually so your child can adapt to the change
3. Develop a special relationship with one key early childhood educator as your child transitions into care. Build this relationship slowly and gently if possible
4. View your early childhood educator/s as an extension of your family, and work together to identify the unique needs of your child and create ways to respond to them that are consistent.

I do have some good news about little girls. They do tend to be better at bonding to key caregivers. In one study, it was noted that if a baby girl was lifted out of her cot, she was more likely to focus on the face of the grown-up who had picked her up than a baby boy was. Given that neuroscience has shown the incredible importance of 'mirroring' due to the presence of mirror neurons, it means that baby girls can form stronger attachments earlier and more efficiently. The phenomenon of smartphones has led to a tendency for mothers to be engaged in what has been called 'brexting', which is either texting, scrolling or engaging in social media when feeding babies. Given the incredible importance of face-to-face connection, this is something to be aware of. However, I do know how incredibly supportive it can be for the mothers of babies and restless toddlers to be able to connect to friends and mother allies in the wee hours of the morning, so it is not all bad!

The longer-term impacts of poor attachment

Much has changed in the last 20 to 30 years in the research around what matters most in the healthy raising of children; however, so much comes from the experiences that impacted us as little ones.

I was once asked to work with a 13-year-old girl who was struggling with her transition into high school. She experienced incredibly strong anxiety and panic attacks, even though she had friends at the same school. When we explored where this may have been coming from, we identified that her transition into kindergarten as a four-year-old had been traumatic. She was very sensitive, and in the first weeks of kindergarten she had clung sobbing to her mother. Her mother stayed beside her for a few mornings to help her settle and after a couple of weeks, the teacher said it was time to be firmer. The next day, she forcibly removed the girl from her mother and sent her mother away. The little girl was extremely distressed and, to avoid the mother from hearing her and to avoid upsetting the other children, the teacher put the girl in a store room and locked the door. As this girl was transitioning into high school, she was being triggered from the emotional memory of that highly distressing experience. We worked closely together with her, her family and the school and gradually, we were able to facilitate a transition that felt safe to her. As a beautiful ending to this story, in her final year at school, this girl had the lead role in the school musical. Her performance was positively stunning and her confidence and perseverance was inspiring.

When I was counselling full-time, I was often asked to work with young girls who were struggling with emotional memories from before birth or at birth. Even before they understand language, they are growing stories or narratives in their mind.

One little girl who was almost four struggled with a lack of joie de vivre. She seemed to be sad a lot of the time and seldom responded with laughter or joy even around times like birthdays and Christmas. When I was working with the mother, I asked her to tell me how her pregnancy had been with her little daughter. At first she said her pregnancy had been healthy and then she paused. She remembered that just after she found out she was pregnant, at around 10 weeks gestation, her best girlfriend had been killed in a car accident. The sudden tragedy had impacted her deeply and she had cried most days of her pregnancy. I suggested that maybe her daughter had picked up the sadness from before she was born, and in some way she was feeling responsible for her mother's sadness. Being marinated in grief while in utero seemed like the most logical explanation for her daughter's sadness.

Up until the age of around five reality and imagination can both appear quite real for little ones, especially highly imaginative little girls. Play therapy and art therapy are definitely ways to help little ones process adverse childhood experiences and trauma. As I had done some training in these therapies, I used a version of colour therapy to help the little girl draw what her sadness felt like and where it was in her body. Then she drew a different picture of how it would feel to be happy, safe and loved. Quite often little girls use the colours of the rainbow and this is what this little girl chose. After that she began learning some simple breath work to release the colours of sadness and fill her body with the colours of the rainbow. Then, using her imagination and with her mother close by, we created an imaginary journey for her daughter. The visualisation involved a simplistic version of her being born into a room full of balloons and being welcomed with enormous love and laughter from her mum and her dad. Afterwards, the little girl was noticeably much lighter. She then drew another picture and it was full of flowers, rainbows and stars. When I caught up with this little girl a week later, the mother burst into tears of joy saying that her daughter was like a different little girl. The sadness had gone and she was finding it easy to laugh and be joyful.

I remember clearly another little girl I worked with who was just five years of age. Her mum and dad asked me to work with her because there were times when she got upset, particularly with her mum, or when life was challenging or when she had friendship issues, she said she wished she could die. Sometimes children use these words to try to express the gravity of their feelings and they are heartbreaking words to hear from little children. I asked for some background of her pregnancy and birth because it seemed that this response was coming from somewhere deeper. The mum explained that she had had a serious drug problem, and shortly after her daughter had been born, she ended up having a significantly difficult two years when she was using drugs and was hopelessly addicted. Eventually, she was able to engage in rehabilitation and she had been drug-free for the previous three years.

Given the understanding around the need for healthy attachment, we decided that the daughter may still be struggling with poor attach-ment with her mum, despite the turnaround in her life. I used some art therapy with this little girl, as well. We did a colour drawing and she released the many ugly colours that represented anger, sadness, fear, feeling unloved and helpless. She then used a beautiful, bright golden colour as the colour of her sense of feeling loved and happy. We did a similar visualisation where she was born into a wonderful loving space with a totally tender and present mum and dad, with lots of golden balloons. Her shining eyes and smiling face are still clear in my mind. As she sat up, she turned to her mum and gently wrapped her arms around her, and they embraced for a number of minutes. Everyone was crying tears of joy. Weeks later, the mother contacted me to say how much happier her daughter was and that when she got upset, she no longer talked about wanting to die.

Over time, emotional memories can create stories in our mind that then create beliefs such as: I am not wanted; I am not good enough;

I am unlovable. These very deep-seated beliefs can unconsciously drive behaviours and choices that we make as a child, and even as an adult. However, it is when puberty happens and there is a significant growth in the limbic brain – our emotional brain – that things can become really intense. This is when that inner critic voice becomes incredibly loud and the self-loathing that many girls experience can trigger anxiety, self-harm and a deep sense of helplessness and hopelessness. Strong, loving attachment in the first thousand days is the best way to prevent these intense negative mindsets. Given how negative mindsets are causing so many of our tween and teen girls so much angst and worry, we need to really focus on building positive mindsets from conception if possible.

Children who are securely attached to their parents are more likely to:

- be able to cope well with stress
- have satisfying relationships
- have healthy self-esteem
- have good mental health
- reach their full intellectual potential
- have fewer behavioural problems
- have fewer discipline problems
- have fewer problems separating from parents when it is developmentally appropriate.

– Robin Grille, *Heart to Heart Parenting* (2008)

Little girls are more robust than little boys

Despite the enormous influence of the shaping of gender through social constructs, research suggests that no-one is completely masculine or completely feminine. Gender identity is not fixed and, even though we are more soft-wired than hard-wired into our masculine or feminine traits, the relationships in the lives of our little ones can have long-lasting impacts.

One of the biggest social constructs I challenged in *Mothering Our Boys* was that boys are tough. Indeed, there is a fragility about our little boys that was seldom acknowledged. Statistically, boys die in utero at a higher rate than girls. They die at birth at a higher rate than girls and they die in the first 12 months of life at a higher rate than girls. When I first read these statistics, I was surprised. How can we call little boys tough with these statistics? This is what can happen when a gender expectation or social norm can be challenged by facts, and it becomes concerning because our expectations influence our thoughts and our behaviour. There is still a strong tendency to speak more harshly to little boys than little girls, and this partly comes from the perception that they are naturally tougher. We often change the tone of our voice when we speak to girls, as though they are more likely to need our help, for example if they fall over. Observe this in your playgrounds, early childhood settings and schools. If grown-ups speak differently to little boys and little girls, it needs be challenged and hopefully stopped. If we speak more harshly to boys it tells them they need to be tougher and ignore their vulnerability. If we speak in sweet ways with girls, we imply they are weak or more helpless, which denies their ability to be strong and brave. If a small child, regardless of gender, falls over or hurts themselves, we need to ask in a warm, concerned tone, 'Are you okay? Do you need a grown-up's help?'

We all come from the same genetic blueprint but a combination of factors including a key protein play a part in determining whether embryos become female, male or in rare cases intersex. Hormones are part of the story and for males, testosterone is key. Well-respected neuropsychologist Dr Allan Schore's research demonstrates that the marinade of testosterone in utero seems to slow down the growth and development of the male baby's brain. This delay can make boys more vulnerable to social stress, also known as attachment trauma, and physical stress. Seen from the other angle, little girls are born a little more advanced and better biologically wired to form healthy attachments to key caregivers from birth, which means the first 1,000 days are an important opportunity to form those attachments.

> The testosterone effects in the womb in the first year of life slows [boys'] brain development (especially in the right hemisphere) so much that they are far more vulnerable than girls to anything that goes wrong.
> – Steve Biddulph, *Raising Boys* (2018)

After birth, there can also be some gender differences in the way that neurotransmitters interact, with boys tending to produce naturally less serotonin and less oxytocin, which have been linked by some researchers to feelings of wellbeing. Maybe this is why girls use communication to ensure connection, empathy and social cohesion more often than little boys, and this could also potentially explain their tendency for greater emotional stability and regulation.

> A girl's parents are lucky; female babies are tougher and more robust than boys. We can only speculate about all the factors that contribute to this imbalance but we can say that cortisol – the stress hormone – and testosterone which boys build up, heighten the vulnerability of the immune system in male infants.
> – Gisela Preuschoff, *Raising Girls* (2006)

As previously stated, the influences of nurture can significantly impact these tendencies because nothing is fixed. Sadly, this is not always a positive thing. The good news is that at any time we can improve the influence of nurture, especially around attachment. In some studies, it has also been noted that parents are more gentle and tender in the care of their baby girls than their baby boys. In one study, grown-ups were placed with a group of infants all dressed in the same yellow jumpsuits and they could not tell which were girls and which were boys. However, as soon as they learned what gender a child was, they reacted differently to the girls and the boys, and labelled the children's emotions differently, for example, seeing anger in an expression when they think the baby is a boy but recognising fear in a girl. Yikes! This is just a small example of how the gender and social conditioning of adults can influence our interactions with our little ones in the first thousand days.

> Maybe this is an unintentional influence of the widespread misapprehension that men need to be toughened up or that maybe boys are not even sensitive in the first place. This is so wrong.
> — Maggie Dent, *Mothering Our Boys* (2018)

Girls are shaped by the interactions of those around them and this is why we need to be mindful of our expectations and social conditionings, even in the earliest stage of life. One area around emotional awareness that needs to change is around anger for girls. It needs to be just as acceptable for little girls to experience anger as little boys. In February 2022, former Australian of the Year Grace Tame met with criticism for showing her anger via her stony facial expression in the public domain. She was quite justifiably angry about how politicians and the media had portrayed her as she fought hard to prevent the sexual abuse of children and to change the culture around silencing victims. Author and ABC broadcaster Virginia Trioli noticed that Ms Tame's anger made many women feel uncomfortable, as it went against their social conditioning to be polite and 'nice'. Anger can be expressed without relational aggression; without name calling, put-downs or exclusion. It is surely time for change.

> After hundreds of years of being raised in the arts of making nice – for safety, for self-preservation, for comfort and for the comfort of others – a new generation of women is stepping into their power fuelled by the unasked-for anger that is the by-product of their trauma. And they want you to see it on their face. And they don't care if it makes you or makes me squirm.

We are going to have to get comfortable with seeing a woman's rage. And if this generation is offering to teach us all the dark arts of refusing to make nice – I want to join their coven.

– Virginia Trioli, 'The reaction to Grace Tame leads to a question: Why are so many of us uncomfortable with the face of an angry woman?' (12 February 2022) abc.net.au/news

Parental stress

There is no question that for the majority of parents today, parental stress is much higher than it was 30 years ago. The digital world has given access to an enormous amount of information that can be helpful for parents; however, it can also add to the confusion. Social media has had positive effects as well as some negatives. Many parents, mums especially, feel social media can provide a platform for parental competition and judgement from others.

PARENTS AND EDUCATORS' SURVEY

At the time, my daughter was 18 months and, of course like any mother, I was constantly following her with my phone to film her.

She was watering the garden with my dad and discussing the process about flowers and watering them. She stopped her conversation with my dad and said, 'Stop taking the picture Mama.' A gentle reminder to be in and enjoy the moment!

Many mums of young babies and toddlers tell me they are drowning in exhaustion and stress. The lack of a village with supportive women is costing mums of little ones in terms of their emotional and mental wellbeing. Being a part of a group on WhatsApp or Facebook that is supportive and protective of members can be a lifesaver for many mothers who are parenting in isolation. But the opposite is also true when an exhausted mother 'doomscrolls' or looks for connection and positivity and instead finds herself negatively impacted by disrespectful online participants.

The first thousand days can definitely be the trickiest as a new parent. The first 12 months of a baby's life is when parents have the most disturbed sleep, and sleep deprivation is one of the biggest stressors of being a parent. Tired and exhausted mums and dads are often unable to meet the needs of their babies and toddlers with calmness and unconditional love. It is very difficult to be joyful and patient when you are exhausted.

Fostering strong, healthy attachment means a child will grow to feel loved and secure in themselves. Unconditional love is not imagining you can have your children grow up in a field of daisies with no prickles. On some days, providing unconditional love means you will need to dig deep inside yourself to find the strength you didn't know you had. It will mean that on the day that your toddler daughter smears your most expensive face cream all over the carpet, the dog, the wardrobe and themselves, you'll be able to take a deep breath and realise that she is a curious toddler doing exactly what she is supposed to be doing . . . exploring the world around her using all her senses!

Healthy attachment requires plenty of human connectedness often, but not every minute of every day. I believe that finding moments to saturate your little girl with loving interaction and respectful, child-centred care in an unhurried, calm environment as much as possible is the key to achieving healthy attachment. This is impossible 100 per cent of the time and parents, particularly mothers, need to stop feeling anguished if they have days when things don't work out as they wished. Try to avoid self-criticism or revisiting every decision you made, especially when you're trying to fall asleep. Good enough is good enough. Everyone will have days when they struggle. I can still remember hiding in the toilet at times, wondering why I decided to have children! Strong, healthy attachment can be formed with imperfect parents who are good enough most of the time. Focus on the good moments, be gentle with yourself, nurture your sense of humour and surround yourself with authentic humans who genuinely care about you. Before you know it, the first 1,000 days will be done and dusted.

I will leave the final words of this chapter to the wise and wonderful Dr Vanessa Lapointe:

When the dance of trust and reciprocity between parent and child is consistent, the child develops the belief that they are worthy of love and that they can simply lean into a parent's enduring embrace – physically and emotionally – to receive that love. Over the years this consistent provision of love from the parent morphs into a consistent provision of self-love from within the child. The greatest gift a parent can give a child is to help them grow into an adult full of self-love.

– Dr Vanessa Lapointe, *Parenting Right From the Start* (2019)

KEY POINTS

- Strong, healthy attachment is as important to healthy childhood development as eating or sleeping.
- Secondary attachment with safe grown-ups who are not parents or key caregivers can have a huge positive influence in children's lives.
- The more words babies and toddlers hear out of in-person human faces, the better.
- Painful emotional memories from early childhood can cause psychological challenges later in life.
- The human mind tends to create stories from our earliest experiences that can create belief systems that lie buried deep in the unconscious mind.

- Invisible negative mindsets can influence behaviour and the development of a healthy sense of self.
- Statistically, little girls are more robust than little boys.
- Parental stress is much higher than it was 30 years ago, especially for mothers.

3

Supporting the growth of a fragile brain

Findings from various areas of developmental psychology suggest that everything that happens to us – the music we hear, the people we love, the books we read, the kind of discipline we receive, the emotions we feel – profoundly affects the way the brain develops.

> – Daniel J. Siegel and Tina Payne Bryson,
> *The Whole-Brain Child* (2011)

The first real-life hint I got that little girls are possibly sharper than little boys happened when my eldest granddaughter, Miss E, was just over 18 months of age. I was watching from the lounge as she stood outside the kitchen in the family's apartment, deep in thought. I don't remember my boys being thoughtful; they were always so impulsive. Then I saw her head towards Daddy and I'm pretty sure I saw her smile sweetly as she asked, 'Can I have a biscuit please?' Now, her mummy was in the kitchen and would have been much closer to the biscuit jar. What Miss E did was ponder deeply before making her approach to the parent who was most likely to grant her request. At 18 months of age!

The second experience that astounded me was with another of my granddaughters, Miss M. When she was around 18 months, her parents had left her with us for the weekend to attend a wedding. It was December, so Christmas decorations were up and my endless Christmas music was in full swing. She was sitting on my rocking chair eating some kiwifruit when she started to sing. In perfect tune, she sang the whole of 'Jingle Bells' without missing a word and in perfect tune!

Brain architecture

In this chapter, we'll explore a simplified version of this growth and development while introducing you to some really significant, relatively new findings that can explain some of the confusing behaviours and experiences with which our little girls can struggle.

Put simply, babies' and toddlers' brain development is about integration of different parts of the brain over time. *The Whole-Brain Child* by Daniel Siegel and Tina Payne Bryson explores how the brain develops from the bottom to the top, meaning that the executive functioning part of our brain in our prefrontal cortex grows very gradually. It is a shame it takes so long to complete its development, as it is not until the mid-20s that it tends to become fully competent! Siegel and Bryson call this vertical brain development. Horizontal brain development, integrating the left and right brain, also takes time.

Let's start at the very beginning. Our babies are born with two billion brain cells, called neurons, with very few connectors. This is really good news because it means the baby's head is smaller than it would be if it had lots of connectors, called synapses. It is definitely something I was grateful for! For a baby to create connectors via axons – long, threadlike nerve fibres – it needs to interpret the stimuli from the environment via the secret ingredient of *experience*.

The Brain that Changes Itself by Norman Doidge explains that this process, happening over and over again when connectors are formed between neurons, creates neural pathways. When a neuron connects to another neuron via a connector called an axon, it begins a neural pathway. The more times that pathway is used, the stronger it becomes, and this is how our children learn everything, from how to walk to how to dress themselves to how to clean their teeth. Imagine your toddler daughter learning to crawl or walk. The brain gradually builds a strong neural pathway that will help her do it automatically at some point. The thing that improves our ability to be able to walk is practice, which in neuroscience is all about our synapses firing strongly so they wire together and form a strong neural pathway, making it easy for the brain to coordinate being able to walk. In a way this is how habits are formed.

This is commonly called the plasticity of the human brain, or neuroplasticity when a brain grows certain pathways. It also has a tendency to prune pathways that it no longer needs. The good news is anything you missed out on learning by the age of five can still poten-tially be learned because of this neuroplasticity.

PARENTS AND EDUCATORS' SURVEY

I am amazed at the questions every day, the willingness to learn and share what she knows. Six years of age.

The early years are when the connectors are built, making brain maps or cognitive maps. Being hurried, overstimulated or stressed impacts negatively on how a child's brain maps form, as well as the emotional triggers that accompany these experiences. Not only are babies and toddlers creating brain maps, they are creating perceptions, beliefs and concepts that shape how they will interpret or make predictions about the world into adulthood.

> Babies create hypotheses, test them and then relentlessly appraise their findings with the vigour of a seasoned scientist. This means that infants are extraordinarily delightful, surprisingly aggressive learners. They pick up everything.
>
> – John Medina, *Brain Rules for Baby* (2014)

In her groundbreaking book *How Emotions Are Made*, Dr Lisa Feldman Barrett explores 'interoception': the process by which your brain makes meaning of all the sensations inside your body like your heartbeat, your breathing and your internal movements, while simultaneously helping you to navigate the outside world so that you don't fall over, you eat when you're hungry, you yawn when you are sleepy and you can climb a tree. It is occurring all the time, *every single moment of the day and night.*

> Interoception is your brain's representation of all sensations from your internal organs and tissues, the hormones in your blood and your immune system.
>
> – Dr Lisa Feldman Barrett, *How Emotions Are Made* (2018)

Dr Feldman Barrett also explores the concept of the 'body budget'. Essentially, your brain has to predict your body's movements, sometimes even before you are consciously aware of the need to move. Neuroscientists and psychologists call this phenomenon *the illusion of free will*. It seems that when we decide to do something, before we do it, our brains have already issued predictions to move our bodies, even before we become aware of it. Those brains of ours are very clever things!

In order to make predictions to keep you safe, your brain is not only constantly scanning the environment, it is spending every second of the day and night monitoring how much energy you are using. Pretend that your body has a bank account for its energy. When we eat good quality food and we sleep well and we keep active, our energy bank account will be quite full. There are many things that drain your perceivable physical energy, however, your body needs to also maintain enough energy in its account to keep your immune system working, your blood flowing, your lungs working and to digest your food. Essentially, your brain is constantly trying to predict how much energy it has in your energy bank.

Have you seen footage of runners in the final stages of a marathon where they are simply unable to walk or talk? This is an extreme example of massive energy depletion. For your little girls, they will sometimes stop eating even your most delicious meal. Or some nights they just do not have enough energy to have a bath before they go to bed without melting down. The meltdown is when the brain perceives that there is simply not enough energy right now to complete that task, and it goes into crisis. Sometimes, a child may stop eating when they're coming down with a virus or when they are constipated or when they are struggling with something emotionally. It makes sense that the brain is preserving its energy to be able to fight the virus or to work on getting that poo to move, or to work out what is happening in their friendship world. Essentially, your brain is always predicting its most important mission, which is to predict your body's energy needs so that you can stay alive and well. Imagine if it ran out of energy and forgot to keep your heart pumping?

Interoception is a whole brain process, with several regions working together in a special way to make sure the energy bank account is not depleted. Dr Barrett's research discovered that these different regions form an *interoceptive network*, which links with other networks like those for vision, hearing, taste, smell and our tactile senses. On top of that, there are the inner body movements for it to monitor. So the part of your brain that is managing your energy bank account, or your body budgeting region, is constantly sending messages and predictions to the body to help the internal environment function, for example to speed up the heart, slow down the breathing, or release more cortisol due to perceived threats in order to keep you safe and alive.

For our little girls, one of the most common ways of depleting energy from the bank account is unmet needs, and these may include:

- Being wet
- Being tired
- Being thirsty
- Being hungry
- Being bored
- Feeling angry or frustrated
- Feeling powerless or weak
- Feeling unsafe or threatened
- Feeling unloved, disconnected and invisible
- Feeling that no-one cares
- Struggling with big feelings
- Feeling unheard and misunderstood.

Self-regulation

Many parents and educators tend to feel that self-regulation is the same as self-control, and it's very important to understand that it is not. Self-regulation is about managing your energy states, your attention, your emotions and your behaviours in ways that enable you to manage and thrive in life. It takes years to develop and some grown-ups can still struggle to self-regulate.

In his excellent book *Self-Reg*, Dr Stuart Shanker explores five different domains that can influence a child's capacity to self-regulate their emotional world: biological, emotion, cognitive, social and prosocial. So, many little things can combine to make big withdrawals from the energy body bank. Check out this list of things that can impact the biological domain alone.

List of Examples of Biological Stressors		
• Allergies • Asthma • Athletic challenges • Autoimmune diseases • Being hungry • Being ill • Being inside too much • Being too cold or too hot • Bright lights • Busy traffic • Caffeine • Car/truck fumes • Chapped lips • Chronic pain • Cigarette smoke or other pungent smells • Clothing (sensitivity to fabrics) • Deep or light touch • Digestive disturbances or imbalances • Eating sounds • Eating sugar/candy • Equilibrioception (feeling 'off balance') • Extreme weather conditions and excessive howling winds	• Eyesight (forgot glasses/eyes not tested/print not clear/ sitting too far away) • Fluorescent lighting, lack of natural light • Food intolerances/ sensitivities • Gastrointestinal issues • Hard chairs • Having cold hands and feet in winter • Having to be too still • Having to sit too long in meetings • Hearing difficulty • Hormonal changes • Humming of power lines • Humming sounds from lights • Inadequate sleep • Infection/illness • Insomnia • Insufficient solitude and quiet • Lack of something such as food	• Listening and feeling of my heart rate • Loud voices • Marathon training • Measuring for high blood pressure • Menstrual cycles • Non-restorative sleep or sleep disturbed • Overindulging • Proximity (too close) • Screen time • Smells (chemicals on floor or in bathrooms/ perfumes/food) • Sore teeth (cavities) • Speech impediment • Thirst • Too many things hanging in a classroom • Tooth pain • Travel • Video games • Dry air

Please see www.self-reg.ca/tools for other stressor examples in the other four domains.

Dr Shanker talks about how the interplay of energy and tension impact how well we will be able to regulate ourselves throughout the day. An example is when you try to put your child to bed at night, it is best if they are in the low energy/low tension state. However, if they are experiencing high tension due to a difficult day, they can find it difficult to fall asleep *even if they have low energy.*

Some children tend to manage their body budgets much more efficiently and effectively than others. Often it is girls who fit this category, as they are more capable of pausing and using their pre-frontal cortex to make decisions. Some children are just much more high-energy, and many parents will suggest they have too much energy! I was a high-energy little girl and I know that I could be really annoying because I just never seemed to stop.

Things that can deplete energy in children that are out of their control include:

- Change, whether expected or unexpected
- Extreme weather events
- Parental stress
- Social dislocation
- Loss experiences
- Arrival of a new sibling
- Natural disasters
- Global pandemic.

Another possible influence on the successful working of a little girl's body budget may be the influence of environmental toxins. Psychologist and family physician Dr Leonard Sax in his book *Girls on the Edge* has expressed deep concerns about endocrine-disrupting chemicals, human-made substances that can mimic the action of hormones in the human body, particularly BPA, phthalates, PET and phenol, which are found in plastics and products we use daily. Sadly, most of these endocrine-disrupting chemicals mimic the action of female hormones, which means girls are especially affected. His research was based in the US, where he writes that about half of all US girls show signs of breast development by their 10th birthday, a significant shift. Dr Sax has also stressed the importance of little girls eating high-quality unprocessed food and avoiding high-fat, high-calorie diets because it can increase the risk of early puberty, even if the girls are not overweight – which has definitely been a contributing factor towards early puberty, which can cause problems later on.

Hopefully with a better understanding of the *body budget process*, as parents and educators we can now be more mindful when we make choices to help girls replenish their depleted bank account. Let it be okay for them to occasionally not eat dinner without an argument, let them skip the bath if you can see they are low in energy or factor in some more rest times or calm times in their busy day. Our little girls will often need some help from their safest grown-ups to successfully manage their body budget, even though they may resist our guidance.

The male vs female brain debate

PARENTS AND EDUCATORS' SURVEY

I can remember my pre-primary little girl (five years old) who could see the story dog (Charlie) was looking a bit anxious after the second day on the job in my classroom. Charlie was cowering and his tail was tucked away. She promptly put some small cones around the chair where Charlie was sitting, and had her stethoscope ready to diagnose his problem. She declared quite emphatically to the class, 'Shush! I can't hear myself think! I am trying to mend Charlie's scared heart!' My assistant and I couldn't keep straight faces! Nice end to the story was she curled up with Charlie on a beanbag and read him a picture book.

One of the things I have noticed with my granddaughters is that they are quite effective at problem-solving, especially around organisational skills. One example was when Miss E was at a coffee shop with her mum and dad, a special family friend, her sister and myself. The grown-ups had all come in different cars for a variety of reasons. Miss E, then three and a half, knew that I was going grocery shopping after the coffee. At one point, she put her hand on my hand and asked if she could come shopping with me. I replied that even though

I would love her to come shopping with me, I did not have a child's car seat in my car so she couldn't come. After a couple of minutes, Miss E put her hand on my hand and said, 'Nanny, I have a good idea. How about you drive Daddy's car, and Daddy drives your car and then I can come shopping with you.' I found that incredibly clever! Needless to say, it was such a good idea that we were able to go shopping together.

On other occasions, my little granddaughters have made suggestions about why one playground may be better than another on certain days. They have also been really helpful at giving me gift suggestions for their mums and dads. I rarely had such valuable, helpful suggestions from my sons even when they were much older! Very generally, I have found little girls to be much smarter and sharper than little boys, though that of course is only based on my own experience. I'm not the only one who has been amazed with their cleverness and their problem-solving capacity, as they were some of the top things mentioned in the survey, along with their excellent memory, imagination, verbal maturity, their caring capacity for people, animals and even dead bugs, and their capacity to tune in to other kids' feelings.

When Dr Louann Brizendine wrote the book *The Female Brain* in 2006, she had already been running the UCSF Women's Mood and Hormone Clinic for over 12 years. In this clinic, she had had plenty of time to gather data about women, biology and how the female brain works, and to explore what's peculiar about it when compared to the male brain. One of her first assertions was that more than 99 per cent of male and female genetic code is the same, but that other 1 per cent impacts everything and makes a big difference.

The male versus female brain debate has to be one of the most hotly debated topics in science. I have been exploring much of the research around neuroscience because I really wanted to find some reasons why our little girls tend to have much stronger imaginations, or why their memories seem so much more efficient, or why they are so much more emotional. It is interesting that when I have sought the help of academics, they noted that due to a concern of appearing sexist, most research around children particularly has avoided exploring the influence of gender. Another consideration about why less research was done around girls and women was the influence of the patriarchy where, for such a long time, being reliable researchers or subjects was not something that women were believed to be capable of! Some suggested you needed to avoid including women in brain research altogether. Dr Brizendine writes that she questioned a professor about why almost all subjects of brain research and studies were males. The answer was that 'women are too fickle because of their menstrual cycle and that would pollute the data'.

In a journal article about sex differences in the brain, lead author Elena Choleris, a professor of neurobiology and psychology, expressed her concern that although there are many biological differences between males and females, females are frequently underrepresented in the research around behavioural neuroscience. The paper makes the salient point that this omission of females from research really hinders any progress in researching possible sex differences in neurobiology and behaviour.

It is important to remember the disclaimer I began this book with – that there is not an 'all boys' or 'all girls' reality. Gender is definitely more fluid and the presence of masculine or feminine tendencies within each of us largely remains a mystery, despite how deeply we can come to explore the human brain. I believe that most of the core differences between girls and boys come from our hormonal differences, biological differences, epigenetic differences – all of which are influenced by social and cultural drivers.

The relatively new field of epigenetics, which shows that predispositions towards anxiety disorders, schizophrenia and autism can be passed on through our DNA, has opened the doorway to the idea that there may be *instinctual tendencies and behaviours which can also be passed on*. There is no question that our social and cultural influences from birth are enormous. While the brains may look the same, the way they interact and function are often dissimilar. Gene expression research is tending to show there are some gender differences, especially in how proteins are made and the consequences of the prevalence of certain diseases or reactions to drugs. It could be safe to say that we turn up with some hardwiring that can be linked to our ancestral lines of gender, however, there is not a one-size-fits-all for children based on their gender identity.

Rob Pascale and Lou Primavera explored the research around the differences that can sometimes happen between genders while declaring that they don't believe one gender is better than the other. In a review of the research outlined in an article they wrote for *Psychology Today*, they proposed that men and women have different strengths. In summary, they found, among other things:

- Generally, men perform single tasks better, while women have a greater capacity for multitasking
- Men tend to use distance and direction when navigating, while women rely more on landmarks
- On average, women have better capacity for social cognition, better verbal abilities, attention and word memory
- Men's sensorimotor speed and spatial processing skills are generally better
- When it comes to long-term memory retrieval, women perform better than men, as well as in fine-motor coordination
- Women orient themselves more towards faces and facial recall is strong; men's is more towards things.

Some of these tendencies can definitely be seen early in life, however, it is the environment around little girls and little boys that shapes their brains the most. When I scanned that list, I agreed with most of it, except that my husband, Steve, is way better than me at having memories of faces. He is certainly much better than me at putting together flat packs from IKEA or Bunnings and, unlike many men, he tends to follow the directions! Let us keep in mind that nothing is fixed in the human brain, even if some studies suggest there is a male and female brain.

I was a little excited when I came across research that showed gender differences in how the brain behaves during negative emotion processing. Using fMRI scans, subjects were shown negative, positive and neutral images. The connectivity between significantly activated regions was then examined with six steroid hormones. Feminine–masculine traits were also measured. The results showed significant differences between genders in brain connectivity during negative emotion processing. The males in the study tended to have a more evaluative aspect of brain response during negative emotion processing. Females had more purely affective aspects of response. Subjectively, the women's ratings on negative emotional images were much higher than in men. I felt this might be research that could validate why our little girls, and women, can be more emotional, especially around negative things and things that worry us, and that it may be a clue to the much higher numbers of our girls struggling with anxiety and mental health issues from eight to 14 and beyond. However, on reading the research paper further I realised it was an extremely small sample of just 25 women and 21 men. Statistically, it is not convincing, but research is continuing.

Some interesting differences

PARENTS AND EDUCATORS' SURVEY

My husband told me today he took our two-year-old to the local café. He said to her that they would buy a coffee for Daddy then go to the park to eat their fruit for morning tea. Our two-year-old replied, 'No, park closed, we stay here.' She wanted to play with the toys in the café! So that's what they did! I love that she knows what she wants and can say it aloud and she is heard.

Given that I was a girl and I am still a female and I have worked for over 40 years as a teacher, counsellor, mother and auntie, I think it is safe to say I have noted that frequently when girls and women get upset, and the limbic or the emotional brain fires up, words of passion often quickly follow! Michael Gurian in his book *Saving Our Sons* shared some information that made a lot of sense. He argued that males and females tend to process big emotions differently in the brain. With males, after the limbic brain fires up, the next part of the brain that fires up is the part that controls the body. Have you noticed how this plays out with boys and men? It sure happens in the movies when a man who is really upset, especially angry, is prone to physically working it out, throwing things around, kicking stuff or perhaps engaging in vigorous exercise.

When females get upset, the limbic brain fires up, then the word centre. The words that come out are sometimes irrational and highly impulsive. For some little girls, the words they use, particularly towards their mums in moments like this, can be incredibly hurtful. Not only do they say, 'I hate you,' they can say, 'You are a bad mummy' or 'I don't want to live with you anymore.' Try to remember that these are words coming from a fired-up limbic brain with a very small immature prefrontal lobe, and it's her way of trying to explain how big her feelings are. Please do not take this personally, no matter how much it hurts.

This may make sense of why little girls can often be very expressive with their big feelings when they are upset. When little girls are toddlers and unable to use words to express their feelings, they can have a tendency to scream and yell, and if they do not feel supported, this can go on for an hour or more. Rather than seeing this as a problem, try to see it as an opportunity to tune in to whatever it is that has overloaded her nervous system. Being told to stop crying or screaming will most likely see things escalate because they have not been heard or understood. This will be explored in more depth in Chapter 5.

Common sense would suggest that the dominance of different hormones for males and females could influence the shaping and development of babies' and toddlers' brains. A study that supports this came from the Telethon Institute for Child Health Research about cord blood at birth. The study, led by Dr Andrew Whitehouse, wanted to explore the difference between boys' and girls' language development since boys tend to develop a little later than girls. The results showed boys with high levels of testosterone in cord blood at birth were between two and three times more likely to experience language delay, which could possibly impact their ability to learn to read when they transition to school. Essentially, Dr Whitehouse's findings give a biological explanation for why language development can be different for girls and boys.

As a young mum, when I looked after my nieces or my girlfriend's little girls, I was fascinated with how much they loved to talk and chat, even when playing by themselves. My sons certainly did not tend to talk as much, and definitely grunted and farted a lot more! It makes sense that, if little girls like to talk and have conversations, they will get very frustrated and angry if people don't make time to listen to them.

Obviously, the development of speech, language and communication skills are enormously variable and not just dependent on gender differences. The nature versus nurture dynamic can have a massive impact on development. It does seem that science is finding some possible reasons for these differences and that hormones may play a part. In a 2019 study it was found that

Generally, estrogen was found to be correlated with enhanced social and verbal skills and to promote the growth of language centers and related areas in the brain, while testosterone had the opposite effect.

– Shir Adani and Maja Cepanec, 'Sex differences in early communication development: behavioral and neurobiological indicators of more vulnerable communication system development in boys', *Croatian Medical Journal* (April, 2019)

Biological drivers and epigenetics

In traditional kinship communities, the gender division was incredibly important to ensure the survival of the human species. Men, given that they had stronger muscles, were mainly responsible for the protection of those more vulnerable like women, children and the elderly. They were also responsible for killing large protein. To be successful at this, they spent a lot of time practising killing because you definitely need some skill to kill a buffalo or a sabre-toothed tiger. The women of the community were responsible for almost everything else; finding small sources of protein, gathering water and fruits and vegetables, sourcing forms of clothing from skins or weaving, looking after children, finding medicines from nature and caring for the sick. Essentially, they were the organisers and multitaskers of their community. Maybe this is where the different wirings in the brain came from in the first place!

If the same biological drivers that have come down from thousands of years are still playing out in our females, that may make sense of why little girls can be emotionally sensitive, or capable of tuning in to other children's feelings more efficiently than boys. In psychology, the term 'tend and befriend' is used to describe the type of behaviour that occurs in response to stress. The 'befriend' part tends to refer to the need to seek out social support during times of stress.

Another better-known response is the fight-or-flight response. Evolutionary biologists tend to argue that males, who are wired more to defend and protect, will tend to respond with a fight-or-flight response much more than the 'tend and befriend' response. Imagine if a mammoth was about to approach a kinship village – instinctively, the men would seek to fight and the women would tend to take care of their kin, especially their children. Maybe these ancient protective responses are still playing out unconsciously and invisibly.

PARENTS AND EDUCATORS' SURVEY

My daughter used to be really skilled at climbing out of her cot. One night, when she'd climbed out and joined me in my room early while I was settling her little brother, I sent a video off to her dad who works away basically saying how fun it is her doing that now, being sarcastic. Meanwhile, my clever little parrot picked up on all the words and emotion I was saying and she copied me, word for word and emotion. I had to laugh at how clever she was! Love my girl! One girl, four boys!

Belief systems and mindsets

According to child psychology, children don't tend to create and form beliefs until around the age of three. However, that may be on a conscious level because they are certainly creating them on an unconscious level earlier. In my counselling work, it was quite fascinating at times to see what 'stories' children, teens and adults told themselves were true or not true.

The human mind is a very complex thing. When a little one experiences something that is not going their way, the brain can often initially go into fight-or-flight as a stress response because our amygdala, our protector, has determined that there is a risk to your sense of survival. Sometimes our brains can act against us and try to convince us that we need to avoid that experience or challenge in the future because it may hurt, or I may fail. We can support our little girls by giving them permission to be less than perfect.

Stephanie Wicker, a child behaviour expert, parenting educator and counsellor who has worked in this field for many years, believes that two of the most important beliefs that we can give all our children are: I believe I can learn to get better at something and I believe that

I can overcome a problem. As a resilience educator, I agree with how essential these two beliefs are to building competence and capacity, especially for little girls, who are often conditioned to believe they are less capable and more fragile. Little girls are more likely than boys to be given subtle and overt messages about the need to be good, well-behaved and quiet.

PARENTS AND EDUCATORS' SURVEY

My strong-willed daughter has mastered the eye roll, and loves to do this at well-meaning friends and family members! It's both hilarious and very embarrassing to have a two-year-old tell someone off with her eyes!

Dr Carol Dweck, in her excellent book *Mindset*, did some research with four-year-olds and found that a significant number had already determined that they were good or bad, smart or not. Some of these children would have been told these things overtly by grown-ups, however, some would have worked it out by themselves. Regardless of our brain wiring or biological drivers, the most important work that happens to shape our little girls' minds *happens after they are born*. Given that they are possibly a little sharper and more mature sooner than boys, we need to prioritise giving them messages about being brave, strong and being comfortable in their own skin – anything that can challenge unhelpful stereotypes that still exist in our world.

I was born after a beautiful sister who was gentle, quiet, very well-behaved and had gorgeous golden curls. She was definitely your ideal little girl. I have no idea how early I realised that I could not be that ideal little girl who looked lovely in dresses but I remember distinctly associating strong negativity with anything girly. I disliked anything pink, I hated wearing dresses, wanted my hair cut short and I con-sciously preferred to spend as much time as possible with my dad. There is a photograph of our whole family at my younger brother's christening. I am four and have been made to wear a dress. I have a scowl on my face and my arms are crossed tightly on my chest in disgust! Before my youngest brother arrived I had decided that I was going to be Dad's little helper. Sadly, my little brother, who definitely had a penis, would slowly take my place beside my father, who was a farmer, because farming was for boys and men. Fortunately, there was plenty of opportunity to spend one-on-one time with my fabulous dad, even with a little brother.

I do remember getting told by folks in the community or at school that I needed to be more like a girl and spend less time playing with the boys. Thankfully, today we are allowing our little ones to find their own expression of themselves, regardless of their gender. It is so much more acceptable for boys to dress up as Elsa and for girls to be superheroes. When we allow them to explore all the ways they can be themselves without giving them very specific messages of what is right or wrong, we are letting our little girls find the pathway to their authentic sense of self.

However, I feel that there is still more pressure put on girls to be good and to behave in a certain way. That pressure to perform can become problematic in the teen years, especially if our girls feel that they only get love when they perform well. The greatest gift you can give a little girl is fierce, unconditional love, so that she can have a mind that allows her to be imperfect and still know she is loved.

Psychologist Dr Renee Cachia in her book *Parenting Freedom* explores some powerful stories of women who have been raised to strive to be their best all the time. The pressure to be perfect is often projected onto our little girls, and Dr Cachia believes that comes with a cost of emotional disconnection. The hunger to control everything to ensure success can become problematic, because life doesn't happen like that. She has found in her work that what children want is quite simple – to feel they are seen, heard and respected not just as a child but as a person. Feeling controlled and pressured does not meet any of those needs.

Emotion coaching for little girls is equally as important as it is for little boys, however, often it may need to be done a little differently.

Girls tend to understand emotions and are often able to articulate them much earlier than boys. However, if they have negative thoughts and beliefs buried in their minds, it will come out in their behaviour, how they learn, how they play and how they grow.

Once you identify that your daughter may have a negative belief or mindset, you can begin emotion coaching by helping her to become aware of it, and how it influences her choices. This needs to happen with great tenderness and care, because if she feels it is a sign that there is something wrong with her, she will tend to resist your support. Thankfully, there are many wonderful picture books around empathy, kindness, being brave and understanding emotions that can help you on this journey. We can change mindsets with competence. For example, if she says she's useless at dancing, we can show that with practice, we can improve. If you can practice with her and show her that your dancing can improve while having lots of fun together, this can definitely change that negative mindset.

Given the power of little girls' imaginations, I'm a huge fan of creative visualisation. This is when you create an imaginary journey, where a little girl closes her eyes and quietly sees herself in a different way. We all run little videos in our mind that are based on our beliefs, and if we can change those videos using the imagination, we can change the behaviour and the outcomes. I once worked with a six-year-old girl who was too terrified to compete in the school running race. It took me a while to realise that she had been teased by her brothers that she was useless at running. She had a little friend who was really happy to help her and come and run with her. I had them close their eyes and imagine being at the starting line, feeling excited and, at the sound of the starting gun, they smiled at each other and took off running. They imagined the sky was blue, they could see their parents cheering them on and they ran as fast as their little legs could take them. This may have taken all of three minutes. On the day of the actual race, both girls were extremely happy and excited to run together and, funnily enough, the little girl who had been so reluctant won the race! As a parent, you can do many creative visual-isations by suggesting a 'let's pretend', closed-eye activity, or you can actually role-play a situation. Both of these techniques will help little girls who genuinely believe something negative that is not true. I have a collection of audios that are particularly suited for girls on my website, including 'Moonlight Magic', 'Accepting Myself', 'Misery Guts Fixer', 'I Am a Good Friend', 'Safe 'N Sound' and 'Sleepytime'.

PARENTS AND EDUCATORS' SURVEY

The sheer delight of rolling all the toilet paper off the toilet roll while dressed in Mummy's heels and covered in make-up, age two.

Fill your daughter's bedroom with affirmations, positive messages and images. The unconscious mind scans our external world and takes those messages on, even if the conscious mind does not always pay attention. Better still, have her create her own posters of positiv-ity for her room!

Regardless of tendencies, predispositions and possible wirings in our little girls' brains at birth, we can create the optimal positive rela-tionships, environment and experiences for them. Every child is born with an enormous curiosity and thirst for life that can be cultivated and nurtured. Little girls can be strong and fearless, and sensitive and caring. Margot Sunderland in her book *The Science of Parenting* wrote about the importance of developing the mammalian brain, also known as the limbic brain, especially the areas to do with caring and nurturing, social bonding, playfulness and the explorative urge. This last attribute which can also be called the 'seeking mechanism' is a bit like a muscle – the more you use it, the more it develops and becomes stronger and more effective. When a little girl has at least one strong attachment figure in their life, she will have the energy required to explore the new and the interesting with an eagerness that will help her grow and thrive. Let her get dirty, messy and sometimes smelly as she investigates everything that her brain finds curious. Allow her to have the autonomy and freedom to ponder, reflect, question and take risks. Resist the need to control her world; rather, imagine you're walking alongside her as she co-creates her own sense of self and identity.

So what else shapes our little girls' minds?

According to the social learning theory, the most significant way that our little girls learn how to be little girls is by modelling on their safest and most significant grown-ups. They are seriously watching everything you do. The mirror neurons in the human brain are designed to facilitate learning, which is why they will sometimes use words that you use (yes, swear words!). If you listen to when little girls use swear words, they are contextually correct with the appropriate tone!

If you want your little girl to feel comfortable in her body, she needs to see her mum, her aunties or her grandmothers being comfortable in their bodies. *She can't be what she has not seen.* The best way to teach good manners to your little girl is not to tell her about them, but to model them to her. If you want her to speak respectfully to other children, then you need to speak to her respectfully.

Very recent research by Dr Lisa Mundy from Murdoch Children's Research Institute and others is showing very clearly that the years eight to 14 for both boys and girls need to be given more attention and concern. In this window, there are some significant hormonal changes in the adrenal androgens that can begin to impact our little girls' mental health. In the CAT study, they found around 20 per cent of kids from Year 3 to Year 5 have elevated symptoms of emotional problems like worry, anxiety and feeling low. When those children are followed through to Year 7, they can be up to a year behind their peers in terms of emotional literacy and capacity to self-regulate.

These hormonal changes are also being driven by the developing brain, and it's useful for parents, key caregivers and educators to understand this as learning how to better see, hear and comprehend the unique needs of our developing little girls. We need to identify those things that are contributing to heightened levels of stress and anxiety, while developing and nurturing buffers and protective factors to enhance their capacity to manage and adapt to an unpredictable world. As neuroscience continues to grow, we will no doubt find out even more about how the human brain works, especially in terms of the creation of the human mind on all levels – conscious, unconscious and subconscious. We all have layers within our personality that are influenced by how our brain grows and develops. Despite all of this knowledge, I believe firmly that deep within every human being is a core of potential goodness and light. Whether you call it the higher self, the spirit/soul, inner compass or the God essence if you have a faith – the name doesn't matter.

An excellent picture book that helps explain the workings of the mind, especially for young girls, is called *Millie and her Mindful of Mess* by Rebecca Kelly. Millie is shown how to manage her Monkey Mind, which is the endless chatter of our inner critic and our ego mind. She is also taught simple techniques to calm her Monkey Mind and to find the voice of the Gentle Turtle, the quiet voice of her higher self, or inner spirit.

We need to teach our little girls how to find this place where they already are enough, they deserve to be loved exactly as they are and their gender does not define them.

KEY POINTS

- Babies' and toddlers' brain development is rapid and involves massive growth in synapses, which are the connectors between brain neurons.
- Neuroplasticity occurs when the brain creates new neural pathways or prunes pathways that it no longer needs.
- 'Interoception' is the process that the brain uses to predict and interpret the world as well as to manage the amount of energy available to an individual.
- When little ones experience unmet needs together with low energy, it can trigger a meltdown.
- Young children do not have a mature adult brain and can struggle to manage their 'body budget'.
- Some children tend to manage their 'body budget' more easily and effectively than others.
- Gender is fluid and the presence of masculine and feminine tendencies exists within every individual.
- Epigenetics and gene expression research tends to suggest that some instinctual tendencies and behaviours may be passed on in our DNA.
- Social norms and conditionings can create mindsets for girls very early in life that can be difficult to change.
- Little girls are significantly influenced by modelling, especially on their mothers.
- As parents and key caregivers, we can help to create positive beliefs and mindsets in our little girls that will help them right through life.

4

Celebrating their wonderful memory

My granddaughters' memories simply blow me away, from little things like reminding me that we needed more milk and Weet-Bix when we're grocery shopping, to a random memory of a trip to a park, to reminding me of a story I told them when they were younger.

One experience that comes to mind that really surprised me at the time was when one of my daughters-in-law and two of my precious granddaughters were heading to morning tea at a café in the countryside. Normally when we go to this café, we turn off the main highway and go the back way as a shortcut. On this particular day, the adults in the car were chatting away and we continued on the main highway instead. Suddenly, there was some loud protesting from the back of the car, as Miss M, aged two and a half, repeatedly announced, 'Wrong way! Wrong way.'

I'm not the only one who has been impressed by our little girls' memories. In the book survey it was one of the top things that amazed parents about their little girls, with 2,973 responses listing little girls' memories as amazing.

PARENTS AND EDUCATORS' SURVEY

My three-year-old reminded me tonight how much they mimic us. I lost my cool for two seconds while trying to get her out of the shower with a screaming newborn. She whipped the curtain open, grabbed my hand and said, 'Mummy, take a breath.' I did so. She looked me in the eye and said, 'Feel better now? It's okay to have big feelings but remember we don't use our loud voices at each when we are upset. Just breathe, dude!'

The possible 'why' about female memory

In my search for answers as to why our little girls have such spectacular memories so early, the best place to start was with those ancestral characteristics driven by biology to ensure the survival of our species. In Chapter 3, I explored the influence of biological drivers from caveman days. The women tended to organise everything except the defending and protecting of the community and the killing of large protein, so they would have to have had extremely good memories to ensure the survival of the kinship community.

In Australia, Aboriginal and Torres Strait Islander people are the First Nations people and belong to the oldest culture on earth. In parts of Australia, there is evidence that they have lived here for over 60,000 years. I once attended a cultural awareness program in Darwin that was run by members of the Yolngu community. An Aboriginal elder woman explained that it was really important that gene pools were kept healthy and that there was a classification of what was called 'skin names'. This was the responsibility of the women and they were able to do this through memory shared via oral tradition for thousands of years. What an astonishing memory feat!

PARENTS AND EDUCATORS' SURVEY
She remembers every type of fruit and any animal in the world!

One study suggests that females tend to recall significantly more stereotypically feminine and neutral items than males; however, males and females tended to perform equally well in the recall of stereotypically masculine items. Another study from 2013, which explored the hippocampus and something called lateralisation, showed that gender differences in spatial memory could be attributed to differences in the hippocampus. The study explored males and females going through virtual mazes, with the results showing that there was a distinct male advantage on spatial memory tasks. Put simply, this means that little girls may start off less advantaged in this area, however, life experience could change that, if they grow up immersed in spatial experiences such as trekking, bike riding or farming. I still seriously struggle with getting lost in car parks, and I once gave my younger brother directions on how to get to an orange farm north of Perth – instead of directing him to go right, I directed him to go left and he ended up on Pearce Airbase and was escorted off by military police!

In a 2018 study called 'The Role of Sex in Memory Function', it reported that females outperform males on autobiographical memory (particularly when the retrieval happens verbally), on random word recall, story recall, auditory episodic memory, semantic memory and face recognition tasks, while other studies have demonstrated female superiority in object location memory tasks. There it is – females have a tendency to be able to find things better than males, with the *exception* of when the males consider the objects to be extremely important. One of my grandsons could name almost every dinosaur that ever walked on our earth and yet could never find his shoes, or remember how to put them on!

The reasons for these differences may be due to how information is organised in the brain or perceived in the first place and things that females tend to do more easily such as semantic clustering and verbal learning tasks. Some research suggested that these differences are influenced neurochemically rather than hormonally. As a mother of boys, I had to keep my conversations short because it was quite obvious that using too many words interfered with their capacity to remember. To help them, I often used very brief communications and included some physical signalling. For example, 'Hey dude,' (point to hat on the floor) 'grab your hat, put it on your head' (signalling hat going on head), followed by a big smile!

Science doesn't have any absolutes as to why our little girls can have such fantastic memories, so let's just celebrate the fact that they do and let them use these wonderful memories to help us sometimes forgetful parents and grandparents to remember stuff. Neuroplasticity in the brain, including memory pathways, needs to be used in order to stay strong. 'Use it or lose it' and 'what fires, wires' are two mantras to keep in mind about maintaining, nurturing or building better memories in our little girls.

The truth about memories

In their book *The Whole-Brain Child*, Daniel Siegel and Tina Payne Bryson explored a couple of the myths about memory. The first myth is that our memory is like a filing cabinet; it is not. The second myth is that a memory is a fixed and accurate reproduction of what took place;

that too is incorrect. It seems that every time you retrieve a memory, you are actually altering the memory in some way because memories are to do with associations. In a way, this explains how siblings can have very different memories about exactly the same experience.

This associative nature of memories, especially in the early years, may be one of the reasons why using play therapy, art therapy or creative visualisation can have such significant, positive results. Imagination and reality are both perceived as real, especially for little girls, and so helping them create realistic, positive imaginings can override a more negative mindset that has been created by their interpretation of their world.

Dr Lisa Feldman Barrett explores deeply how the brain is constantly working at predicting things in her book *How Emotions Are Made*. The brain takes previous similar experiences and makes instant predictions on how to cope with the current experience.

> The theory of constructed emotion – in every waking moment, your brain uses past experience, organised as concepts, to guide your actions and give your sensations meaning. When the concepts involved are emotion concepts, your brain constructs instances of emotion.
>
> Dr Lisa Feldman Barrett, *How Emotions Are Made* (2018)

Given the incredible volume of stimuli and experiences that flood our little girls' brains, there is a strong tendency for the brain to register memories when there is a heightened state of emotion. Eric Jensen in his book *Enriching the Brain* writes that memories are anchored much more deeply when there are strong emotions present. This would make sense in terms of powerful, scary memories and how they anchor so deeply in the brain. This is great news for the happy times, especially the peak moments of success that we experience in the early years of life. Do you remember when you were first able to ride a bike without training wheels, or when you conquered the long monkey bars, or were able to swim a significant distance for the first time? These are all really helpful memories that can increase our sense of confidence and courage because they are a peak moment of success. Sadly, the opposite is true too. The time you fell off the trampoline and broke your arm, or the time you were excluded from a game in preschool, or the time you were hit by a parent with a wooden spoon for disobeying a request. They all get anchored more strongly than the day-by-day stuff.

I still remember the bitter disappointment I got on a couple of Christmases when my gifts from Santa were not very impressive. I mean, who wants a new school bag from Santa?

Given that little girls have such good memories, it makes sense that some of their emotional intensity is linked to their ability to remember the bad stuff. One of my granddaughters frequently reminds me of how she hurt herself on a certain piece of equipment in a certain playground, and *it happened a couple of years ago*. Another tells me about finding a dead bird on a path and often when we walk along that same path, she reminds me. This is simply not my experience with my boys. Heck, one of my lads as an eight-year-old came and asked me where the socks were and I told him that I'd had the same sock drawer for 15 years, and that he could possibly go and look in that!

PARENTS AND EDUCATORS' SURVEY

I have three children – girl, boy, girl. My son is worried about starting kindy because his little sister will miss him. And Miss Two-and-a-half said, 'I will not miss finding your hat and your shoes every time we go anywhere. How will you remember anything without me?' My girls dote on my son (my two-year-old gets my five-year-old dressed and puts his lunchbox in his bag every day).

When we look after our granddaughter and grandson, who are 18 months apart, we have been staggered by how our granddaughter remembers so much. She helps us know where to put bowls and glasses out of the dishwasher, she knows where to put the towels in the cupboards, she knows which medicine her brother needs and how much and she is incredibly helpful when we go shopping. She knows which aisle the bread is in, where to find the eggs, which shampoo Mummy prefers and reminds me when I forget things. As a consequence of learning about little girls' memories from Miss E, I suggested to one of my sons that he ask his four-year-old daughter to help him remember things when he goes shopping. He thought I was being funny! Needless to say, he was pretty amazed that she remembers everything he suggests, and it has become habitual for him to do that now. Not only does he remember more, but his little daughter feels valued and important and helpful, and that's a win for sure. There have been times when she asks him to check whether he needs more fuel and it is usually when he is quite low in fuel!

PARENTS AND EDUCATORS' SURVEY

I remember when my son was about four months old, my daughter would have just been two. She was a very hands-on little girl, mimicking me being a mother to my baby. She'd have her baby doll and carry it around like I'd have mine. This one night, I had her in the bath and I placed my son in with her and she was holding him between her legs and she used her arm to push me away, pointed to the door and said, 'Mum, I've got this under control. I can bath Ned.' She was two! To this day, she has her brothers under control – she is six and the boys are four and two. She is like their second mother. Don't get me wrong, they have their moments but overall, she is very good at instigating play with them, will read to them (they have to sit on the floor and she be the teacher) but yes, she is my sidekick!

Explicit and implicit memories

There is another fascinating side to memories that can help you to understand how your little girl becomes a unique human being rather than a clone of her parents or siblings. There are two types of memories – implicit and explicit – and these interweave and work together.

Think of driving a car, something that we do almost without thinking after we have had a lot of experience. This 'knowing' becomes largely automatic and is known as procedural or implicit memory. The ability *to recall learning to drive*, however, many years ago, is explicit memory. Also, forming habits in childhood can be either a positive or a negative. Certain things can become automatic easily for some and not for others – think cleaning teeth!

Most of the time, when we are recalling past experiences and predicting how to behave, we tend to be using our autobiographical or episodic memory, which is a conscious recognition of what happened in the past. In many ways, it's the autobiographical memory that can cause our children to have emotional meltdowns and irrationally big, ugly feelings. I have worked with little ones who have experienced significant pain and discomfort during a medical crisis and subsequently become incredibly distressed if they need to go anywhere near the hospital where it happened.

Many adults who struggle to remember their childhood sometimes mistakenly think that maybe something awful happened, which the mind has suppressed to protect them. More likely they had a bland and quite normal childhood without an abundance of peak moments of suffering or joy. Common sense would suggest that we need to prioritise significant moments of joy and delight in the first five years of life, especially as it can help wire the brain to create memory pathways of anticipation of good things rather than painful things.

Making memories that matter

Parents instinctively want to give their children positive experiences and that is what family rituals are all about. If we do family rituals often, they will be remembered more than the very occasional ones. Birthdays, for example, are a time to celebrate a child's life in a way that can create positive memories. Creating family rituals around what happens on birthdays needs to happen when children are quite young. What happens when they first wake up? Do you have a special birthday hat that they can wear at breakfast? Where do they find their presents? Do you have a treasure hunt with clues so they can find their presents? When do they unwrap their presents? Maybe they choose what they have for dinner on their birthday?

Interestingly, children have told me that sometimes their birthday has made them sad because they did not get the dress-up outfit or a new tiara or art book they really wanted, yet the parents had got them heaps of other gifts that were quite expensive. On further investigation, the girls told me that they had requested these gifts sometimes as early as a year before the birthday and they were genuinely disappointed that their parents had not remembered the gift request. It could be helpful to keep a gift reminder memo maybe on your phone so that you will remember what she requested, if it is reasonable and affordable. On the other hand, not getting what you want is one of life's lessons that builds resilience!

Maybe having a party is one of your birthday rituals. While we're on the subject, I would like to add a note to be mindful that a party can be a trigger for a major meltdown, especially for sensitive kids, because it is simply too much stimulation. Children's birthday parties often become overwhelming, especially for young children under five, and they can end up in tears and tantrums because our precious little children are not always very good at social and emotional intelligence.

I remember being at a little girl's dress-up birthday party, and two girls became extremely upset because they had chosen the same outfit! At another party, two little best friends became very upset when the other didn't wear a matching dress. Our little girls can be tricky, can't they?

There are so many mini rituals or fun habits that can help to create the happy memories you want your little girl to have, and which will benefit her memory pathways. Rituals for when you leave the house for the day are a great idea – maybe there is a special farewell like 'See you later alligator' or maybe one parent kisses inside the right hand and the other parent kisses inside the left hand!

I'm a huge fan of bedtime routines and rituals because they build predictability and they tend to help children prepare for bed and sleep. I especially like rituals that remind children how loved they are. My personal favourite is:

> I love you more than every star in the night sky.
> I love you more than every grain of sand on every beach in the whole wide world.
> I love you more than all the hairs on all the bears.

It is especially beautiful when they personalise the bedtime ritual, as two little girls did when they asked if Mummy loved them more than all the hairs on Daddy's back!

We were lucky to live next door to a family who had two beautiful little girls. Every night, these two little girls would go down to the bottom of the garden and leave breadcrumbs for the fairies. We could often hear them as they headed off down the back path. What was really lovely was that after they had delivered the breadcrumbs, the dog went down and ate them, so they believed their offerings were being eaten by the fairies at the bottom of the garden. They will have fond memories of those afternoon delights and the invisible fairies.

Building memories that anchor deeply in the brain occurs when you repeat significantly positive experiences. There are many families who return to the same campsite or the same family farm for repeated holidays throughout childhood, not just because they can't think of anywhere else to go, but because memories are made and reinforced by doing the same fun thing year after year. Think bike riding around the campsite with a heap of kids that you only ever meet at that time each year, swinging off the flying fox into the river, climbing trees, building cubbies, hunting for prawns in the estuary in the dark, playing spotlight or fox holes on the beach with lots of kids (and often quite a few dads), or playing on the swings from dawn till dusk – this is the stuff that builds positive memories that your child can draw on later in life as evidence that they had a fabulous childhood.

Families who like to visit different places on their holidays can still lock in the same strong memories by taking their holiday rituals wherever they go. I can still remember the double chocolate ice cream that we walked to get at the nearby deli after dinner on holidays. The same goes for family games like Scrabble or Monopoly, kicking a football outside, playing cricket, going fishing, bush barbecues in the back paddock or yard, collecting field mushrooms or heating marsh-mallows over the campfire on a chilly winter's night. I am deeply saddened that many of these wonderful memory-making moments are at risk of disappearing as our children spend hours on iPads and tablets rather than playing with other children and the adults who love them the most. Without plenty of happy memories to draw on, our children can be more vulnerable to negativity and despair as adults.

Given our little girls have amazing memories, please do all you can to consciously build memories that matter in the first five years of life. When one of my great-nieces was young, she had a beautiful ritual with her daddy. Some nights when it was warm and clear, after locking the chickens away, they would lie on the lawn and watch the stars. Hopefully at her 21st birthday, her daddy will remind her of the magical times they had together when she was very little.

Parent memories and how they influence our parenting

PARENTS AND EDUCATORS' SURVEY

Those meltdowns that you realise the universe gave you, by par-enting a tiny version of yourself, and by using it to remember to pause. Thank you.

If there is one thing for sure, it is that we all had parents of some sort and a childhood and no matter how fabulous our parents may have been, we all come with scars from our childhood. Now that you understand how memories are formed and how they influence our behaviour, especially implicit memories, you may appreciate why parenting is so challenging. In any given moment, a mum or a dad may be triggered by an experience that makes them react from an unconscious place deep within their mind, and they can make a choice that they deeply regret later. Essentially, we all have unfinished business from our childhood, and it is not until you live in close proximity to children who you are helping to raise that these buttons tend to be pressed.

In her book *Parenting Right From the Start*, Dr Vanessa Lapointe explains that as a mother and a practising psychologist, she has discovered the following:

> Over time I've come to understand the two most powerful influences that affect how we parent; one is how we were parented and the other is our family's history.

Mothers and daughters are born female and regardless how they identify with gender later in life, they have a lot more in common than fathers and daughters. My mum was not the mum I wanted, as my two main love languages are quality time and safe touch. My mum was emotionally unavailable and a poor communicator, so being frozen out and ignored were two very significant wounds I experienced as a little girl. When I reached my teen years, I was pretty angry, aloof and struggled with profound self-loathing and self-hatred despite the confidence I displayed.

When I became a mum, I remember choosing to be present and to be as loving and as available as I could be. Then one afternoon, when my oldest son at two and a half was throwing a particularly spectacular tantrum, I swung round to hit him in the head, stopping my arm midflight with a hideous thought, 'Oh no. I have turned into my mum!' That single experience was enough for me to realise that I needed some help to become the mother I wanted to be rather than the one I had been mothered by. I needed a lot of professional help to release the pent-up anger, rage, sadness and remorse from my challenging relationship with my mum. I spent many weekends over several years doing personal development programs; I went to counselling and therapy and explored the story of my childhood. My story was that I was obviously broken, flawed and completely unlovable. Catholicism also taught me I was a sinner, a heavy burden for a little girl to carry. I now understand that I was a very challenging child for my mum because I was a highly spirited, strong child and I questioned her behaviour and choices loudly. I was secretly jealous of my older sister who was the perfect daughter who never got into trouble.

While my relationship with Mum was challenging on some levels, she was an excellent cook, a good sewer, a competent gardener, an avid reader, a passionate bird lover and a highly intuitive woman. All these wonderful and positive attributes are very much a part of the women my sisters and I have become, and for that I am deeply grateful. After I had worked through much of my emotional baggage, I remembered so many more beautiful memories with my mum. Helping her to bake and eating some of the mixture, helping in the garden with the flowers and the veggies, and helping her to bottle fruit from our orchard were all memories that I had buried under my emotional pain. I remembered a couple of beautiful dresses that Mum had sewed me too that I had completely forgotten about. In time, I came to a profoundly peaceful place with my relationship with my mum when I realised that she had done the best she could, with what she knew and with what she had experienced being the fifth of 12 children raised in a challenging time in history. Forgiveness came easily once this realisation anchored in my brain.

To be the best possible parent for your child, I encourage you to honestly explore the story you have in your head by reading good books, attending seminars and workshops, and finding a professional who can help you with the most challenging moments that you experience as a parent. This will enable you to parent from a grounded and loving place, rather than a reactive and defensive place. With more knowledge, understanding and a bucketload of compassion, we can really rewire the memory pathways in our own minds so that we can navigate a better and more loving journey in our own homes.

Ancestry and trauma

PARENTS AND EDUCATORS' SURVEY

Me: 'M love, can you help me remember things? I'm very forgetful.'

Six-year-old: 'Mum, I already decided to do that but forgot to tell you.'

Dr Bruce Perry, a renowned brain development and trauma expert, is just one of the experts teaching parents and educators about the long-lasting impact that trauma has for both individuals and for generations. In the book he wrote with Oprah Winfrey, *What Happened to You? Conversations on trauma, resilience, and healing*, Winfrey shares her abusive childhood and how it turned her into 'a world-class people-pleaser for most of my life'. When powerful, frightening and traumatic experiences happen to young children, they are stored deeply inside their brain. Dr Perry argues that the most important question to ask someone is not 'Who are you?' but rather 'What happened to you?' Even though we know that children younger than three are not mature enough to create linear narrative memory, some form of memory still remains buried deep that can be triggered by a seemingly random sensory experience. For example, if a child under three was molested by someone with black hair, years later, they may experience a panic attack because a man with black hair sits next to them in a movie theatre. This is a trauma response.

Dr Bessel van der Kolk was a pioneer in exploring trauma. His thesis centred on how the brain responded to a traumatic event, and the changes that occurred in the body as a result, arguing that the brain quite urgently needs to suppress the memory of the experience, by hiding it or through self-blame, to ensure an individual's survival. Trauma is a form of psychic wound that hardens you psychologically so you can survive, then interferes with your ability to grow and develop in healthy ways. The most important message from van der Kolk's work is that emotional distress is stored in the body, and it does not dissipate. For much of my childhood, I was a chronic bedwetter and a frequent sleepwalker, and several therapists suggested that these physical behaviours had a lot to do with the fear that was buried in my body.

Deb Dana in her book, *The Polyvagal Theory in Therapy*, explores how our autonomic nervous system is wired for us to survive in moments of danger and thrive in moments of safety. Because we are social beings we are wired for social engagement, and we are wired to do anything we can to be able to connect to others. This means there are times when we will make choices that will avoid us having conflict with others because that has been conditioned into us as little girls or little boys.

- What will other people think?
- Don't speak unless you're spoken to.
- I'm so disappointed in you.
- Stop making things so difficult.
- What is wrong with you?
- Just be nice to people.

- Now don't think too highly of yourself.
- Do as I say, not as I do.
- You just need to try harder.

Does this make sense of why sometimes our little girls deny their own voices and sense of self in order to please the grown-ups? Or to avoid parents being disappointed in them? Or to avoid others noticing them – except when they're being nice, of course!

These messages and experiences of shaming can create long-term psychological harm. Shining a light on them, especially on secrets, can make a huge difference. If the wounding has been painful but is not traumatic, having deep, honest, raw conversations with safe people – whether family or best girlfriends who can hold a safe, confidential space – can be enough to start healing. However, for deeper wounding, more may be needed.

Everyone has an autonomic nervous system that is constantly working in the background. I explored this in the previous chapters under the concept of interoception and the body budget from the work of Dr Feldman Barrett. This highly efficient nervous system is shaped through our experiences over time, and sometimes it can store challenging emotions in the body so that they are out of the way and the system can keep functioning.

Early in my counselling I noted that a person's body might start trembling or shaking as they revisited a painful traumatic experience, so I trained in therapy that helps the body release trapped trauma and distress. The energy therapy, which was called EFT (emotional freedom technique) but is now more commonly just called tapping, was a game changer in my therapy room. Tapping on acupressure points allows significant amounts of emotional tension to leave the body in a short space of time and enables the participant to come to a very calm place after they had gone to a very dark place. This is a technique I used with children and adults in combination with narrative therapy and visualisation.

There are many other therapeutic tools that can help with releasing difficult emotions and processing trauma. I also trained in TRE – Trauma Release Exercises – and found that the shaking that often happened spontaneously created significant shifts in clients' emotional and mental wellbeing. I have also found some helpful techniques in NLP (neurolinguistic programming), and EMDR (Eye Movement Desensitisation and Reprocessing) is a similar technique now used in psychotherapy. Kinesiology also uses some excellent techniques that can release emotional stress and tension from the body.

PARENTS AND EDUCATORS' SURVEY

I was teaching visualisation meditation imagining waves washing over the body. After a few days in a row, I asked her to tell me what colour the wave was and where on her body it washed over. She replied, 'It is a colourful wave crashing over my vagina.'

I want to add a trigger warning here before I tell this next story – it contains some graphic detail of a suicide so please skip ahead to the next paragraph if you are concerned. Many years ago, I worked with a five-year-old girl who found her daddy after he had shot himself. Her mum was a solo mum with a new baby and was herself traumatised by the sudden death of the father of her children. The little girl started coming to me once a week. Early on, I had a sense that she had 'split' from her body, which meant that she was experiencing her thinking and feeling sensations outside of her body, not inside of her body, as she struggled to process what she had seen. One of the techniques in NLP helped to hide the image of finding her daddy on the floor and that was the first area I focused the therapy on. Each week I chose to follow the same pattern of therapy, using the same music, the same calming essential oil, art therapy and breathing while holding her head in an emotional release position. She also used my

'Moonlight Magic' relaxation audio most nights before she went to sleep. Over six weeks, her vacant look and her disconnected sense of self gradually shifted. Over the next year I saw how, bit by bit, the shock of that traumatic event seemed to dissipate, and she returned to being a lively, chatty little girl. I saw her mum many years later and she thanked me for that experience because at the time she had no energy to look after her daughter as well as the new baby, and she also had to grieve and heal.

These therapies can be very important because without addressing trauma and difficult emotions, children are more vulnerable to various problems. Dr Gabor Maté is a world-renowned expert on addiction, trauma, ADD/ADHD and other mental health–related areas who argues strongly that there are neurobiological roots to addiction that stem from trauma early in childhood, and he believes addiction is linked to childhood trauma.

A key message from the experts in the trauma field is that we need to allow our children to have big feelings following difficult experiences, especially ones that they could perceive as traumatic. How often do little girls feel the need to shush, to stop crying or to stop expressing other big feelings? Dr Maté argues that this pressure can lead our little girls to make the decision that it might be easier to suppress big feelings in order to be acceptable, to be a good girl. Indeed, he argues that many grown-ups have similar dysfunctions as a consequence and overcompensate for them, all in the name of being 'nice'.

I myself had to work on overcoming a tendency to never hurt anyone else's feelings, which meant I was doing a lot of people-pleasing and denying my own truth. It can be really hard to say no, especially to people who I value and respect! Fortunately, I have found it easier to focus on being generous and kind, which is quite different from just being nice. It took many years of deeply exploring myself, and the stories I had convinced myself were true, until I felt I could speak up on important issues even if I might have others disagree with me.

Allowing our little girls to have an authentic voice when they are little is beyond important, even if it means they aren't always nice. Encourage them to speak their own truth even if you disagree, and allow them to discharge the emotional tension in the nervous system following really difficult experiences.

One of the best books I have read on this topic is *Raising Girls Who Like Themselves* by Kasey Edwards and Dr Christopher Scanlon. They have wonderful suggestions on how to raise your daughter to have a power perspective about herself and life in general. They also explore ways to build her independence and mastery over herself that are excellent and highly practical. I recommend it to anyone raising a girl.

Ancestral influences

The study of epigenetics has found that trauma can be passed on via the DNA. In his book *It Didn't Start with You*, Mark Wolynn, a world leader in the field of Inherited Family Trauma, explores many such stories from his extensive experience in therapy. Dr Norman Doidge, author of *The Brain that Changes Itself*, also supports the idea that we can relive family traumas and that psychotherapy might often be about 'turning our ghosts into ancestors'.

Much of the research around epigenetics happened with mice across many generations. The research continues to find ways to show transgenerational epigenetic inheritance or the notion that behaviours can pass from one generation to another.

PARENTS AND EDUCATORS' SURVEY

My girl is Indigenous and wants to be white due to no family connection and seeing white girls at school being invited to all the
birthday parties etc.

Sadly, intergenerational trauma impacts many First Nations peoples
around the world. Following massive dispossession of their home-
lands, denial and destruction of their culture, murder, massacre and
the stealing of children, First Nations communities around the world
struggle with poor physical and mental health, dysfunctionalism and
high suicide rates. Many members in these communities may have
experienced difficulties with attachment, disconnection from their
extended family, and are dealing with the impacts of trauma.

Many of the children who are struggling in our school environments can be struggling with the impacts of adverse childhood
experiences (ACEs) and trauma. The work of researchers like Dr Ross
Greene, Dr Mona Delahooke, and Deb Dana shows that *children will
behave well if they can,* but children who have experienced trauma
are often in a hypervigilant state with high levels of stress before they
even start their school day. So many of our children impacted by
trauma are punished, suspended or expelled, which further heightens
the trauma response. This needs to change.

The science isn't completely clear on why little girls seem to have an
innate ability to remember, however, I encourage you to use it, and
be mindful of it, from as early as possible. If your daughter experiences a traumatic event, allow her to express all the big feelings and
emotional tension in whatever way works for her. When she is ready,
have a conversation about what distressed her so that she can make
sense of it in her mind. If it is a really big thing that has upset her, she
may need to revisit it many times; that is absolutely fine. You should
certainly seek professional help if the trauma involves any form of

abuse or a loss she is not recovering from in good time. Otherwise, though, it is not our job as parents to fix these big moments, but to be a safe space and support our daughters as they make sense of it all, and release the enormous emotional angst that the experience may have formed inside their bodies.

KEY POINTS

- Little girls' memories are noticeably more effective than little boys'.
- Memories tend to be anchored more strongly when there are strong emotions present.
- Consciously create memories that matter – family rituals can be really helpful here.
- We all bring stories from our own childhood that influence how we parent – both good and bad.
- Trauma experienced in the early years of life can create layers of buried emotional distress that can unconsciously create challenging behaviours and choices later in life.
- Many little girls are conditioned in the early years to be people-pleasers and to put others before themselves.
- We need to encourage our little girls to have their own authentic voice and to avoid silencing them.
- Trauma and adverse childhood experiences can create difficulty for children in managing stress.
- Celebrate your little girl's memory and give her the responsibility of reminding you of things.

5

Her emotional world

Let's start with the basics around emotions: all emotions are valid and normal. There are no good or bad emotions. Emotions are triggered by our brain's response to experiences both real and imagined and, due to the immature brain architecture of little children, it is developmentally normal for them to struggle with containing the flood of big feelings.

It is important to remember that no matter how nonsensical and frustrating our daughters' feelings may seem, they are real and important to them. When any child gets really distressed, they are often unable to reach their logical left brain and they instead display emotions through gestures and in other non-verbal ways such as crying, yelling and throwing things. We must remember that *our children are not being bad or naughty*; they are struggling to cope with their world. A key message to remember around little girls and big emotions is the three As – *allow, acknowledge and accept them.* This can be really difficult, especially because most mothers had experiences as little girls where their emotions were made to feel wrong, bad or unnecessary and grown-ups tried to stop them expressing their feelings.

For a very long time, it was thought that emotions have fingerprints; this means that emotions such as anger or sadness present in the same way for everyone, and can therefore be easy for us to identify. The groundbreaking work of Dr Lisa Feldman Barrett in her book *How Emotions Are Made* has shown this to be incorrect. Everyone experiences emotions in their own unique way, based on their experiences from the first years of life. Since our brain functioning is mainly about prediction, how little children are supported and guided in the early years is critical to their future emotional wellbeing. I have come to believe that with more awareness about how to emotionally coach our little girls in the first years of life, we will be able to better support them to navigate their own emotional world as teens and as women. Experiences are constantly building neural pathways in our little girls' brains, so we can recognise that by helping them to identify the emotion, acknowledge the emotion, feel the emotion and release the emotion. We can help our girls build strong emotional literacy and confidence, possibly for life.

From the responses in the survey, the most challenging part of raising little girls seems to be their emotional world. These were the top concerns (noting that respondents could choose more than one):

- Meltdowns/tantrums (67 per cent)
- Resistance to things (49 per cent)
- Anxiety and irrational fears (30 per cent)
- Her moods (29 per cent)
- Sensitivities (25 per cent)

For girls aged four and older, the top concerns were:

- Friendship dramas (40 per cent)
- Anxiety and irrational fears (34 per cent)
- Meltdowns/tantrums (34 per cent)
- Resistance to things (30 per cent)
- Her moods (21 per cent)
- 'Mean' behaviours (21 per cent)

Before I dive into exploring the emotional world, let's dive into what makes our girls happiest.

- With family/with Mum and/or Dad (5 per cent)
- With her friends, playing, laughing (16 per cent)
- Playing: imaginative/toys/dolls/games (13 per cent)
- In nature, outside, park/with animals, pets (12 per cent)
- Hugs, cuddles, roughhousing, tickles, touch (9 per cent)
- Being active: sports, dancing, bike riding, trampoline (7 per cent)

PARENTS AND EDUCATORS' SURVEY

Whenever she sees anyone cross, she comes up to them and says in the sweetest voice, 'I can see an angry face.' She has the biggest smile on her face and everyone starts laughing – she's four.

There is little conclusive data to show a significant difference between how our little girls and little boys manage feelings or emotions. One study showed that there was a difference in interpreting emotional understanding, the ability to understand, predict and explain the feelings of others and oneself. Anecdotally, the picture is quite different. Overwhelmingly, from my survey and my work around families, schools and communities, most girls show significant differences in their emotional worlds compared to most boys. They can be more intense emotionally for much longer than boys – much longer!

Building emotional intelligence and understanding

Daniel Goleman, in his book *Emotional Intelligence,* argues strongly that having emotional intelligence may be equally as important, or more important, than intellectual intelligence in helping people to live healthy, happy lives. A person with emotional competency would, for example, have patience in queues, be able to resolve conflict without verbal or physical abuse, be capable of loving, caring relationships, overcome setbacks more effectively than others and enjoy being themselves most of the time. No-one is born with all the attributes of emotional intelligence, but they can be nurtured or cultured, especially in the early years of life.

- Knowing your emotions and feeling states
- Managing your emotions
- Motivating yourself
- Having an ability to accurately empathise with others
- Handling relationships
- Having the ability not to be swamped by your emotions
- Believing in your ability to cope
- Persisting in the face of frustration
- Being able to delay gratification
- Feeling hopefulness.

– Maggie Dent, *9 Things: A Back-to-Basics Guide to Calm, Common-sense, Connected Parenting Birth–8* (2014)

Daniel Siegel has explored emotionally mature behaviour as being a function of the middle portion of the prefrontal cortex, or the last part of the executive brain to develop. We must keep in mind that the logical, rational prefrontal cortex is gradually growing until we reach full maturity in our mid-20s. It has the ability to coordinate essential skills such as:

- Regulating our body
- Attuning to others
- Balancing emotions
- Being flexible in our responses
- Soothing fear
- Creating empathy

- Having insight
- Having moral awareness
- Using intuition.
  – Daniel Siegel, *Mindsight: Change your brain and your life* (2012)

As parents, the best way to help our little girls to develop these attributes is with strong attachment with consistently loving grown-ups modelling good behaviours and emotional coaching.

Strong attachment: am I loved?

PARENTS AND EDUCATORS' SURVEY

My daughter is the most snuggly, caring, compassionate little girl who is really in tune with others (especially Mum, Dad and big brother). She is always offering cuddles and telling us that she loves us!

With their little brains growing by constantly making predictions about their world, while simultaneously managing their 'body budget' energy, we need to be attuned to and conscious of the environment we create around our little girls. We all tend to function better when we experience harmony and predictability rather than a state of chaos.

The key fundamental thing to remember is: does she feel loved by and secure with her key caregivers? Whenever you are really struggling with your daughter, always go back to this basic – *relational safety trumps everything*. Unless that is strong and secure, a little girl is technically in a stress response.

Many times in my counselling, I came across girls, little, tween and teen, who were absolutely convinced that their parents did not love them when in truth, they loved them a lot! Michelle Mitchell has worked with girls for more than 20 years and found that they were more likely to describe their relationship with their parents as distant if the girls themselves struggled with emotional regulation and fought a lot with their parents. It seemed that the big emotions get in the way of what was most important – feeling loved and connected.

Parents often think it is obvious how much 'I love you' because of all the things they do for their children, and because they genuinely do love them. Keep in mind that little ones, who have very immature brain architecture and very little access to a logical brain, can decide that because you have not given them the treat, the biscuit before dinner or the toy at the supermarket that you can't possibly love them. When we talk about strong attachment, we're not talking about these moments; we're talking about how safe a child feels most of the time to have their basic needs met, to be soothed and reassured when they are feeling distressed. It's about their face lighting up when they see their parents.

It can be handy to think that inside our little girls is a love cup. Over time, using emotional intelligence, you can help your little girl work out how she can sense how loved she feels, possibly by using a positive colour to represent love. In my work, so many little girls choose the colours of the rainbow for when they are feeling loved. If you notice she is feeling sad or angry, you will need to work out the best time to talk to her about how her love cup feels. For some little girls, after they have had a verbal vent and become calmer, they can be ready to talk about it quite quickly. Others may need to take themselves to a safe place to allow themselves to become calmer before they can have a conversation.

One of the best books I read when I was a parent of young boys was *The 5 Love Languages of Children* by Gary Chapman and Ross Campbell. There are five ways that we fill our children's love cups. Learning this was one of the most significant lightbulb moments that I have had, not only for my parenting but also for myself. The authors believe there are five love languages and that we all have a unique need for certain kinds of loving connection. My love languages are quality time and physical touch, and as a little girl I was especially disadvantaged with my relationship with my mum because she was not warm and tender. I have no memory of being held or hugged by my mum. She avoided physical touch right through her life. The five love languages are as follows:

1. **Physical touch.** Close physical proximity, plenty of safe touch, loving her hair being brushed, sitting on you rather than beside you, co-sleeping with their arms and legs wrapped around you.
2. **Words of affirmation.** Hearing words of love, encouragement, guidance and appreciation works for some children. They are sensitive to tone and criticism, and often very sensitive when feeling ignored and not acknowledged.
3. **Quality time.** If this is the primary way your daughter feels loved, she may sometimes drive you nuts with wanting your full attention – a lot. These girls value eye contact, one-on-one time, real conversations, lots of questions, endless chatter, sharing feelings and bedtime rituals.
4. **Gifts.** These little girls are very attached to the gifts you have bought them over the years and, rather than be concerned with cost, size or shape, they are more tuned to the thought you put into purchasing the gift. Be very careful about buying meaningful gifts as opposed to bribery and manipulation, as your daughter will know the difference!
5. **Acts of service.** These little girls respond to acts of service and notice and mention when you cook their favourite meal, come to watch them play sport, how you wash and take care of their favourite outfits or make their school lunch with their favourite foods.

One of the things that we can do unconsciously as a parent is to offer the love language that we prefer and thrive on receiving, *rather than figuring out the love language our little girl prefers*. I strongly recommend that you explore with your daughter her preferred love language, and how you can build on her feelings of being loved.

Modelling

> Children have never been very good at listening to their elders, but they have never failed to imitate them.
>
> – James Baldwin, American novelist and essayist

Humans are social beings, which means we are meant to live in relationships within systems, within communities. Given that our little girls have such amazing memories, we need to be mindful of what we are modelling to them. If we shout at them and expect them not to shout back or at their siblings, they simply won't buy that because you did it first! If they don't see you clean your teeth well, they may really take some convincing as to why they have to clean their teeth well. If they hear you complaining about our appearance or our body weight, they will internalise it. If your little girl sees you enjoying physical activity like playing netball, yoga, running with the dog or riding a bike, you will normalise this for her at an early age.

In a way, I was a little girl who was not conditioned in traditional ways partly because I spent most of my childhood either on the farm or at school. I spent a lot of time with my dad, so I became a repairer of broken things, and I was comfortable with tools and spending hours outside often working. I rarely wore make-up until my early 20s mainly because it was just something I had not seen or had modelled to me *as being important*.

One of the things that can be really helpful to model for little girls is thoughtfulness and empathy. The wonderful optical mirror neurons suggest that children learn empathy best by observing people who are caring and compassionate. Our behaviour towards others becomes a template for our children, and taking the time to develop a sense of morality and empathy can really help our little girls navigate life in the 21st century. It can be really helpful if at times you can give your daughter hypothetical situations to consider. For example, would it be okay to run a red light if there was an emergency? Would it be okay to push a child over who was running too close to a busy road? What would you do if you saw a child steal something out of your friend's schoolbag? How could you help a new student who doesn't have any friends? Giving our little girls opportunities to be problem-solvers is important, especially when we are building their capacity for empathy and learning to see the world through other people's eyes.

When we have conversations with our daughters, rather than us telling them how they need to think or feel, we are creating a 'social reality'. Dr Feldman Barrett explains that this is so important because if you as an adult perceive a baked good as a decadent cupcake or as a healthy muffin, you not only condition your daughter to have the same reality, there is research to show that your body metabolises the cupcake differently! This is one of the reasons why dieticians encourage us not to label food 'good' or 'bad', because our mind then sets it up to be a problem. 'Discretionary food' or 'occasional food' is a much better way to describe food that has lower nutritional value. There is a mental food war going on in the minds of most women. 'I can eat this piece of cake because I'm going for a run later'; 'I can eat this bag of potato chips because I'm having a Diet Coke with it.' Being mindful of the words we use to describe things around little girls can help give them positive rather than negative modelling.

Emotional eating tends to start in the early years of life. Children who are struggling to feel loved and connected – or who may be dealing with high levels of stress due to abuse, abandonment, deprivation or trauma – can use food to help them lift their neurochemicals to find comfort. In my experience of working with a number of girls who were classified as obese, all of them had major emotional trauma buried deep in their minds, hearts and bodies.

Reframing is an excellent way of changing possible negative words that have been commonplace over time. Reframing is the art of seeing things differently so that your perception may change to enable you to respond more favourably in your communication. So often our parental triggers come from negative thought patterns that have been embedded in us from our own childhoods. Take for example: 'My daughter is such a sook; she is always crying about something!' Not only is that unhelpful for your daughter, it will also feed your frustration and build your negative feelings towards her. Thanks to the incredible growth of the science of child development, we now know that children do not use emotions to manipulate their parents, and they are not trying to be bad or naughty. If you have a sentence like this that you are using around your daughter and you want to change it so you can have more empathy and understanding, it will be helpful to understand what your trigger is by exploring your own inner world. Once you understand the emotional charge you have around these words, then you can reframe the thought that accompanies the emotional trigger. Instead of, 'My daughter is such a sook; she is always crying about something!' you could reframe the thought to be, 'My daughter is having a really hard time right now and needs my help.' With practice, the spontaneous irrational trigger can be disarmed and weakened, and you can model a very different way of seeing the world.

- Overdramatic could become sensitive
- Annoying could become persistent
- Bossy could become assertive
- Mean could become insensitive or unkind
- Loud could become spokesperson
- Picky could be decisive
- Emotional could be passionate
- People-pleaser could be thoughtful or considerate
- Attention-seeking can be connection-seeking.

It is not until around three years of age that children become more aware of and responsive to the gestures, facial expressions and actions of others. They then become capable of connecting these interpretations to what another person is feeling. Technically, this is when they become capable of socialisation with other children. This is the time where our little girls are linking what they see on people's faces with how they feel, and when they create their perception of reality. Dr Feldman Barrett calls this the *'theory of constructed emotion'*, meaning that every individual from around that age is constantly using their past experiences – especially through the influence of significant grown-ups – to create concepts that your brain then uses to construct an instance of the emotion.

> **MAGGIE'S MAIN IDEA**
> Emotions are not reactions to the world, they are your brain's responses that will guide your actions and give all of your sensations meaning.

To give our little girls a sound and reliable base for her emotions, we need to keep her world as safe and secure as possible, and we need to model respectful behaviours. Finally, we need to spend time with her and to help her learn the world of emotions so she can make meaningful predictions around human behaviour for the rest of her life.

> **PARENTS AND EDUCATORS' SURVEY**
> My worries for my daughter: friendship dramas, sensitivities, her feeling unheard, other children's use of emotional manipulation and bribery that challenges my child's agency (i.e. she will give in to placate the other child).

Emotional coaching

I have often found that parents have too high an expectation of little girls and their ability to navigate their world. Just because your daughter can make her bed, put away her toys and clean her teeth without needing to be asked some days does not mean she will have the energy to do it every day. On the days that she is unable to do what you expect her to do, rather than express your disappointment or remind her that she can do it, it is best to validate that she is having a hard time today and that is okay. Check the two lists in the previous section about emotional intelligence (pages 76–77) and see if you are modelling those behaviours. Remember that little girls are conditioned to be good and to do as they are told, so *they can feel stung by parental disappointment*. Given that our little girls have incredible memories, they can accumulate clear memories of repeated moments of disappointment and when they are feeling sad or unloved, they can revisit all of these experiences and get stuck in what we call 'a mood'.

> **MAGGIE'S MAIN IDEA**
>
> The first place to start in building emotional intelligence in your daughter is to explore the environment around her and the expectations that you have of her.

I was definitely a little girl who was 'moody', and I can remember clearly that there were many times when I was attacking myself on the inside for being unlovable, not good enough and flawed in some way. Given that females tend to ruminate and run repeated thinking cycles, we learn early in life to be our own worst enemy. Helping our little girls identify when they are feeling stuck in a mood, and helping them work out ways that they can escape the mood, can be a really helpful life skill. This does not mean you need to jolly them up or rescue them; it means you help them to discover their own pathways out of negative moods. It may be helpful to put a different connotation on moods. Maybe you could explain we can have happy moods too, and that we can really enjoy being in these emotional states.

Remember that the rage, fear and separation distress system is set up at birth to support a baby's survival, not to cause their parents distress. These systems were designed to ensure that our little ones were not eaten by predators or harmed by any other potential danger in their world. These days, our little ones' distress systems can be triggered when a door slams loudly, when they are unable to dress themselves, when you walk out of the room unexpectedly or when you cut their toast into four pieces instead of three!

A simple way to help our little ones understand sudden triggers to their amygdala is by *making statements of observation* like:

- That door slamming frightened you.
- You wanted your toast cut in three pieces and Mummy cut it in four pieces.
- It is frustrating when your little brother smashes your Duplo tower.
- You want to stay at the playground and Mummy needs to get home to cook dinner.
- It hurts when your friend doesn't want you to play.
- You are thirsty and want to drink and we left your water bottle in the car.

This might sound incredibly simplistic, however, over time, this helps our little girls recognise how experiences can trigger big feelings. Gradually, they will learn to make better predictions about how they can respond. Following this statement, pause and remember the three As about what she is feeling – *allow* the feelings, *acknowledge* the feelings, *accept* the feelings. Then you might help your daughter recognise the emotion she is needing to express. Given how clever our little girls are from such a young age, be prepared for her to argue with you about which emotion you think she is feeling! You may suggest that she is feeling frustrated about something – be prepared for her to tell you she is just really angry! Also keep in mind that beneath anger often lie other feelings that are being clouded by the anger. These can include sadness, fear or embarrassment.

Here is a list of some picture books that might be helpful to look at with your daughter from when she is around two years old:

- *The Way I Feel* by Janan Cain
- *Let's Talk About Emotions* by Dr Libby Aitken
- *Sometimes I Feel* by Dr Samantha Seymour
- *How Big Are Your Worries Little Bear?* by Jayneen Sanders
- *My Feelings Matter* by Sara Stace
- *Some Days* by Ash Bisdee
- *Little Big Chats* by Jayneen Sanders

Acknowledging irrational feelings, helping our girls understand them and allowing our little girls to feel loved is all incredibly important. Minimising big, ugly feelings denies an opportunity to teach our children how to manage such feelings. This is essentially what emotional coaching is and why it is so important.

PARENTS AND EDUCATORS' SURVEY

Emotional manipulation by others ('I'm not your friend if you don't . . .' or 'Swap with me, go on, swap with me' until she gives in just to keep the peace). Being an early childhood educator, I have taught my children how to recognise emotional manipulation and how to deal with it, but it still influences my empathic, gentle, kind daughter and really places her in a position of conflict.

Every little girl is a one-off unique little miracle, and your job as a parent is to work out how you can attune to how she is feeling – her physiology and even the look on her face are not always reliable indicators of that. Working with your daughter after she has had a meltdown or a tantrum helps her work out what may have triggered it, and what may have worked in supporting her to process the emotional tension that flooded her body. Co-regulation is about you offering a safe base for her to truly express her authentic self – no matter how ugly that may be in the moment – and to do that with unconditional love. Dr Mona Delahooke in her latest book, *Brain-Body Parenting*, explains that these spontaneous moments of emotional flooding are all pathways that a little girl uses to protect herself, not to deliberately misbehave. When she feels safe she is in the green zone. When she is flooded with stress she may discharge outwardly with a meltdown or tantrum – this is the red zone. Many girls shut down instead and are often mistakenly thought to be OK because they are silent, but they are actually in the blue zone. Whether it is the red or the blue pathway, *a little girl's brain is working closely with her body to ensure that she survives*. What really does help is that parents have the awareness to keep ourselves in the green pathway so we can support her to cope.

PARENTS AND EDUCATORS' SURVEY

Can be quite emotional but this seems to be mainly linked to tiredness.

Take a parental pause

I have created a simple technique that can help to form a habit for parents to enable them to stay calm while the storm within your daughter runs its course. This allows you to respond rather than react to any hidden triggers we have from our own childhoods.

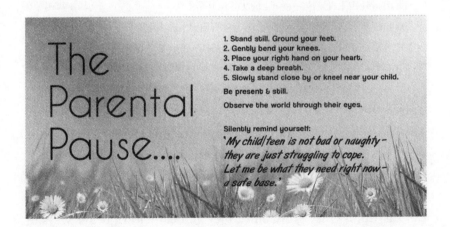

The Parental Pause....

1. Stand still. Ground your feet.
2. Gently bend your knees.
3. Place your right hand on your heart.
4. Take a deep breath.
5. Slowly stand close by or kneel near your child.

Be present & still.

Observe the world through their eyes.

Silently remind yourself:
'My child/teen is not bad or naughty – they are just struggling to cope. Let me be what they need right now – a safe base.'

Emotional triggers for grown-ups

Sometimes adults will find certain things trigger us more than others depending on our own childhood experiences. Dr Vanessa Lapointe believes that we run a program, consciously or otherwise, that has been buried within us since we were young. For example, if whining triggers a strong emotional reaction, it is likely that you were shamed or scolded for whining as a child. 'You never do as you are told!' can be another trigger when kids don't do what you ask! Many little girls were told quite simply, 'Behave and be a good girl' and were often left to flounder in heightened emotional states without any understanding or support.

Pam Leo, in her podcast *Healing the Feeling Child*, explores the importance of being able to discharge these feelings spontaneously in the moment while still being loved and supported. *Essentially, the way we talk to our little daughters, while refusing to let them feel their feelings, becomes the inner voice.*

Invalidated: There is nothing to cry about or there's nothing to be frightened of.

Shamed: Don't be a sissy or you should know better.

Threatened: I'll give you something to cry about.

Placated: I'll get you a new one, or let me fix it.

Distracted: Let's go get a cookie instead.

Isolated: Go to your room, or ignoring the child.

The message 'don't express your feelings' can become 'don't feel your feelings'.

– facebook.com/DanceWithMeInTheHeart (12 October 2021)

The trigger for an emotional meltdown or tantrum in a little girl is often a cluster of unmet needs that coincides with a lack of energy or too much tension in her body. So much of this response is spontaneous and unconscious as her body works with her brain to ensure she can survive. As they grow older, they gradually learn better ways of understanding how to take care of themselves and to meet some of their own needs.

Coaching little girls to understand unmet needs

When we encourage our little daughters to become problem-solvers of their own unmet needs, we are building an incredibly important capacity within them. At the same time, our little girls are still *little* girls, even if they are capable of logical thoughts and conversations, so coach gently and with compassion.

You might say to her:

- 'Will a hug help?'
- 'Here is a drink of water. Does that help?'
- 'Do you feel sick? Let me feel your head.'
- 'Let's go outside for a while.'
- 'Can I help you with something?'
- 'Take three deep breaths and think about how you really feel.'
- 'Tell me what you need right now.'

Or you might take an action:

- Offer a safe base to enable a calming of their amygdala.
- Kneel nearby and offer a calm, kind presence.
- Go sit in a favourite spot – a comfy chair or couch – and hug her favourite soft toy, i.e. mimic soothing.
- Take three deep breaths or three big sighs together.
- Quietly start singing a favourite nursery rhyme or bedtime ritual.
- Quietly lie down on the floor nearby and be still.
- Put some nature sounds/calming music on.
- Send her rainbows of love.

The best way to help a child build a healthy emotional intelligence is for us as the primary carers to work on our own capacity to love and feel safe about being our own authentic self. Life experiences will create plenty of opportunities for you to grow emotionally, mentally and socially. Enjoy the ride and try to keep your heart open.

Things that can help in 'hot' moments

> **MAGGIE'S MAIN IDEA**
> One of the things that we do need to accept as the parent of a girl is that emotional intensity is quite normal and not a sign that there is something wrong with your little girl, or something wrong with your parenting.

Parenting is really like an endless guessing game. This list of suggestions may give you some ideas and new insights into helping your relationship with your little girl, and help her through her highly emotionally charged 'hot' moments. Keep in mind as you read that you, the parent, are the person who knows your child the best, so choose the suggestions that best suit your little girl.

1. **Communicate respectfully as you would with your best friend.** Your daughter from birth is a whole person with her own mind and her own unique needs. Like many first-time parents, I believed that my newborn was completely helpless, needy and totally dependent on me. I had no idea that he was capable of being communicated to, and responded to, in a far more intelligent and responsive way until he was about nine months of age. He walked early and one day, I suggested he take his towel and put it in the laundry, having absolutely no expectation that he could understand me! A short time later, I found the towel in the bathroom, and my whole perception of raising little ones changed forever. When we see our little ones as capable, aware, intuitive and able to understand language and abstract ideas, we change the way we communicate.

Whenever adults speak, we are being role models for the children in our presence. What we speak is what we teach. Children record every word we ever say to them or in front of them. The language children grow up hearing is the language they will speak.

– Pam Leo, 'Teaching Children Respect',
connectionparenting.com (13 June 2020)

Imagine you are out for lunch with your best friend. If she spilled some food on her shirt, what would you say? If your little daughter did the same, what would you say and how would you say it? Imagine saying to your partner, 'It is time to do the dishes, 5–4–3–2–1, now off you go.' Other disrespectful behaviours that our little ones tend to get a lot are criticising, lecturing, ridiculing, bribery, shaming, screaming and threatening. Given that our little girls have a heightened emotional awareness, and very long memories, communicating to them disrespectfully is one of the main ways we create the negative inner voice that becomes very loud when they become adolescents. If you want to help your daughter to learn to love and value herself, focus on respectful communication.

2. **Help her understand her own unique strengths, challenges and needs.** Given the pressures on our girls to be 'perfect', we need to build a strong foundation of awareness about authenticity. Help her to identify the things that bring her joy and happiness, as well as the things that cause her to struggle so you can support her to build strategies to manage her challenges. You can help her to build a healthy attitude and mindset to learning and life. Some of her 'hot' moments will come from failure and setbacks. Check Chapter 16 on resilience, because it can be nurtured from toddlerhood.

3. **Connect and redirect.** If you need your little girl to come to the table for dinner or to go and clean her teeth before bed, rather than calling out a command across the room, try coming alongside her and connecting warmly before making your request respectfully.

The same can happen when you need to leave a playground that she is enjoying. Come alongside her and maybe whisper quietly that you will need to leave soon. Commanding and demanding our children can often trigger a stress response in them because it can threaten their own autonomy. It is exactly the same in the classroom as it is in our home.

4. **Seek their help.** Toddlers and infants like to be helpful and to be treated as capable. If the play room has toys everywhere and you would like it cleaned up, ask your daughter what she thinks would be a good way to do that. If you run out of groceries, ask your daughter to remember certain items for next time you go shopping. Ask her to help you remember lots of things because she can be really good at it and it helps her feel valued and important. When your little girl feels powerless or that she doesn't matter, her stress response can be triggered, which increases the chances of meltdowns and tantrums.

5. **Name it to tame it.** This is an excellent technique that comes from *The Whole-Brain Child* by Daniel J. Siegel and Tina Payne Bryson. When our little girls experience something painful, disappointing or frightening, the amygdala can flood and the fight-or-flight response can be activated. Supporting her to identify her feelings is helpful, *if you can do it before she becomes emotionally overwhelmed*; otherwise, wait until she is able to calm down. Ask her to retell the story of whatever experience frightened her. This allows our little girls to explore their feelings within the story and an adult may then be able to help explain any bits she can't understand. Some little girls may need to tell their story over and over until they make sense of it themselves. This can be tricky because the sooner you go over the story, the better, but if it's time to cook dinner, pick up other children, or you are about to leave for work it can be like a red rag to a bull. Little girls need to be heard when they need to be heard, not just when parents have time to listen.

This technique is really helpful to explore further through the work of Dr Lisa Feldman Barrett, who I have mentioned before. Her research shows that our emotional world and how we predict future experiences in our life is built on our experiences. Without a safe grown-up to help a little girl make sense of her big emotional feelings, and then help her release them, many little girls end up with emotional tension buried somewhere in their body or nervous system.

6. **Accept and validate that all emotions matter.** It's so important to teach our little girls that emotions are meant to be experienced and it is okay to feel them. Reframe any messages that suggest that girls are more dramatic because they express their emotions verbally more than boys. It's important girls understand that our emotions exist because we are human, not because we are weak, bad or naughty. 'It's okay to not be okay' needs to be affirmed for our little girls. Telling her at times, 'It's okay to be angry at your brother for breaking your Duplo tower', 'It's okay to feel a little bit worried about starting big school'. Keep reminding her that you hear her and you are here for her.

PARENTS AND EDUCATORS' SURVEY

Six-year-old. She is very caring towards her friends and has a very emotional side to her. She cries at almost every movie, with a happy or sad story in it. Lots of emotions – it makes me smile.

---

7. **Helping them express 'hot' emotions safely.** While is it important to validate that expressing emotions is okay, we also need to teach our girls that there are some boundaries around how they express big feelings. Hitting others is not okay when we are really angry. If your daughter feels the need to hit, give her a big cushion or suggest that she hits a soft couch. Tapping on the K27 acupressure point (google it!) on the thumb side of the nail on her middle

finger can release emotional tension from the nervous system. Try it yourself next time you are upset.

Tell her that running away is okay when you're at your home, however, running while out in public is not okay because she could run onto a road or get lost.

PARENTS AND EDUCATORS' SURVEY

As an educator of a child with additional needs, my colleagues and I have been introducing the concept of a visual card 'Solutions' Box with children in order to better manage emotional needs and difficult situations. Indie approached me after engaging with a particularly 'challenging' friend, proudly holding up a sign she'd made depicting an outline of a boy with a large cross across his body. Indie explained, 'When . . . annoys me, I hold up this sign so he knows to leave me alone and don't go there buddy!'

---

8. **Attitude matters.** Given that we know about how beliefs, mindsets and how we predict the world are all formed in the first five years of life, we need to do everything we can to help our little girls develop a healthy and positive attitude to life. Dr Martin EP Seligman explains that optimism is not just positive thinking; it's more about the way you think about things. There are three different dimensions that we can explore to help little girls make sense of both the good and the bad that will occur in life. They are permanence, pervasiveness and personalisation.

MAGGIE'S MAIN IDEA

Our thoughts not only create our own version of reality and our map of the world, they create our emotions as well, so helping little girls to build healthy attitudes makes sense.

A) **Permanence.** If you have noticed that your daughter is using words like 'worst', 'never', 'devastated', 'always' or 'everyone', it could be a sign that she is wiring herself to see the world through a negative lens. 'It always happens to me! Everyone hates me.'

When our girls spend time watching other girls catastrophise, they are more likely to act more fragile and powerless than they normally do.

– Kasey Edwards and Dr Christopher Scanlon, Raising Girls Who Like Themselves (2021)

After they've had a good vent, we can help our daughters pause their thinking by asking them questions. This technique interrupts their mind from looping a familiar negative story. When our brain hears words suggesting permanent awfulness, it automatically winds up the emotional intensity. It can be helpful to keep reminding your little girls that how you feel right now won't last forever. Indeed, you could burst into the famous song from *Frozen*, 'Let It Go', to help her understand this. Try asking:

- 'Is that really true?'
- 'How do you know that is true?'
- Substitute words like 'occasionally', 'sometimes', 'some people', 'a little bit'. Remember, our inner voice can become a habit and habits take time to change. If this is happening with your daughter, help her to create some fabulous posters for her bedroom and bathroom that show positive attitudes to counteract her negative views.
- You could model to her that she can interrupt those thoughts by tapping on the side of your head: 'Delete, delete, delete'.

B) **Pervasiveness.** This means that if you believe a cause is pervasive, you tend to project its effect across many different situations in your life. This is a really common way of building a negative attitude to yourself and life and it is something that little girls are expressing a lot. 'I am always useless.' 'Nothing ever goes right for me.' 'Everything is unfair.' This is the pattern of the catastrophiser, and it is something that can become incredibly debilitating in the tween and teen years. Spend some time deconstructing and reframing the pervasiveness that you hear from your little girl. Some really positive affirmations that you can help your little girl adopt include:

- I am enough exactly as I am.
- I am, I can, I will.
- Everybody matters – no matter what.
- I am so much more than this experience.
- Stretching my comfort zone will make me grow stronger.
- I can deal positively with anything that happens in my life.
- No matter what happens, I am still a worthwhile person.
- I matter in this world.

C) **Personal.** The third dimension is the 'personal' where individuals decide where the fault lies. When bad things happen, individuals can blame themselves (internal) or they can blame other people or circumstances (external). Blame can become a really toxic influence later in life if we turn it outwards inappropriately, therefore avoiding accountability and responsibility. Conversely, we can also tend to become our own worst enemies by blaming ourselves for things that are not of our doing.

Depressed children and adults are forever blaming themselves and feeling guilty over things that are not at all their fault, and being a self-blamer increases a child's chances for depression.

– Martin Seligman, *The Optimistic Child* (2011)

9. **Teaching emotional release techniques.** It can be really helpful to support our little girls as they work out how to discharge emotional

tension in a way that suits them. Not all girls like to talk about big feelings. As a little girl, when I was upset, I took off for the bush or the paddocks and would only come home when I felt calmer and happier. If you can model techniques, like taking some deep breaths when you feel stressed, your daughter will copy you. If you sometimes recognise you are becoming too stressed, and you let your daughter know you're going to sit in the calm-down chair, or you're going to have five minutes in your bedroom to calm down, your daughter will copy you.

I am a huge fan of tapping on the body's acupressure points to release emotional tension. I have been using this technique for more than 20 years and it is still my go-to when I am facing a big emotional challenge. It could be grief, anger or frustration. I tap on my K27 point, near the clavicle on the chest, for a couple of minutes while taking some deep breaths, and I can feel a noticeable difference with my emotional intensity. There are other acupressure points on the head, fingers and hands that we can teach our little girls how to use from a young age.

Creative Visualisation (CV) is another way to help build healthy pathways in your daughter's mind. Imagining going for a walk on the beach, sitting under a full moon or eating an ice cream on a holiday will trigger the same feel-good endorphins that would be generated if the event was really happening. CV is also effective at shifting negative mindsets and negative attitudes, especially for children under the age of eight. Thankfully, mindfulness has now become mainstream, and learning and incorporating these techniques into our lives can benefit grown-ups and our children.

10. **Family meetings.** Given that a family is a system and all systems need leaders and opportunities for their members to be heard, having a family meeting, either regularly or from time to time, can make a huge difference in the lives of children. Rather than the parents being the sole problem-solvers and decision-makers,

creating a cooperative climate is not only respectful, it can improve predictability, cohesion and connectedness within your family.

> **MAGGIE'S MAIN IDEA**
> Family meetings can be really helpful for younger kids as well as they get to see adult communication and, most importantly, have the opportunity to be heard.

I encourage using a talking stick so that only one person can speak at a time. This ensures that the quieter ones can be heard and it can teach our children to become respectful listeners. In many families, sometimes something quite small might be triggering emotional tension and conflict can fester and become a much bigger issue. This can include siblings fighting over chores, poor boundaries around personal belongings or a sense of unfairness in the way grown-ups are making choices. To be truly respectful in our parenting, and to give children the best possible opportunity to understand relationships and how to overcome conflict, they need to experience it.

Given how important it is for our little girls to be heard and respected, to be seen as creative thinkers and problem-solvers, a family meeting can be your excellent way of giving them that space. It's a great idea to keep the meeting short and to finish on a challenge that the whole family needs to consider but which can be resolved at the next family meeting. This encourages deeper thinking and usually some incredibly creative solutions are found.

The *Exploring the Decline in Wellbeing for Australian Girls* report from August 2021 shows that young female people are significantly more likely than their male peers to have anxiety and depression, lower self-esteem and, some evidence suggests, lower resilience. Building a healthy emotional intelligence can be a significant protective factor in their future health and wellbeing as our little girls grow up. We cannot put all the blame on a changing world and social media; we need to look at building a stronger foundation in the first five years of life, before our girls transition into big school.

Emotional coaching can make such a difference, by building healthy attitudes towards themselves and others. We can avoid the conditioning that can teach our girls to be people-pleasers or that their needs must always come behind the needs of others. Helping to give our precious little girls a predictable foundation can make an enormous difference to their mental, emotional and physical wellbeing, especially during the turbulent adolescent years.

What is equally important is giving them a safe place within themselves where they can retreat and make sense of what is happening around them. Their imaginary world can be very helpful here. See more about why in Chapter 12.

PARENTS AND EDUCATORS' SURVEY

We've focused on emotional regulation development. My daughter will also consider others' feelings, especially when it comes to inclusion, in every aspect of life. Whether that is sharing Christmas presents so everyone has an equal amount to unwrap and play with, changing a game so everyone has the opportunity to play or standing up for those who aren't comfortable.

KEY POINTS

- All emotions are valid and normal; there are no good or bad emotions.
- Most girls tend to have *more emotional intensity* than most boys.
- No matter how nonsensical and frustrating our daughter's feelings may seem to us, they are real and important to her.

- When children get distressed, they are unable to reach their logical brain and we need to remember they are not bad or naughty – they are struggling to cope with their world.
- Since our brain functioning is mainly about prediction, the better supported and guided our little girls are around their emotions the healthier they will grow to be.
- We need to remember the three As about emotions – allow, acknowledge and accept.
- The parental pause is an excellent strategy to help you stay calm when your daughter is having an emotional storm.
- We need to help them identify the emotion, acknowledge the emotion, release the emotion and make sense of what triggered the emotion.
- Safe grown-ups need to model ways to calm emotional tension and stressful moments.
- With emotional coaching, our girls can develop emotional intelligence that can help in so many ways right throughout life.
- Every little girl needs to feel loved and to have a sense of feeling safe and secure.
- Nurturing a sense of empathy and a 'social reality' is important in the early years.
- Be mindful of the words we use around our daughters and learn the art of reframing.
- Emotional attunement and co-regulation can really help our girls manage their emotional world more easily.
- We can encourage little girls to become problem-solvers of their own unmet needs.
- We can teach little girls emotional release techniques.

6

The influence of temperament

Imagine that, when a child is born, they come with a little blue chip that is encoded with unique information as to who our little one is meant to be. It will have the instructions for what age they'll start walking, if they'll have blue or brown eyes, flat feet or dimples. This blue chip also has a determination of the temperament your little one will have.

Temperament can be seen as a continuum. At one end, you have your feisty, strong and confident 'roosters'; at the other, you have your gentle, sensitive and often empathetic 'lambs'.

For optimal growth and development in terms of temperament, we would like our children to be in the middle of this continuum rather than stuck at either end. We all want our children to be capable of being strong and confident and thoughtful and considerate. Many children are a mix of rooster and lamb from birth.

Characteristics of rooster girls

Our roosters can:

- have a heightened sense of their own importance
- yearn for independence and autonomy and prefer to do things for themselves
- often be loud
- often be very stubborn about making their own choices
- often be early wakers and among the last to go to sleep
- be capable of arguing over almost anything – clothes, food, toys and chores
- be manipulative and selfish
- prefer to go first
- struggle to share
- be very impatient and impulsive
- learn really fast and often learn best by making their own mistakes
- get quickly frustrated and angry, especially with grown-ups
- ask endless questions and yes, they will question your choices and decisions
- be entertainers quite early in life, or 'party animals'
- be fearless and brave at taking risks and embracing challenge
- cope with change and adventure with gusto
- sometimes disappear at large public events because they like to explore
- enjoy the company of older children and adults
- often make you feel you are the worst parent ever!

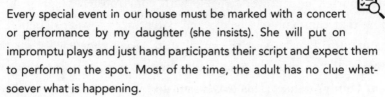
Even as toddlers, our rooster girls have a drive to grow up as fast as possible. I clearly remember my sister calling me after she had an enormous argument with her 20-month-old daughter about what clothes she wanted to wear. Given that my sister had been a sweet lamb, she found this feisty little girl a bit of a mystery! As soon as you identify that your daughter has strong rooster traits, it is a good idea to weave as many choices as possible into her day. Having choices feeds her hunger for autonomy and independence, and can save many arguments. *This does not mean that she should get her way all the time.* As girls tend to have superior verbal skills earlier, our little rooster girls can tend to manipulate situations and parents masterfully. They often do this by exploiting your guilt and yes, they can do this while they are still toddlers! Their capacity for 'pester power' is exceptional, and there will be times that you will have to find your 'parent swagger', as Canadian psychologist Dr Vanessa Lapointe names it, and hold your ground. Creating a strong connection of love with your rooster girl is the key to being able to hold those boundaries.

Dr Lapointe, in her excellent book *Discipline Without Damage*, writes beautifully about the importance of parents needing to be in charge:

Children need us to be in charge. Not in a scary, power-hungry way but in kind, subtle, intuitive and compassionate ways. They need us to channel our inner Hulk in order to feel that somebody capable and trustworthy is at the helm.

Some days, you will manage this effortlessly and other days, you will find yourself in a power struggle with your rooster daughter. One thing that can definitely help when parenting a rooster daughter is the mantra 'Don't sweat the small stuff'. Save your energy for the times that you need to hold a firm boundary that is important to your family's values. This may mean that if your daughter has been intentionally rude to a sibling or friend, after appropriate warnings, she receives a consequence that may be uncomfortable. Rather than shaming or excluding her, you might give her an extra chore or she might lose a privilege of some kind. Interestingly, this only needs to happen a few times and your daughter will realise that there are certain things and certain times when she doesn't get what she wants and she needs to accept that. Shaming and excluding, without warm discipline, tells children they are bad and wrong and that will become a child's inner voice as a teen and adult.

PARENTS AND EDUCATORS' SURVEY

One of my daughters is in a kind of a triad of friendship with one girl who is adored by her and the other girl. There is a lot of jealousy and attempted controlling behaviour at play every day, particularly by the other girl vying to be the 'best friend', who doesn't have the same level of emotional maturity and problem-solving skills/communication skills as my daughter as she's quite a bit younger. My daughter ends up being very hurt by controlling behaviours and thoughtless words.

Sometimes our rooster children can struggle to consider other people's feelings because they value their own so much. Empathy can be nurtured or encouraged, and the sooner the better. Modelling being considerate and thoughtful is incredibly important, and reading picture books where characters model empathy is also helpful. If our little girls are shouted at or shamed when they lack consideration or empathy, we are simply teaching them to shout at and shame others.

One of the things that helps build empathy in our rooster children is to get a small pet, like a guinea pig, kitten or puppy. The repeated stroking and cuddling of a small pet can help to strengthen the neural pathways in the brain that encourage tenderness and gentleness. Pretend play where little girls pretend to be mothers of babies has also been shown to help build the empathy pathways.

When our rooster girls stay stuck in a self-absorbed, self-important state, especially when they become overly dominant and narcissistic, the friendship dynamics can get really difficult in the formative years. When I was counselling full-time, I worked with a number of little girls who struggled with friendships because of their tendency to dominate and be bossy, and I also worked with many little girls who lacked assertiveness. Growing social and emotional intelligence takes time, guidance and practice with other children in the real world. Prioritise play with other children as much as possible, especially children of multiple ages, as that is the best way to nurture the development of both our rooster and lamb girls. Much of sibling angst is normal and helpful at teaching our children about needs, wants and boundaries. The screen world has displaced many precious moments where this education was happening. I have created a creative visualisation called 'I Am a Good Friend' that helps to build social skills via the imagination for children who struggle.

What can help our rooster girls grow healthily?

PARENTS AND EDUCATORS' SURVEY

My two-year-old wild one was doing a lovely clay craft activity at a recent family camp. Together, we made her creature out of clay and she was excited to get the red paint out. Not only did the creature get a lovely coat of red, but finger painting was the obvious next choice. The table, chair, floor and Mummy were also painted red. It definitely made everyone laugh.

As soon as your little girl is talking, speak to her like you would an adult, especially an adult you like. Little girls are attuned to the tone of adult's voices, especially parents! All of our children are biologically wired to resist being told what to do and rooster girls are especially sensitive when they are commanded to do something.

MAGGIE'S MAIN IDEA

Making a request politely and gently, as if you were asking a grown-up you like, then pausing, can make a whole world of difference to rooster girls.

The pausing gives her some time to consider your request. If you have a hurried expectation that they need to do as they're told, especially if immediately, this can be like a red rag to a bull.

What can also work really well is giving her an option of when to do your request. For example, 'Can you please brush your teeth – before we have a story or after. Which works for you best?'

One of the unfortunate and very unhelpful parenting habits from the old days when behaviourism ruled is giving our kids threats. When our children don't do what we command, or ask them to do nicely, so often we resort to a threat. 'If you don't eat all of your dinner, you won't get dessert'. I can still remember vividly an experience from when I was around six. I hated peas. My mum said I had to stay at the dinner table until I ate them. Given that I was a stubborn rooster, I fell asleep in the chair around 10:30 pm.

It is usually our rooster girls who are most resistant to doing as we ask. Threats to rooster girls, especially towards the end of the day when they are tired, can trigger the most massive tantrum. Rooster girls see threats as an attack *on their heart*. This can damage your relationship with your rooster daughter for a long time, especially if repeated. Even if you seek to repair the damage done, they tend to hold on to that emotional pain for a very long time. Threats may give you temporary compliance, the same as a timeout or the threat of a smack, however, the long-term cost of making our girls feel unsafe or anxious is simply not worth it. It can also set our girls up to become people-pleasers, something many women struggle with later in life.

What works best is nurturing the relationship and showing respect. Have genuine conversations with her about things you see in the world that can shape not only her sense of self, but also how she sees herself and others. For example, if you see a hurt or upset child in the playground, you might chat about that in the car on the way home. You might check what she observed and ask how she felt the grown-ups could have helped that child better. Then you might ask what she would have wanted you to do, if she had been in that situation. Talk to her about values and expectations, and always take the time to hear her. Invite your rooster daughter to help with problem-solving, from little things around the house to bigger things that impact the whole family. You will be surprised at how clever they can be! We need to be careful to avoid talking *at* our daughters, especially our rooster daughters, and recognise that conversations occur when both sides are being heard.

PARENTS AND EDUCATORS' SURVEY

My daughter is eight, and she has always been very lively since birth. The way she cheers up her little brother with a funny voice or a gentle song always makes me smile.

Given that our rooster girls can struggle with patience and hate to lose, try to prioritise playing games where they will learn to take turns, to wait, to lose well and to win graciously. The more time you invest in card games and board games in the early years of her life, the better she will cope with disappointment and failure right through life. To be honest, I would like to see birthday party games like musical chairs and pass the parcel return to only having one winner. This will give families more opportunities to help teach how disappointment feels and ways of overcoming it in a controlled environment. Learning to recover from setbacks and disappointment is one of the keys to becoming a resilient young woman.

Our rooster girls particularly honour being respected and trusted. If you can find small opportunities where your rooster daughter can do something that other children of the same age are unable to do, this builds authentic confidence. She might be the only child in the family who checks the letterbox or the only child who can make their own snack. Remember your rooster daughter may not be the oldest child, however, *she may be the more capable child*. Sometimes she is going to ask to do things that make you nervous. It may be to audition for a part in a musical, or to play in a sporting team with older children or to climb a tree that you think is far too tall. Please take some deep breaths and allow her to stretch and grow.

When your rooster daughter makes a poor choice, allow her to express her big feelings without judgement or a need to shut them down. She needs to be able to acknowledge and feel all the big feelings so they can leave her body. Your next job is to reassure her that you love her exactly the same as you did before. Many rooster girls I have worked with who were very successful academically or in sport shared that they felt they have been loved *conditionally*. When they didn't win or succeed, or they expressed their extreme disappointment or frustration, they definitely felt unloved by their parents. So please reassure your rooster daughter that your love is fiercely unconditional – no matter what, no matter when, no matter why.

Many rooster children have high levels of energy, so have conversations about the need to discharge excess energy in their bodies in healthy ways, whether that's jumping on a trampoline, going for a bike ride, playing chasey or just running or jumping. It's important for them to know they can release the tension they feel in their body. It can be helpful to talk to your preschool daughter about 'arousal states' as explained by Dr Stuart Shanker:

Those arousal states are:
1. Asleep
2. Drowsy
3. Hypo-aroused
4. Calm and alert
5. Hyper-aroused
6. Flooded (tantrum)

— Dr Stuart Shanker and Teresa Barker, *Self-Reg* (2016)

The optimum state for us is number four – calm and alert – and this is when we learn best and play best. When we lose energy, our arousal states head towards drowsiness and lethargy, and when we have too much, we head towards being overly aroused, which can easily tip into being flooded. Roosters have a much stronger tendency to move towards being hyper-aroused and flooded due to having higher energy. It can be handy to describe arousal in terms of the metaphor of a cup. When the cup is full we are in number four – calm and alert. When we lose energy, the cup empties and we can feel depleted and sometimes that presents as whingey and whiny. When we have too much energy, the cup overflows and children can become irritable and restless. We simply have to keep in mind that children in either the depleted state or the overloaded state are not bad or naughty; they are just struggling to keep their energy levels in check and will need a grown-up to help.

Time in nature

One thing that helps all children, but particularly our high-energy girls, is time spent in nature. There is a wealth of anecdotal and scientific evidence that shows us that simply being in nature is restorative; it takes us out of our routines, away from the ordinary, and captures our attention without requiring mental effort. Prioritising time every day for little ones to simply 'be' in nature helps them to develop calm pathways in their brain. The early years of our children's lives are when they exist in a naturally mindful state with very little understanding of the concept of time, so it's important to allow children unrushed opportunities to explore the natural world. The exponential growth of their fragile brains through exposure to all nature's sensory inputs is just one of the gifts spending time in nature gives. Have you ever noticed how fascinated toddlers and little ones are over seemingly uninteresting things like a dead leaf, a rock or a broken shell? To them, they all seem interesting, especially if they have not seen them before and they discovered them themselves – even better.

The natural mindfulness of early childhood can allow our precious children to sink into moments of natural transcendence. This is an exquisite state where time stands still and they are in complete oneness. The more times our little ones are able to experience this natural state, the more likely they are to seek it later in life. It can become a source of refuge and of mental and emotional sustenance, which is especially important for our rooster girls learning to settle themselves. I was raised on a farm and spent many hours in nature in an unhurried way. As a rooster girl who was often shouted at and shamed, I used nature as my friend, my safe base and a sanctuary to restore my mind, heart and body.

PARENTS AND EDUCATORS' SURVEY

One early morning my little seven-year-old climbed into bed with me and said to me 'Open up your arms Mummy and let me come in.' She wanted to have a little snuggle.

The search for authentic identity

Professor Susan Greenfield, in her book *ID: The Quest for Meaning in the 21st Century*, writes about her concerns that the busyness and the 'fun-focused' pressures on childhood can impact how our children's brains and minds are shaped. To create a unique sense of self, she argues, children need to be marinated in mindfulness moments and child-led experiences – like independently exploring nature – so they can pause, ponder and think deeply. This creates opportunities for the natural 'aha' moment where they can make connections or see their experiences in a different or wider context. Over time these experiences gradually shape and personalise the brain, and guide the growth of a girl's unique identity and sense of self – her mind. Professor Greenfield has strong concerns that the immediacy and instant nature of screens, together with the absence of time spent pondering and exploring, is changing how our children's minds are being formed. Children need a diversity of experiences to learn how to *think deeply* and develop their mind.

If we're serious about creating an environment that allows our girls to discover who they are, and find meaning and purpose, then we need to ensure that girlhood has time to develop. Rather than schedule too many activities and expectations, maybe we need to allow spaces to dawdle, to explore, to ponder, to discover and to create.

The search for identity can take a lifetime, however, we can nurture this in our little girls from a young age. In fact, it is essential, given that so many girls grow up believing their identity is about their appearance rather than their whole being. In his book *The Inner Self*, social psychologist Hugh Mackay writes that if we are truly *to respect* who we are, we first have to work out *who we really are*. In the science of child development, the concept of 'theory of mind' means we begin to shape this in the early years. Around the age of five, children realise that the way they see the world – their beliefs and desires – is unique and different to how others see it.

We can help our rooster girls understand what is unique about their temperament and how it can shape their identity, while nurturing their ability to develop empathy and self-awareness.

Characteristics of our lamb girls

Lamb girls are typically quieter, more patient, considerate and accommodating and less demanding. As babies, they tend to love sleeping and seem to be less energetic in their toddler and preschool years.

Our lambs can:

- dislike noise and too much stimulation
- be very sensitive to being sanctioned or spoken to with loud voices
- keep their comforter like a blanket or a teddy bear well into childhood
- often like their own solo quiet time
- be very patient and can wait while roosters go first
- get distressed easily by strange people, places and things
- prefer routines and predictability in their lives
- tend to prefer smaller numbers of children to play with
- take longer to adjust to change

- take longer to warm up in social settings even if they are familiar
- tend to withdraw when they feel frightened or upset
- often like to hide in their bed or a cupboard when distressed
- struggle with social dislocation more than roosters, especially starting a new school, different teacher or change of home or relationships
- lack assertiveness and be slower at making decisions
- struggle with 'shyness'.

One of the key messages for raising our little lamb girls is to resist the temptation to want to toughen them up. Forcing them to be braver *before they can be braver* can create even more anxiety, which can make them even more fearful in the future. You can help your daughter grow in confidence by role-playing scenarios as she grows in courage in her own time. If possible, avoid calling her 'shy'; labels can take quite some time to remove.

One of the best ways to build her personal courage and confidence in social situations is to create opportunities where she plays with the same children, preferably multi-age children, in a familiar environment with familiar grown-ups. Over time, she will build confidence and often unconsciously copy behaviours of the older, more confident children.

One of the most common mistakes I see parents of lambs make is they assume they are weak just because they are sensitive. When lambs are nurtured with love and connection, they can be very determined and capable. They can also grow to be fearless and brave without needing validation or celebration from the wider world.

It can be tempting to compare your little lamb to rooster children, whether they are siblings, friends or classmates. Your precious little girl is a one-off miracle and your job is to create an environment that will allow her to grow and flourish. This may mean making choices that others may question, and you need to trust your parental instincts. For instance, you might choose to delay her starting big school because you feel in your gut that a little more time may help her transition with more bravery and confidence.

I have worked with many lamb teens who struggled to live in a family with shining, confident rooster children. Identifying and supporting their strengths to grow early on can give them confidence and a strong inner sense of self that will help them stand tall in their own shoes rather than endlessly comparing themselves to their siblings. Look for small opportunities to develop mastery as early and as often as possible. Simple things like dressing themselves, tying shoelaces and making their own snacks all build inner confidence and competence. Gradually keep adding other competencies in the playground and house, like cooking pancakes, helping grandparents with simple tasks and helping younger siblings.

MAGGIE'S MAIN IDEA
Every new experience of mastery will make a difference in your lamb daughter's sense of herself and her abilities in her world.

The truth about rewards and praise

Another mistake I have seen parents of sensitive children make, even though it is coming from a place of great love, is the overuse of praise and rewards. Parents may say things to their children like 'good smiling' or 'that's an awesome drawing'. Many parents tell me that they overuse praise because they cannot remember being praised as children. Others have told me that they don't want to damage their sensitive child's self-esteem by telling them no, or expressing displeasure.

Sadly, in many homes and schools, we have been conditioned to believe that rewarding our children with stickers, certificates, treats and trophies is the way to improve their behaviour. This rewarding of good behaviour and punishing of poor behaviour comes from the work of BF Skinner and was called 'operant conditioning'. The science of child development has come to show that this is not effective long term and can compromise the fundamental need of children for connection and relational safety. In fact, little girls, who have emotional maturity often much earlier than we could possibly believe, can also feel manipulated by too much praise! Dr Helen Street, a social psychologist and a leading advocate for positive psychology in our school communities, has argued strongly that many school-based practices in Australia are based on misconceptions and are ineffective and unhelpful.

Alfie Kohn certainly doesn't hold back in his concerns about the damaging effects of giving children extrinsic rewards or praise to encourage better behaviour. In his book *Unconditional Parenting*, he proposes that we need to encourage children to develop an inner locus of control, which means they do things because they are motivated by themselves rather than by something external. Children do not need to be rewarded for sitting down to watch their favourite cartoon show or to play a favourite game, because the immediate reward is of feeling good and experiencing a positive emotion.

Kohn argues that, in the long-term, praise tends to set our children up to not only need a sweetener to do more challenging tasks, but also to look for our approval when they make decisions. Our words of praise don't just tell our child what she has done well, they show her that we approve of her actions. Maybe this is one way our little girls learn that they should do things to please others, or for approval, instead of for themselves? They can also form negative beliefs and mindsets about their worth and value that they will carry forward in life.

Kohn cites quite convincing research that children who are praised often become 'praise junkies' and even as adults continue to rely on other people for validation because they are unable to give it to themselves. Indeed, he quotes one study that showed that if you praise a child for being kind you actually reduce the chances of them being kind again. Ouch!

The good news is that regular acknowledgement and encouragement are better ways to let little girls know that our love is unconditional, regardless of the choices they make. This also encourages them to make choices that make them feel good.

We still want them to know the difference between good choices and poor choices, and often non-verbal encouragement is easier and more effective. The more connected and valued that children feel, the less they need to seek external praise and validation.

Encouragement can be such a deceptively powerful influencer in all our lives. Giving our children permission to give things a go and to be persistent are wonderful traits to model. It's also okay to ask if they need our help to master a task that is beyond them, rather than just swooping in to help (much as we want to!). Ways to give positive acknowledgement include:

- Smile often at them, wink and give a thumbs up
- Say hello using their name or term of endearment
- Say, 'I'm glad to see you' or 'I missed you today!'
- Suggest, 'Let's go play together'
- Ask them to show you how to do a puzzle
- Give them a gentle pat on the head/back
- Hug them if appropriate
- Ask about their favourite toy
- Sing together, especially favourite songs
- Hold their hand or put your hand on their shoulder
- Have welcoming, farewell and bedtime rituals.

Say things like:

- 'Thank you for helping me clean up the toys'
- 'I noticed you washing your hands after going to the toilet'
- 'I know how hard it is to be patient when you play with others'
- 'I can see how much effort you put into that – well done'
- 'Disappointment sucks – and it's okay. Everyone has moments of disappointment.'
- 'You are so much more than grades and test results!'

Let me make a confession. I did use praise as a parent, though not endlessly, and (oh dear) I was also known to offer bribes using chocolate – both things researchers now warn us against. Transitioning from a praise and reward system to positive acknowledgement can be difficult, and it takes time. Keep in mind the 80/20 rule – it's what we do 80 per cent of the time that matters, and in that 20 per cent of the time, we teach our children that there is no perfection in life, and that good enough is okay.

Soothing those frightened butterflies

Many lambs have a stronger need to be comforted and reassured. As early as possible, prioritise spending time building comforting patterns with your little lamb daughter, whether that be through soothing lullabies, nightlights, white noise, teddy bears, special blankets, massage and bedtime routines. All of these can help to build stronger neural connections that help calm the developmentally normal anxieties of early childhood. The more that we prioritise meeting the unique needs of our little ones in a soothing manner, the stronger their stress-regulating systems will grow. The more distress our girls experience in the first five years of life, the more likely they will be to struggle more with stress in later years.

Be mindful not to think they may be too old for some of their comforters as they grow older. I have met many teenage girls who still cuddle their teddy bears when they feel sad or worried. Maybe we need to reassure our little lamb girls that you're never too old for a teddy!

Safe place to be

Sensitive children tend to struggle more with social dislocation than more confident children. By this I mean change that involves new environments with new people, whether that be starting big school, moving house, moving suburb, parents divorcing or living through a pandemic! Spend time explaining to your sensitive child that feeling anxious when change happens is normal and okay, and that you are always there to help them in these difficult times.

There are times when our lambs can find the world too stimulating or overwhelming and need a safe place to retreat. I have heard of many lambs who hide under their beds, in their beds or in cupboards when life just gets a bit too much. I encourage parents to help them create a space where they can seek refuge. Maybe a cushion she can rest her head on, or a special small soft toy that waits for her in a special space. The more positively we see this behaviour, the more soothing it will be for the child. Many lamb children quite simply have less energy than their rooster siblings or friends. When they feel low, time for a pause or rest can help them restore their energy.

It can also be helpful to find a safe place to be outside the home. I had a special place under a fig tree that always welcomed me and made me feel safe. I also believe having a resting chair somewhere around the home is a wonderful thing. This resting chair needs to be comfortable and in a quiet space. If grown-ups can sometimes be found on that resting chair because they were feeling a little stressed or unhappy, we model for our children that it's okay to find a place to pause, to rest, to reflect and to regroup.

> When our children perceive us as steady and calm – regardless of their mood or behaviour – they can relax, knowing that they can rely on us to get them through challenging moments of their life.
> – Susan Stiffelman, *Parenting Without Power Struggles* (2012)

Given that our sensitive little lamb girls can be less brave and confident, it is important to gradually stretch their sense of comfort rather than to completely avoid social situations. Taking her to familiar places is a great place to start. If possible, taking her with you to the one coffee shop rather than different ones will gradually build her sense of confidence. If she has an older sibling, taking her to day care drop-offs, school assemblies or extracurricular activities can be helpful, even if she has to be on your hip!

Small playgroups are wonderful for our sensitive lambs. They often struggle with large numbers of children at any age, so it can be helpful to allow gradual stretching and growing. As with our rooster girls, I am a huge advocate for outdoor play opportunities with multi-age children. For our little lambs and neurodivergent children, this can be especially helpful if it is with familiar adults and in familiar places. In these settings, children can gradually step away from their parents when they are ready because the other grown-ups are already familiar. The children are also familiar, and younger children often learn a lot more from older children in play settings than they do from their parents! Sensitive girls may frequently revisit their safe grown-up before returning to play many times. As the wonderful Circle of Security program shows, this is a natural way for our children to grow in confidence in social settings outside of the home.

Another suggestion is to explain the difference between assertiveness and aggression. She will experience dominating rooster children – and grown-ups – throughout her life. We need to help her learn to speak up for herself and be assertive when she feels she is being treated poorly, disrespectfully and hurtfully. We also need to reassure her that sensitive lambs are just as deserving of love, affection and acceptance as rooster children, even if they don't attract or desire as much attention.

The good news for our sensitive girls is that they are often born with a temperament that is inherently caring and considerate, and often there is a deep-seated desire to help others. Make sure they see this as a strength, and give them opportunities to build on this capacity to be caring. We need to also remind them that they need to prioritise caring for themselves, not just everybody else! This is one of the girlhood conditionings that many older women still struggle with. As we cannot give from an empty cup, parents and especially mothers need to model a cup-filling activity that they do each week. It might be a coffee catch-up, a yoga class, art or music. This also needs to be done guilt free!

Even though our temperament tendencies come from our DNA, and we can identify that we have a strong rooster or a gentle lamb, we need to help our little girls to develop the positive and healthy attributes of both archetypes. If they stay stuck at the rooster end of the continuum, they can become self-absorbed, arrogant and have a tendency to bully others. If they are stuck at the lamb end of the continuum, they can become victims and feel powerless to stand up for themselves or create a positive life. There is no question that the world celebrates confident roosters who can cope easily with life. A key message for our rooster girls is that they can be fierce and strong while still being thoughtful and considerate. We also need to encourage our sensitive little girls to recognise that they are equally valid and just as important. Experiences and guidance can help your daughter create a unique personality, whatever her dominant temperament.

PARENTS AND EDUCATORS' SURVEY

She always snuggled into her middle brother's cot when he was a baby.

KEY POINTS

- We want our children to be capable of being strong and confident and thoughtful and considerate. Many children are a mix of rooster and lamb from birth.
- Social expectations and norms are an incredibly powerful influence on our little girls.
- Rooster girls can be very challenging to raise and helping to build empathy in the early years is really important.

- It can be helpful to speak to roosters the same way you would speak to an adult who you love and respect.
- Avoid using threats with roosters, especially at the end of a long tiring day.
- Focus on nurturing the relationship, modelling kindness and thoughtfulness and show her respect.
- Lamb girls are typically quieter, more patient, considerate and accommodating and less demanding.
- Avoid too much praise and too many rewards.
- Many lambs tend to have a stronger reliance on ways to be comforted and reassured, and we need to respect this for as long as they need it.
- Allow lambs to stretch their sense of comfort at their own pace, with small steps of mastery.
- Avoid comparing lambs to roosters.
- Many lamb girls can be sensitive and yet very strong.
- Emotional coaching can help girls navigate the world, regardless of tendencies of temperament.

7

The dandelion
and orchid influence

One thing I have discovered as a parent, counsellor and teacher is that some children just seem to cope with life more easily than others. Many years ago, I read W. Thomas Boyce's *Orchids and Dandelions: Why Some Children Struggle and How All Can Thrive*. Dr Boyce had been a paediatrician for over four decades and became aware of the differences, or 'unevenness', in individual children's health and development right from birth. Some children just seem to have a special capacity to thrive, even in the presence of adversity, while others appear to struggle much more even with small challenges.

His research suggested that the variance he noted was attributable 'not to innate traits that a child is born with, but to differences in children's relative biological susceptibility to the social context in which they live and grow, both the negative and the positive'. Put simply, some children have a kind of 'biological indifference' to adverse experiences because their stress response circuits are just not as reactive as those of more sensitive children. Boyce labelled the children dandelions and orchids, as dandelions are flowers that exist in almost any environment and tend to thrive regardless of hardship, while orchids can be tricky to grow and are very delicate, as well as susceptible to more diseases and challenges even in nurturing and safe environments.

Much research has built on Boyce's work since he first put forward this theory in 1995, and the good news is that the research shows that while there may be a genetic predisposition towards sensitivity, the influence of nurture is really significant. With awareness and conscious choices to support our children (particularly our orchids), they can all thrive.

We can imagine this sensitivity as another continuum that you may need to consider when trying to understand your unique little girl. Not only will she have some rooster/lamb tendencies, she may also have some dandelion/orchid characteristics. Rather than being concerned with labels, you can simply be more mindful of the characteristics, tendencies and influences that your daughter may be displaying *so you can meet her needs*. Creating a supportive environment with realistic expectations and strong relational safety are the keys to raising your daughter to be her healthy unique self.

Little lambs and dandelions

I do not explore lamb–orchid girls in-depth in this chapter. Orchid tendencies tend to align with lamb tendencies, which include being less brave and more sensitive. Much of what I wrote about lambs in Chapter 6 will apply to the lamb–orchid. All parents want to build competence in all the areas that can impact their children's lives, intellectually, emotionally and socially, and from early in life, the special needs of the lamb–orchid little girl will be easy to spot. See Chapter 16 for key strategies that can help these gentle souls.

As for our dandelion little girls – whether they are roosters or lambs – they will tend to adapt and cope with life with little effort. They will thrive if they have secure attachment to safe grown-ups and live in an environment without the threats of abandonment, abuse and/or deprivation. Resilience research shows they will also survive these adverse childhood experiences and trauma better than orchid children, provided they have one person who always has their back and never gives up on them.

Your rooster–orchid little girl

When the sensitive, tricky nature of orchids combines with the feisty nature of roosters, we find ourselves faced with the rooster–orchid child, a combination that most parents find challenging.

Rooster–orchid girls can struggle emotionally, particularly around feeling invalidated, not good enough and ignored. For a rooster, these orchid traits of feeling vulnerable can create some serious inner emotional turmoil.

You will know if you have a rooster–orchid girl by the frequency and intensity of her distress in highly emotional times. These little girls can have long meltdowns over very small things and it can be really confusing and frustrating for their parents to work out how to help. From ages two to four, which is a time when they are seeking their own sense of identity and autonomy, the tiniest bit of *perceived resistance* from parents can mean the whole nervous system completely discharges excess stress hormones and neurochemicals. This can happen with the wrong colour cup, not being allowed to get into the car seat by themselves (a favourite in our family), or resisting the much-needed afternoon nap. The rooster part of the personality is about seeking their *own choices*, even if they are completely irrational because they are still young children, and this is developmentally appropriate. The orchid part of the child will tend to be less resistant to the body's messages of needing a nap. Let's be honest, it can be incredibly frustrating for a parent of a rooster–orchid girl who has chosen to resist a routine that helps her manage her life better! One of my granddaughters fought her afternoon nap at around three years of age and for many rooster children, that is coming from a serious case of FOMO. They just want to make sure they don't miss out! My son would take her for a leisurely drive in the early days of her resistance and most times, she fell asleep. However, it did not take her long to realise that that was exactly what Daddy was trying to do and no matter how tired she was, she refused to fall asleep on those long drives. She even would make suggestions on which roads she thought her daddy should take while he was trying to get her to fall asleep!

PARENTS AND EDUCATORS' SURVEY

Our fourth child and daughter is not one to be left behind. With a 10 year gap between our eldest and her she wants to be a big kid too. We found her on the toilet – she had seemingly decided to success-fully toilet train herself as she gave up waiting for her parents to see that she was ready. Age two-and-a-half years.

The rooster–orchid meltdown

I often hear from parents worried about a normally confident rooster daughter who may still be having extremely volatile meltdowns lasting up to an hour. While meltdowns and tantrums are developmentally normal in the early years, as children grow in their ability to manage big feelings with immature brain architecture, these meltdowns seem particularly hot (and often involve piercing screaming). The first thing we need to keep in mind is that this is a sign that a little girl has a flooded nervous system full of the stress hormone cortisol. As we explored in Chapter 3, every child is trying to navigate their body budget, or how much energy they have available in each moment. This process involves the brain and the body in a constant feedback loop. When our daughter's body budget is depleted or empty, she can become completely flooded or drained. She is biologically wired to release this hormone and, provided we create a safe enough environment for her to do so, this can still be seen as a normal part of early childhood.

There is still a perception that a little girl should be learning to control her big feelings better from three to six and that after this age, *there is an intentionality to her meltdown and that she should be able to stop.* If you have a daughter who is struggling with this, please remember she is not being bad or naughty – she is struggling to cope, and it is probably because she is more of an orchid than a dandelion. With the knowledge that orchid children can particularly struggle with high levels of stress and tension, we can understand that children aren't intentionally choosing to have a meltdown. *Orchid children seem to have a higher reactivity and sensitivity to when their body budget is struggling*, because their brains are often triggered by a small threat in the same way they are by a serious threat to survival. When a child is in this red zone of distress, they can struggle to hear because the sympathetic nervous system is in full flight. Indeed, a parent trying to talk to a child in this state can often escalate the distress. We should also be aware that some orchid girls may have a different response to distress; instead of a meltdown, they may become hypervigilant, which sadly can show up as overcompliance where a girl becomes desperate to please others.

Interoception gives us some fabulous insights into why some children – possibly those with a strong capacity for understanding and managing their energy levels – thrive, while others struggle. I have had many occupational therapists who specialise in the area of sensory integration explain that there are so many things that can overload a sensitive child's nervous system. Some have sensory processing challenges, while others have difficulty recognising and understanding things in the world around them, which impacts their capacity to predict how they can stay safe. This can exhaust them, and we know that tired children have a harder time coping.

Endless reassurance and strengthening her connection to her safest grown-ups are the best way to help her manage these really big, hot releases. She needs to be heard, and sometimes her sensitivity can make it hard for her to make sense of her world. Please prioritise having unhurried, real conversations with her one-on-one.

If these major meltdowns are happening several times a day, please have a chat to your family doctor or health professional who specialises in the area of regulation and anxiety just in case there is an underlying health issue. Vision issues, sensory issues, hearing issues, tonsils/adenoids are just a few examples of things that may impact on your child's capacity to cope. Trust your parental instincts and never be afraid to explore things more deeply.

Love bridges and micro-connections

The number one fundamental need of all children is to feel loved and secure. Dr Delahooke explores the complex interaction between the brain and the body via the nervous system, which constantly influences the way we all feel, act and think. She calls this *the platform*. This is useful in understanding dandelions and orchids and their sense of feeling loved and safe.

> A sturdy platform supports optimal behaviours and strengthens the child's capacity to be flexible, think and make decisions. A vulnerable platform on the other hand increases a child's wariness, fear and defensiveness.
>
> – Dr Mona Delahooke, *Brain-Body Parenting* (2022)

One of the ways a parent can strengthen an orchid girl's platform is through warm connection. The sensitivity around feeling less loved or unloved can be addressed through building 'love bridges' through micro-moments of loving connectedness.

Dr Gordon Neufeld and Dr Gabor Maté have written about the concept of having 'soft hearts' towards our children, and teaching them to have soft hearts, which means *they feel their feelings* rather than simply *having their feelings*. Our orchid daughters certainly benefit from soft hearts from their key grown-ups. The authors believe that so much of the way we live our lives today creates experiences of separation for our young children, rather than creating experiences that connect and bond us to our children.

PARENTS AND EDUCATORS' SURVEY

I always find little 'I love you mumma' notes scattered through my work book and diary.

If you have been struggling to find large amounts of quality time with your little ones, then I certainly have some good news. Micro-connections are much smaller connections of love and tenderness that can be spread throughout the day. Sometimes just joining their pretend play for a short time, by being a patient while they are playing doctors, or by ordering an ice cream if they are playing shops will be a much-needed top-up to their love cup.

MAGGIE'S MAIN IDEA

There are many ways, some really tiny, that build a heart connection.

Sharing little chats and conversations is another way of micro-connecting with your daughter. I was blessed to spend hours of my childhood in the farm ute, driving around the farm with my dad as a captive audience for my endless chatter and questioning him about everything. No wonder he struggled with his hearing as he got older! However, I knew I was loved.

PARENTS AND EDUCATORS' SURVEY

Age six. I love the random chatter and stories she comes up with on a daily basis. Can be really hard to know what is true!

Building love bridges with your little girl

Children who feel loved through having a full love cup or a strong heart connection will feel safer and more secure. The more loved they feel, the safer they feel and the calmer their nervous system will be. Here are some ideas for making a micro-connection:

- Wink at her more often, make funny faces, give her high fives or thumbs ups – non-verbal messages of connection.
- Give small symbols to hold on to in your absence like a kiss in her hands or hearts drawn on the back of her hands.

- Create a bedtime ritual. 'I love you more than . . .'
- Send her imaginary rainbows when you are away.
- Create a small jar of captured kisses from all the people who love her.
- Create an imaginary giant protector/guardian angel to watch over her.
- Have a picture of you with your child in a locket or plastic sleeve she can keep in her bag when at day care or school.
- Record readable stories or bedtime rituals on smartphones if you're away and have them on the phone of the parent who is staying home.
- Take small bites out of her toast or a bite out of her sandwich and say there is a love bug in the house.
- Leave notes or funny pictures in her lunchbox or on the bathroom mirror or write messages of love on a banana.
- Create moments of lightness and laughter often.
- Hide special messages of love and hope around the house when you go away.
- Spontaneously join in dress-ups, drawing or colouring in.
- Join her on the couch randomly to watch a favourite show (or many episodes).
- Engage in spontaneous hugs, cuddles and tickles.

If you have an orchid daughter, prioritise filling her love cup. This may mean at times you step over the washing pile, ignore unanswered emails, resist checking the latest news on Insta or WhatsApp and instead build some love bridges with your precious sensitive daughter – it is never too late!

Emotions that rooster–orchids can struggle with

Your highly spirited rooster girl can really struggle with emotions like feeling unnoticed, excluded or ignored – this is again a combination of the rooster and orchid influence. She perceives that she is not being recognised as being important enough and this can trigger really big emotions, and her ability to manage them is less efficient than a dandelion child.

One of the key things that can trigger big feelings is jealousy – sensing *she is loved less* than a sibling or friend, or that there is one parent who is not loving her enough. If her nervous system is already overloaded with other stressors like unmet needs, even a small perception of invalidation can trigger the meltdown. This meltdown may have more to do with what happened at day care or school than what happened at home, and she may have held a lot of emotional tension in until she could get to her safe place – home.

Another emotion that can be triggering for the rooster–orchid child is embarrassment. This can happen quite spontaneously where they feel they are being seen as less capable, less important or that they have made a mistake. Externally this looks very similar to when they feel incredibly jealous and it important in your emotional coaching with your rooster–orchid daughter that you help her work out the difference between the two. She may learn to navigate these big emotions in similar ways, however, she needs to understand the differences. In Chapter 16 there is more information about helping her learn to sail through these moments and recover.

Some rooster–orchid little girls can struggle with emotional intensity, even with positive emotions like anticipation, excitement and enthusiasm. The lead-up to a birthday party or Christmas can be quite volatile because their enthusiasm can exhaust them or overstimulate the nervous system. Parents can help by tempering their own enthusiasm and excitement as a model for our little girls. I have had a few parents comment on how disappointed a toddler daughter was when their baby sibling arrived. The parents' enthusiasm about the upcoming birth had filled their daughter with anticipation, but in reality it takes quite a long time before you can play with your sibling!

While there is some research that suggests girls can understand and articulate their emotions more easily than little boys of the same age, sometimes the expression of their big ugly feelings in the moment can feel really hurtful for parents. Some intense, feisty little girls can verbalise how much they hate their parents, how they would like to live somewhere else or how they never want to speak to their loving parent ever again! These words are often expressed very loudly and frequently.

Heartbreaking! It can be helpful to remember that these words are your little girl's way of trying to communicate how *big* her ugly feelings are. Remember that as orchid children, they are particularly susceptible to responding to many sensory inputs and many of these pressures are invisible to them and their parents. Often, blaming their parents can be a way of coping. We need to be careful not to see these moments as a sign that we are failing as parents or that there is something wrong with our daughter.

I know of some little girls who have discovered for themselves that running to their bedroom, slamming the door and snuggling on their bed with their favourite comforter blanket or teddy helps them better than a well-meaning parent trying to soothe them. Remember that while they are in a volatile storm, our main task is not to join them in the storm but to create a safe base for them to return to once it's passed. In time, your daughter will work out what works best for her and that too may change as she grows older and matures.

MAGGIE'S MAIN IDEA

Even though our little girls are generally better able to articulate their big emotions than boys are, they can be further triggered by their parents' well-meaning verbal attempts to help.

Keep in mind the metaphor of a glitter jar which, when shaken, spontaneously sees the jar flooded with glitter. When allowed some calm-down time, the glitter will settle on the bottom. When your little one's emotions have settled, it is a much better time to chat to her about her distress. This is also an opportunity to problem-solve with her some strategies that might help the next time the glitter jar gets all shaken up – ways she may manage those big feelings in a less volatile way. Notice, I did not suggest you tell her what she needs to do next time. Instead, help her work out her own solutions to these challenging moments.

> **MAGGIE'S MAIN IDEA**
> Taking immediate deep breaths, bending knees and placing a hand on their heart and imagining breathing in a sky-blue colour will soothe their reactive nervous system.

I also suggest teaching these strong, sensitive children to tap frequently on the side of the nail on the middle finger with their thumb. This can help diffuse tension especially around frustration and anger. See www.eftdownunder.com for more on tapping.

I have noticed that these often-volatile little girls, when regulated, can be very empathetic and pick up the emotional distress of others, including their parents. They will often start crying if a younger sibling has been hurt, if they witness distress in a parent, or if a friend is sad or angry. As they grow older, they will learn ways of managing healthy boundaries around the big feelings of others. However, it does take time.

PARENTS AND EDUCATORS' SURVEY

At a birthday party with an ice cream cake our six-year-old daughter asked if we could save one of the spare pieces for her little brother (party still going and he was >20mins away at home). I had to smile – how heartwarming is the innocence and kind heartedness of our little girl!

Perfectionism in the rooster–orchid

Many rooster children, especially little girls, are wired to strive to continually better themselves. They are often dissatisfied with achieving the same level as others, whether that be an academic goal, sporting goal or a bettering their sibling goal. There is definitely a healthy sense of self striving for improvement that we can encourage in our girls. However, they have been getting messages for a long time about what they need to do to be accepted.

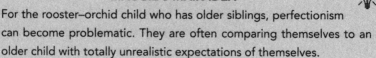

MAGGIE'S MAIN IDEA

For the rooster–orchid child who has older siblings, perfectionism can become problematic. They are often comparing themselves to an older child with totally unrealistic expectations of themselves.

A sign that your rooster child may be striving too hard with unrealistic expectations is that they are seldom content with any tasks they attempt. I know of rooster–orchid children who do a homework task many times, striving to do it better each time. This can be a sign they are developing *an unhealthy sense of perfectionism*, which can happen when they have been overpraised about outcomes rather than the process. An example of this is being told that a little girl is 'clever', which does seem quite harmless. However, even clever girls can make mistakes, because cleverness is not fixed. In her work exploring mindsets, Dr Carol Dweck found that some children who were told they were clever could struggle significantly in high school as academic expectations increased.

Having a fixed mindset or belief can definitely create problems in the adolescent years. Sometimes these can create unrealistic expectations when children compare themselves to others. Keep reminding your rooster–orchid daughter that practice can improve performance and that sometimes good enough is good enough – this is a more flexible mindset. If your daughter is striving for perfection with her homework and it is taking a lot of time, please communicate with her teacher so that both of you can help her feel more comfortable with her genuine effort. Unhealthy perfectionism can also increase the chances of procrastination with your daughter, which can create a whole new level of anxiety.

Another sign that your rooster–orchid is overly invested in striving to be better is that they seldom seem content in their life. Not only might they express negative feelings about themselves, but they can often get into a pattern of blaming others for things they are unhappy about – especially siblings, parents, teachers and coaches. Blame is a scapegoat that needs to be tamed for our rooster–orchid kids. Sometimes this type of unhealthy perfectionism shows up as endless whingeing and whining.

I have worked with a number of girls whose perfectionism was driven by a need for parental approval. Given that managing stress and pressure at school are consistently given as two of the main challenges of being an adolescent, according to Mission Australia's Annual Youth Survey, we need to have a serious conversation with our little girls about effort being most important. Please tell them that we will love them fiercely and unconditionally even if they don't graduate high school or win the swimming carnival, or if they need to be picked up from a party because they got drunk. This is the message every child needs to hear, especially in our heavily competitive and award-driven world.

What can help our rooster–orchid daughters to thrive?

The best place to start in empowering your sensitive rooster daughter is to start early in steeping her in opportunities to fail, and as often as possible. This will help her build strategies to manage setbacks and disappointments that she can take forward into life. It is fantastic if her parent or parents model how they manage disappointment. If you have spilled some milk, or dropped something, in as light a tone as possible say, 'Oh dear, whoopsie!' or 'Oh no, never mind', or even, 'Now that's interesting!' Avoid at all costs the OMG! response, or using a loud, expressive voice. We can temper our emotional response with what we say after we fail or muck up. The more expressive our response, the more our nervous system floods with stress hormones. The calmer our response, the less our nervous system floods. Essentially, it is what we do as humans *after* we experience failure that really matters.

Some other things that you could teach your daughter to say in these moments are:

- 'Ah well, that didn't go as planned'
- 'This won't go down in history as my finest hour'
- 'Must've forgotten my lucky undies today'
- 'This too will pass'
- 'Now, I never saw that coming!'

Memorise one or two of these to say to yourself as quickly as possible after you have experienced a poor choice or mistake that can trigger feeling inadequate and incapable. These suggestions can work with our lamb–orchid little girls as well.

Our rooster–orchid girls can be very deep, and it can be really helpful to create regular opportunities in similar locations to have the big chats. These chats may take quite some time, and you may go over things several times before the clarification that you or your daughter are seeking occurs. Bath chats, pillow chats, cubby chats or one-on-one chats while walking or in the car. The key is it has to be one-on-one and not be rushed, and you need to be fully present. Ensure your phone is nowhere nearby because an alert from your phone could create some serious feelings for your sensitive, strong little girl. These chats are incredibly important at helping your little girl build an understanding of how she can be sensitive while keeping her heart open and her spirit strong. Remember to remind her of her unique strengths when you have these conversations, and avoid making them about things she needs to improve or she will simply stop participating.

The importance of lightness and laughter

In resilience studies in homes, schools and communities, having a sense of humour has been recognised as a protective factor. Helping our orchid children to cultivate a healthy sense of humour can be incredibly important to support them in emotionally challenging moments. Put simply, laughter triggers positive neurochemicals in the brain and it can help to release cortisol after it has been triggered. Indeed, laughter can transform negative emotional states faster than almost any other strategy or technique.

We know our children are happy when we hear them giggling and laughing. It is one of the most magical sounds you will hear in your life. Just like anything that children learn, they need to hear it and play with it and experience it in order for the brain to know what it is and to anticipate it in a positive way. That means encouraging laughter and lightness in the home.

PARENTS AND EDUCATORS' SURVEY

My little girl is three. She has such an infectious laugh that she can start laughing and everyone joins in.

Funny picture books and riddle books are a great way to bring laughter into your family. I think it's a great idea to have a couple of funny, age-appropriate books in the toilet because little children can take quite some time in there, and reading a few good jokes would be a great way to wait for that poo. To be honest, having a few riddle, fun facts or joke books in the toilet would probably be good for many stressed parents as well! A few of my favourite jokes are:

'No man has ever been shot while doing the dishes.'

'Five out of four people have trouble with fractions.'

'If one synchronised swimmer drowns, does that mean all the others have to?'

'Be careful not to be too open minded – your brains might fall out.'

Seriously, did you have a small smile when you read those? Our orchid girls can often get stuck in their big feelings, so nurturing their sense of humour, and using humour with lightness and laughter, can make a huge difference to their ability to cope with their world.

PARENTS AND EDUCATORS' SURVEY

When she was around two and three, her vocabulary was amazing and her dad came home from work one day and said he was '&$#*ing knackered'. From then on, she would tell everyone and in many situations – supermarket check outs etc. – that she was '&$#*ing knackered'! She is now four-and-a-half.

Sharing simple riddles and jokes with young children is an excellent way to nurture a sense of humour. With my grandchildren, I deliberately change the words of songs that are very familiar to them. In the song 'The Wheels on the Bus', for example, I sometimes sing, 'The cow on the bus goes woof, woof, woof!' The first reaction is always, 'No, they don't, Nanny!!' Then there's always a smile and I keep singing equally ridiculous things.

Another way I have helped my little sensitive grandchildren particularly is to change nursery rhymes. These are some of their favourites:

Jack and Jill went up the hill
to fetch a pail of water
Jack fell down and broke his crown
and Jill said, 'What did you do that for?'

Another one:

> *Little Miss Muffet sat on her tuffet*
> *eating her curds and whey*
> *along came a spider*
> *and sat down beside*
> *and she said, 'Rack off, Hairy Legs!'*

A positive gauge of the wellbeing of a child can be how often they smile and laugh. It is something that is very difficult to fake. As adults, we need to treasure these exquisite moments of joy. The capacity to laugh deeply and in an uninhibited way is another life skill that takes developing and can create an incredibly helpful layer of protection for our sensitive orchid girls.

PARENTS AND EDUCATORS' SURVEY

Her joke-telling ways crack us up. She makes up jokes that make no sense! It's hilarious and we all laugh and giggle.

However, we do need to spend time teaching our children that *laughter works best when we are laughing with people, not at people.* We have to teach them about inappropriate humour that is sexist, racist and misogynistic and that is not something we start teaching them in their tween and teen years. We must start having small chats with them from the time they start developing their sense of humour so they learn that making fun of other children or people is not acceptable.

PARENTS AND EDUCATORS' SURVEY

When she ran down the shopping centre ramp to hide and scare me. She jumped out too early and scared a poor old man. He did see the funny side but it still makes us laugh. We love to jump out and scare each other whenever we can. (Six years old)

The joy of pets

Pets can open our hearts to tenderness and kindness in a way that humans can't, which can be especially important for our rooster–orchid girls who may struggle at times to feel secure with their parents' love and attachment. Pets become a part of the family and they can be incredibly good teachers in the areas of care, tenderness, responsibility and – the big one – unconditional love. No wonder animals are brought into aged care facilities, classrooms and hospitals to help make people smile and feel happy!

I am particularly passionate about having a good dog. A good dog has a special ability to love unconditionally, no matter what happens from day to day. They never have favourites and they don't hold grudges. Indeed, a good dog can be an incredible asset in your home because they can teach without saying a word and they can be the best playmate. A good dog can meet our children's natural exuberance and excitement without any effort. They can chase, run and jump insatiably when we grown-ups have collapsed on the ground. I enjoyed many a calm cup of tea while our fox terrier, Jess, ran the gunk out of my sons' motors – she could dispel any excess cortisol that was in their system.

The act of patting and stroking an animal you love is incredibly calming and connecting. After a tough day at day care or school, our little ones will seek out the family dog and quietly hug and stroke them, and this is exactly what their brain needs to trigger the calming neurochemicals of serotonin and other endorphins.

If you do have space in your home for a pet, please consider getting a good dog who will definitely be an unconditional ally to your sensitive orchid daughter.

PARENTS AND EDUCATORS' SURVEY

When is my daughter happiest?
Cuddling my dog while drawing.

Despite the challenges in raising these strong yet sensitive little ones, know that they are often tomorrow's leaders, change-makers, inventers, entrepreneurs, entertainers and healers. They will have the strength to stand up to the wrongs of the world and find ways to make the world a better place while considering and respecting others. The world needs rooster–orchid children no matter how challenging they can be as children. It will be worth it eventually. I should know . . . I am a rooster–orchid child all grown up!

PARENTS AND EDUCATORS' SURVEY

Her friends call her bossy boots as she has leadership qualities and cares for everyone around her and this gets misunderstood by peers.

Our orchid daughters who have caring, warm and incredibly patient parents and other adults who spend time building their understanding of their 'body budget' can become less reactive and much more like dandelions. There tends to be a significant positive shift when our little girls turn six and that's partly due to increased brain growth in the prefrontal cortex, more experiences in life and a gradual recognition of the things that nurture and support them. There is nothing quite like life experience to both challenge orchids and help them grow new strengths and capacities.

KEY POINTS

- Some children just seem to have a special capacity to thrive even in the presence of adversity while others appear to struggle much more even with small challenges.
- Just like temperament, these tendencies can be influenced enormously by nurture and the experiences following birth.

- Rooster–orchid little girls can be particularly confusing to raise as they can be feisty and strong, and yet extremely sensitive with a high level of emotional volatility!
- Orchid children seem to have a higher reactivity and sensitivity to when their body budget is struggling and they have run out of energy, or they have too much energy or tension in their nervous system.
- Sometimes sensory processing challenges can contribute to some of these additional emotionally distressful times.
- Prioritise having unhurried real conversations with your rooster–orchid little girl, so that she feels noticed, heard, valued and loved.
- Prioritise building micro-connections or love bridges with your sensitive strong little girl as it can continually put more energy into her nervous system.
- Jealousy and embarrassment are two emotions that rooster–orchid little girls can struggle with intensely. They can also struggle with excitement, anticipation and enthusiasm.
- Remember while they are in a volatile emotional storm, our main task is not to join them in the storm but to create a safe base for them to return to once it has passed.
- Remember the metaphor of the glitter jar! Let the glitter settle before exploring whatever may have triggered it.
- Perfectionism that is unrealistic can also become a problem in the lives of our rooster girl, particularly the rooster–orchid girls.
- Help to cultivate a healthy sense of humour in our orchid children.
- Having pets can also be a positive influence in the lives of our orchid daughters especially.
- Real-life experiences with other humans are the best way to help our little girls come to understand the world around them, despite their temperament tendencies.

8

Introverts, extroverts and optimum attention

There are a few other influences that may be helpful in discovering the final pieces of the puzzle that make up your special daughter. These ideas add another layer to our discussion of the rooster–lamb and dandelion–orchid continuums, and they help us understand our little girls with even more nuance.

PARENTS AND EDUCATORS' SURVEY

My daughter will transform herself into a different animal every day. She whispers to me and says what animal she is and what her name will be for the day. She is a delight . . . my sunshine! She is three.

Sensory sensitivity

As a little girl myself, I enjoyed playing outside in nature, especially with imaginary animals and companions. I also spent a lot of time playing with my siblings. In the 1950s and '60s, children played together for many hours at a time at community cricket games, tennis clubs, football games and local golf courses. We tended to play completely unsupervised by adults, and were supervised by the older children in the group. I found myself happy in these places and yet, during adolescence, I didn't enjoy large social happenings with friends and peers! As a teen, I avoided socialising outside of school. It took me a long time to realise that I am much more of an introvert than an extrovert – I wish I had known earlier! I struggled to understand why I declined most invitations to gatherings and parties with my peers and friends. If my energy cup was full, I could navigate familiar environments with familiar people easily. If I was enthusiastic about an event or activity, I could have enough energy to appear like an extrovert but if environments were noisy, I would lose energy and need to leave.

Given that over the last 20 years, I have spent most of my time speaking to large audiences, there may be some people who find this hard to believe. I am so lucky that I am married to a good man who understands and protects my boundaries. After a presentation, I have an absolutely empty cup and unless I can spend some significant quiet time by myself, I am unable to engage socially. I rarely speak to my good man following a speaking event. I am unable to go out for dinner and at conferences, I will decline social invitations. I simply cannot find the energy to navigate a different environment that could be noisy.

In her book *The Highly Sensitive Child*, Elaine Aron writes that around 15 to 20 per cent of every animal population is especially sensitive to their inner and outer environment. She argues that this is because it is helpful for the survival of the species that some of its members are sensitive enough to be able to pay attention to the more subtle warning signs in our environment. Take my sensitivity to sound. Background noise that is quite loud simply drains my energy and overloads my nervous system, and I can seldom stay for more than 15 minutes in such an environment. However, I can enjoy a concert or a theatrical performance, provided the noise level is not too high. Occupational therapists explore the role of how we develop our sensory processing sensitivities, including sound sensitivity. Given that I spent so much of my childhood surrounded by nature – which has a profound quietness – it makes sense that my neural pathways around sound were formed with a sensitivity to background noise. I find all the noisy appliances in our homes today – like the dishwasher, the refrigerator, the microwave and the washing machine – particularly annoying.

Every child has a different way of processing their senses through their sensory receptors, and this can be especially challenging for our neurodivergent children. This is why you may notice neurodivergent children wearing sound-cancelling headphones when in social situations.

Children who are on the sensitive side often have thinner filters through which they perceive the world, which means that lights may seem brighter, sounds may seem louder, smells may seem stronger and looks or comments that might go unnoticed by other children can hurt deeply. Please be careful to avoid urging your daughter to 'toughen up', 'lighten up', or speak to her in ways that make her feel ashamed for being who she is. Highly sensitive children will tend more to the orchid–lamb end of the continuum, however, not always.

Some children are only sensitive to one sensory processing system, while others are sensitive to more than one which can be more difficult. For example, an orchid daughter can be struggling with more than one sensitivity, which is why it so important for parents to help her to identify this and develop coping strategies. Be gentle with your daughter while helping her learn the skills and tools that she can use to navigate environments where her senses are challenged. There are occupational therapists who specialise in sensory processing issues and regulation and I would recommend having your daughter assessed if she is struggling to cope, especially with familiar environments.

Introvert tendencies

As we explore these tendencies, keep in mind that there is never a one-size-fits-all scenario. Your sensitive daughter may have some of the attributes of introversion, but not all of them. There is no question that some children are wrongly labelled 'shy' but – when it suits them and when they feel their energy cup is full – they actually have significantly capable social skills. The main trait of introverts is that they need significant time away from people to renew their energy. Many little introverts can struggle with large settings of children in long day care unless they have a safe space to escape to. This is why I've always recommended a quiet corner or an area like a cubby where introvert children can spend some time alone. Sometimes, an introverted child can fill up their energy cup surrounded by other children, but only if they are completely absorbed in their own creative project or play. Indeed, little girls who choose to play by themselves are often seen through a deficit lens, as though there is a problem. If your little girl is in early childhood and has a tendency to do this, please have a conversation with the educators about the possibility of your daughter being an introvert rather than a child struggling with social skills.

The research suggests that up to 50 per cent of the population are introverts. Sometimes, introverts can be like me, behaving confidently in large social settings. Sometimes they are more reserved yet have the same fundamental needs. I am an introvert who does like to come out and play, especially when there is no background noise to exhaust me!

In her book *The Hidden Gifts of the Introverted Child*, Dr Marti Olsen Laney argues that introverted children are often misunderstood. Their fundamental need to spend time alone, often quietly, gives them plenty of space to ponder, reflect and to 'be'. When they don't get that time and feel overwhelmed or exhausted by their environment, they can appear aloof and unmotivated.

Prior to the digital world arriving, much of their recharge time would have been spent reading, drawing, creating or being mindful. The introverted child can use their quiet time to concentrate and think deeply about some of the complex and confusing things they may discover in their world. They spend much of their time daydreaming or playing in an imaginary world.

Sometimes introverted children have a higher need for their own physical space. I have worked with some children who have pushed and hit other children because they felt crowded. Helping your introverted child to create and respectfully maintain boundaries that suit them is helpful.

PARENTS AND EDUCATORS' SURVEY

She pushes notes under the door of her brother's bedroom while I'm putting him to bed. She wrote me a note last week: *Mum, just letting you know, the cat has a ball of poo hanging from its tail, thanks.* I laughed silently, nearly dying, while I was stuck under a barely asleep toddler.

Dr Laney believes that the signs for introversion or extroversion appear around four months of age. I found this interesting because I once had a conversation with my mum and she told me that sometimes, when she went to pick me up out of my cot, I would turn away and prefer to be left! Apparently, I was the only one of six children who chose my own company at such a young age.

Given that introverted children tend to spend more time thinking and pondering, they can have a higher emotional intelligence (EQ) and be more in touch with their feelings. Sometimes this can be a good thing, but it can mean they drown in big emotions that are difficult to manage.

Dr Laney suggests that introverted children tend to be serious observers of life, including other people and activities. They are much less impulsive and can appear hesitant and cautious, and more energetic and talkative at home where they feel safer. Given this strong connection to the inner world, the introverted child is less likely to follow the crowd, be impacted by peer pressure or try to fit in with social groups because they prefer to trust their own values and standards. Again, this can be misinterpreted when seen from the outside.

Introverts are capable of developing friendships, although fewer friendships and deeper friendships suit them better. Even if they have been playing with their friends, they might wander off on their own when they need to recharge their energy. Given that they have limited social energy, be mindful not to expect them to spend full days playing with other children. This could lead to tears and meltdowns as their nervous system becomes depleted.

PARENTS AND EDUCATORS' SURVEY

Katherine has a friend who has disabilities and cannot speak or walk. When Katherine was two to three and her friend was four to five and didn't have a wheelchair yet, Katherine would bring toys to her, get things and generally help where needed during play so she didn't feel left out. She would also imitate her friend and sit and shuffle on her bottom alongside her rather than walk/run, so they were always at the same level.

Dr Laney argues that introverted children are often better listeners and they might look away when speaking as they gather their thoughts. Introverted little girls can remember conversations in great detail, even ones they are listening into from a distance.

If your daughter has introvert tendencies, reassure her that these are not a deficit or a negative. Help her to work out ways to maintain her energy, especially when she is in large social settings like classrooms and school grounds, and remember to celebrate the gifts that come with being an introvert.

Extrovert tendencies

PARENTS AND EDUCATORS' SURVEY

A concert for a three-year-old kinder with all the other kids standing and singing, while my daughter jumped and danced around while singing her heart out. She'd just turned four. Have the best photo of her in midair with such a mischievous grin!

The world tends to celebrate confident, extroverted personalities, yet children who are extroverts can still struggle to navigate their world.

Extroverts are our social butterflies. They are outgoing, often energetic and they thrive when they are with people. If your daughter is an extrovert, you will know that she will get bored and frustrated if she does not have other children or grown-ups to play with. She fills her energy cup with company and social interaction. Many extrovert children prefer to spend time with older children and grown-ups rather than children of their own age, finding it easy to socialise and mix with children and adults alike. At a family wedding, one of my great-nieces who was aged just 18 months spent a couple of hours on the dance floor with the grown-ups because she is an extrovert rooster. She could also really dance and loved being the life of the party; she seriously shone in her own light.

PARENTS AND EDUCATORS' SURVEY

My almost three-year-old loves to sing 'Let It Go' from the movie *Frozen* and likes to work the dance floor to spend her energy.

Extroverts also tend to be risk-takers who seek new experiences. They often become very enthusiastic and deeply engaged in activities or hobbies they enjoy. Where your introvert child may hover at the edge of social situations, your extrovert child will be the centre of attention within minutes! Many little girl extroverts like to talk a lot, and then some more, and they tend to be verbally good communicators. I have heard some parents tell me their daughter continues to talk in her sleep because she doesn't seem to be able to get enough words out during the day! They seem to be able to function on less sleep than introverted children too, and they often resist falling asleep because they crave social interaction.

Rather than being deep thinkers, extroverts are often quick thinkers and sometimes impulsive. It's like they're in a hurry to live

all of life as soon as possible! They are comfortable being spontaneous and love a challenge, and many extrovert little ones have a
serious case of FOMO. They don't want to miss out on anything
and you can struggle to accommodate all of their desires. If you
have an extrovert daughter, you will feel like you are always organ-
ising her social calendar. Fortunately, they often have more energy
to manage their extracurricular activities than the more sensitive
introvert children.

> **PARENTS AND EDUCATORS' SURVEY**
>
> So many times she makes me laugh out loud with the things she
> says but I forget them. I do remember her singing: 'Grandpa has
> coronavirus, Mummy has coronavirus' etc. to the tune of 'Baby Shark' in
> the middle of Bunnings. Whoops! Haha.

Given that you won't always be able to create fun social activities
and happenings for your extrovert, they can struggle with boredom.
One of the big attractions for extrovert children who get bored easily
when they don't have anyone to interact with is being able to play
in online platforms. As it is not a substitute for real-life interactions,
it's important to limit online interaction until children are at least
five years old or even older. But provided this is done responsibly
and respectfully, and with careful monitoring, it can be a lifesaver
for some parents of extroverts, especially if they are a solo child in
the family.

> **PARENTS AND EDUCATORS' SURVEY**
>
> She is the funniest, most caring little girl. One day, her older male
> cousins were doing pretend karate moves on each other. She sat
> watching for ages. Then she stands up and says, 'I've studied you boys.
> I know what to do now. Can I play?' We all watched them for hours while
> she 'took on the boys'.

Receiving optimum loving attention

Our job as parents is to create the unique environment that best suits our children so they can thrive, be safe, and have their needs met while we love them as unconditionally as is possible. Hungarian paediatrician Emmi Pikler and the wise and wonderful American early childhood educator Magda Gerber both promoted a philosophy of respect and trust when raising small children. We need to respect that *they are already whole beings* and we need to trust that together we can create the relationship that allows our little ones to grow well and healthfully.

Many years ago, I read an interesting article based on the work of these two wise women called 'The philosophy of respect'. The article explored that for each individual, there is an optimal amount of attention – optimum, not maximum. If an individual can get enough attention through connection in warm, respectful relationships, then satisfaction is achieved for both the individual and the primary carer. However, an individual who does not get enough will seek it in a variety of ways early in life by:

- Being attractive to look at
- Being sweet and kind
- Being smart, skilled, capable, competent or talented
- Misbehaving
- Being loud
- Talking a lot
- Talking little
- Being outgoing
- Being shy
- Being sick
- Being helpless.

– Maggie Dent, 9 *Things: A Back-to-Basics Guide to Calm,*
Common-sense, Connected Parenting Birth–8 (2014)

This is most relevant if we have a daughter who is trying to communicate certain unmet needs through her behaviour. As a little girl in a very large family, my need to be loud and to talk a lot makes sense, and I see these various behaviours through this lens.

It is never too late to better understand our children and to guide them to better understand themselves and their own unique strengths and challenges. This is the path to self-acceptance and self-love so our young girls can walk in their own shoes, speak with their own voices and love with their own hearts as openly and honestly as possible.

PARENTS AND EDUCATORS' SURVEY

Our little Miss Three wandered up, placed her little hand firmly on the ironing board I was using, looked me right in the eye, sang, 'A Dream is a Wish Your Heart Makes' at the top of her lungs, finished and promptly said, 'Okay, Mummy, you can clap for me now.'

Birth order

There has been much written about the influence of birth order, but recent research has shown that this influence is much less important than the role of attachment with key caregivers. The New Zealand neuroscience educator Nathan Wallis argues that the firstborn child in any family is at an advantage because they are exposed to more one-on-one experiences with parents, and they would have heard more words. Essentially, he believes any future children in the family are at the same, mild disadvantage. More recent research shows that firstborns can have an intellectual advantage over their siblings, however, there is no statistical evidence of the effects on extroversion, emotional stability, agreeableness, conscientiousness or imagination.

I have shared these extra considerations to help you discover the unique attributes and characteristics of your daughter so you are better able to meet her individual needs and celebrate her gifts and talents. Your next most important job is *to teach your daughter who she really is, and that she matters exactly as she is.* Let her know that you will love her fiercely and unconditionally as she navigates this strange thing called life.

KEY POINTS

- Every child has a different way of processing their senses through their sensory receptors, and this can be especially challenging for our neurodivergent children.
- Please be careful to avoid urging your daughter to 'toughen up', 'lighten up' or speaking to her in ways that make her feel ashamed for being who she is.
- Highly sensitive children can find it harder to handle life's ups and downs without your support.
- Introverted children have different ways of filling up their energy or their 'body budget' than extroverted children.
- Many introverted children feel overwhelmed or exhausted by their environment and can appear aloof and unmotivated, rather than in distress.
- Introverted little girls tend to be serious observers of life or can be called 'the noticers'.
- Extroverted little girls are often social butterflies who are outgoing, energetic and they tend to thrive in the company of others.
- Many extroverted little girls can have a serious case of FOMO and worry about missing out.
- The firstborn child in any family is at an advantage because they are exposed to more one-on-one experiences with their parents.

9

Nurturing her gifts

PARENTS AND EDUCATORS' SURVEY

I am amazed by my daughter's problem-solving capacity, verbal maturity (i.e. use of big words and expletives so appropriately), tuning into other kids' feelings, caring capacity (i.e. for pets, animals, dead bugs?), fine-motor skills (i.e. doing up buttons, turning pages, using scissors), and physical ability – gross motor skills (i.e. sitting, standing, running, jumping, climbing).

In his 1983 book *Frames of Mind: The Theory of Multiple Intelligences*, Howard Gardner proposed that there are eight different intelligences. Since then, critics have argued that his definition of intelligences was too broad and that the eight categories he suggested more likely represented talents, personality traits and abilities. Even so, these eight categories can be helpful in allowing us to understand the innate gifts or talents of our little girls.

Elsewhere in this book, I have explored the metaphor that every child is born with something like a unique blue chip somewhere within their DNA that brings with it certain gifts . . . and often challenges. The sooner we can identify our little girl's unique gifts, the sooner we can create opportunities in a positive environment for her growth. This strength-based approach of parenting is much more effective than the deficit approach, where parents identify what their children can't do and how they can fix it. Giving priority to strengths allows parents to better nurture their little girls and better understand their wants, needs and hidden potentials.

The eight categories of intelligence that Gardner suggests are as follows, including a description of qualities which people who are strong in these intelligences tend to have:

Logical-mathematical intelligence. Good capacity for reasoning, recognising patterns and logical analysis of problems. Tend to think conceptually about numbers, relationships and patterns.

Linguistic-verbal intelligence. Able to use words well in both written and verbal communication. Typically good at writing stories and reading, as well as memorising information they have read or heard.

Visual-spatial intelligence. Good at visualising and particularly skilled with directions and seeing patterns. Can interpret charts, graphs, maps, pictures and videos well. Often enjoy visual arts.

Musical intelligence. Strong capacity for thinking in patterns, rhythms and sounds. Good appreciation for music and also often good at musical composition, singing and playing instruments, and remembering songs and melodies.

Bodily kinesthetic intelligence. Good at body movement, physical control and performing physical actions such as dancing or athletics. Excellent hand-eye coordination and dexterity.

Intrapersonal intelligence. High awareness of one's own emotional states, feelings and internal motivations. Enjoy self-reflection and analysing strengths and deficits. Thoughtful, often tend to explore relationships with others, and engage in critical thinking.

Interpersonal intelligence. Excellent at 'reading' other people, understanding what drives them. Great communicators with capacity to see different perspectives and resolve conflict. Often have positive relationships.

Naturalistic intelligence. Highly attuned to nature, often engaging in outdoor pursuits that nurture and explore the environment. Love learning about plants, animals and ecosystems. Tend to be animal lovers and environmentally aware.

Over time, Gardner identified one more intelligence, and that was existential intelligence, which is a sensitivity and capacity to tackle deep questions about human existence such as what is the meaning of life, why do we die, and how do we get here? Yikes! . . . That sounds a bit like something I used to ponder as a little girl!

Children who find academic learning quite easy could have a combination of logical-mathematical intelligence, linguistic verbal intelligence and visual-spatial intelligence. Then again, school-based learning won't necessarily identify or further the strengths of children who are more gifted with interpersonal and intrapersonal skills, yet these can be incredibly important in our personal and professional lives. Many of us have met doctors who have what we call 'poor bedside manner' because, while they are excellent at their job, they are lousy communicators. This means they may have all the intelligences to help them to be clever, and not the one that helps them communicate in compassionate and caring ways. None of these intelligences are fixed, and we can become more competent in the areas we are not naturally gifted in – which is what the nature versus nurture argument is all about.

In this chapter, we will explore some clues that may help you to identify any of these innate, hidden traits in your daughter – what medical doctor, psychiatrist, clinical researcher, and the founder of the National Institute for Play Dr Stuart Brown calls a 'core truth'.

Working with her to strengthen these skills is an excellent way to build her confidence and competence early in life. It can also help later in life as she makes choices around work and hobbies.

PARENTS AND EDUCATORS' SURVEY

Her dress sense. At about 20 months old, she insisted she had to wear her red dress to day care with her blue tutu underneath and dress herself. Part of the red dress was tucked up in her tutu and she wouldn't let anyone fix it. Then she put on her runners.

Music in her soul

A couple of years ago we had the honour of having one of our granddaughters – then two – stay for a couple of days. She would spontaneously burst into song and could sing 'Jingle Bells' and 'Mary Had a Little Lamb' with expressions to match. She has been making sounds in a rhythmic way since she was a baby, and seems to have music in her soul. Now, as a five-year-old, she often sings as she plays her imaginary games and she's taken to picking up her mum's guitar.

PARENTS AND EDUCATORS' SURVEY

She loves to dance and especially loves to dance in front of the mirror with no clothes on. She will often say, 'Come on, Mummy, dance with your whole body like this'. She's so free and happy.

In our current parenting landscape, where the 'schoolification' of children is such a priority, I wonder if there are children who have music hiding in their souls but don't realise it. When I was in primary school, we did a lot of singing in class – although, sadly for me I was asked to leave the choir in Year 3 for 'not being able to sing'. We also did folk dancing, and there was always a real person playing the piano!

The national emphasis on STEM has me a little worried. Don't get me wrong – science, technology, engineering and maths are important, and our girls particularly need to be encouraged in these areas where they've traditionally not been nurtured, but so too are the arts. We need to keep that A for art in this initiative – STEAM – and this includes music. The research is very strong about the importance of music on the developing brain and for the development of healthy self-regulation. With the overcrowded curriculum, music and singing have been squeezed out to the edges.

Dr Anita Collins has explored what's happening in the first five years of children's lives. She identifies musical elements in the way we speak, with our pitch, rhythm, sound dynamics and timbre all influencing how our little ones come to understand sound and how the brain begins to organise its neural pathways to interpret human voices and sounds in the world around them. Dr Collins argues that sound is food for the brain, especially for babies and toddlers. She calls it a 'cognitive nutrient', with other nutrients including touch, facial expression and eye contact.

Dr Collins also explores the importance of 'parentese', which is the unique way that we speak to babies. The tone is different and there is a distinct melody to how we communicate which is incredibly important in the first year of life. She says significant new research shows how music, especially singing, and using 'parentese' . . .

> . . . may be the most powerful way that we as humans develop connection to the point where it turns into pro social behaviour, the ability to feel empathy and then agency to help others in our tribe. It starts early and simply but it may have a more powerful impact on the humans we grow into than we will ever know.
>
> – Dr Anita Collins, *The Music Advantage* (2020)

In the first years of life, we need to be mindful of the sound environments that we create for our young children. They need sound variety, however, we need to be careful of excessive background noise, as it can tip our little ones into auditory overload. This is one of the reasons some of our sensitive children have spontaneous meltdowns. It took me until my 50s to realise I am extremely sensitive to background noise. Please keep this in mind as you watch your little girls grow. If they put their hands on their ears from time to time, they may be struggling with sound sensitivity.

Music and listening to other people singing has always been a significant part of my wellbeing.

MAGGIE'S MAIN IDEA

Songs and certain pieces of music can evoke positive emotions within us and, in our stressful and busy world, we need to build these healthy neural pathways that connect us quickly to our joy and our delight. Music can do that with the touch of a button.

When I was teaching in high schools, my students were allowed to choose a class song that they could play sometimes during class. The songs were life-enhancing and upbeat, and a student could put the song on when they were feeling flat. I can still remember some of those songs when they come on the radio. Music can link us to memories effortlessly.

PARENTS AND EDUCATORS' SURVEY

She makes up lovely songs about any situation we are in. Singing about butterflies and rainbows and anything beautiful.

When she was three, my daughter got on stage at our church camp and sang 'Twinkle Twinkle Little Star' into the microphone. When she was done she didn't want to let go of the microphone or leave the stage.

My grandfather was a musician who played the piano and the piano accordion at local country dances. Apparently, my siblings would often be asleep in a pram not far from where my grandfather was playing the piano. Sadly, his innate gift failed to pass through into my gene pool. I gave up the recorder in Year 3, which is just as well as I'm sure it scared the family dog and gave my parents headaches! Just because there is music in the family does not mean there is an innate sense of music within the children born in the family.

But there are those who have music as a core truth. Dr Brown shares a beautiful story of Gillian Lynne, who as a child struggled as a classroom learner. She was sent to visit a wise paediatrician who, on completing his assessments, decided he would try one last thing. He put a piece of music on and left the room and, as he watched through a two-way mirror, he saw Gillian begin to move naturally and freely. His recommendation to Gillian's parents was that she needed music and dance in her life. As soon as she took up music and dance, her learning improved. What is particularly beautiful is that as an adult, Gillian Lynne became a well-known dancer and choreographed two of Broadway's most famous shows, *Cats* and *The Phantom of the Opera*.

> When people know their core truths and live in accord with her 'play personality', the result is always a life of incredible power and grace.
> – Stuart Brown, *Play: How it Shapes the Brain, Opens the Imagination, and Invigorates the Soul* (2010)

Please observe your little girls, especially if they naturally move when music is playing or spontaneously burst into song without any provocation. They may have music in their soul and for them to become the best expression of themselves, they need music, singing or dance to become a valuable part of their lives.

PARENTS AND EDUCATORS' SURVEY

My daughter thinks she is Pink!. She wears crop tops, practises acrobatic manoeuvres on our yoga swing and sings at the top of her lungs despite inheriting my terrible voice. I hope she never loses her confidence.

Dance classes

There are so many incredible benefits to little girls doing dance. One of my daughters-in-law is a passionate dance teacher and we have had conversations about the wonder and magic of artistic expression that dance can bring into the lives of little girls. We have also had conversations about concerns that some dance schools are ignoring the damaging effects of sexualising dance. These concerns are shared by Mary Bawden, an American dance teacher and founder of Soul to Sole Choreography and an advocacy and education movement to stop the hypersexualisation of children in dance called DA:NCE (Dance Awareness: No Child Exploited). In an article published by the US-based National Center on Sexual Exploitation, Bawden states her concerns:

> Many young children in dance classes are exposed to sexual moves, sexual ideas, sexual music and sexual costumes that not only sexually objectifies them, but also educates and exposes them to pornographic sexuality.

Mother of a six-year-old girl Inbar Niv discovered that not all dance classes are the same and wrote about her experience for *Child* magazine online. Her own experience as a little girl was quite magical and innocent, and when she signed her daughter up, she was expecting the same experience. At her first dance concert she noticed that:

> All the kids look identical in their sparkly costumes, matching hairdos (most with hair extensions), bright red lipstick, blush and blue eye shadow. The slightly older girls are also sporting eyelash extensions and fake tan. On show are mini-adult costumes, crop tops, feathers and sequins reminiscent of showgirls. They're moving their tiny bodies to Beyoncé and Britney Spears, blowing kisses to an adult audience who understands every word uttered by the divas of pop. The choreography is formulaic, adult and uninspired. It's a mixture

of emotions; some children clearly relish the experience while others appear overwhelmed and even fearful.

As I sit there, I experience a sinking feeling, which soon turns to guilt and eventually anger.

Niv was so concerned by that experience, she eventually set up her own dance school where she ensures there is no early sexualisation, and children are allowed to experience the true magic of dance in its creative and artistic expression. If you are signing your little girl up to a dance class, see if they have photos of previous dance concerts to check that the school has a respectful culture and no pressure to sexualise little girls' experience.

The gift of 'taste'

PARENTS AND EDUCATORS' SURVEY

My daughter asked me the other morning when I was dressing for work if she can have my stockings when I die. (Aged four)

No, this is not the ability to taste different foods. It is the innate ability to appreciate design and fashion from an early age. My good friend, child psychologist and parenting expert Dr Vanessa Lapointe, grew up in rural Canada where, as a little girl, she would spend hours choosing what to wear and how to do her hair. I have seen this in little girls today, some as young as 18 months, who have decided they must wear necklaces when they go out because they want to look 'dressed up'.

I missed this innate gift too, and it wasn't until one of my beautiful nieces, who was 17 at the time, took me aside and gave me some coaching that I started to enjoy clothes. From a very early age, my niece dressed carefully and had an ability to choose certain styles and colours for her bedroom! For those of you who are nodding your head because you have such a daughter, taste is one of her core truths.

Many little girls like to have their fingernails painted, their hair done in certain ways, or to wear certain clothes, and these interests need to be accepted and encouraged. There is no problem with your daughter wanting to be dressed up all sparkling and pink, or like Elsa from *Frozen* or the sadly recently retired Emma from The Wiggles. She can still climb trees or jump in puddles in her sparkles and tiaras! It only becomes problematic when our little girls are drawn to choosing some of the sexualised clothes that are available, such as crop tops, micro shorts, high heels and even padded bras, and are allowed to without hesitation.

If you do have a little girl who has taste, encourage her by asking for her suggestions if you plan on getting some new cushions, clothes or shoes. Please avoid buying her clothes, shoes or even hair ties without her input (and maybe even seek her input on yours!).

Are the arts in her soul?

Does your daughter love putting on shows for you? I love these spontaneous shows that grown-ups get invited to. Yes, they can go on for ages, and we have to wait to the very end – before the final bow – before we can applaud. But this is a sure sign that your daughter has the arts in her soul!

Sometimes you can identify if your daughter has arts in her soul through her love of books, colouring or an eagerness to write for herself. Many little girls love to colour in and can do it for ages without any encouragement from parents. I've noticed that as their ability to draw independently starts to take shape, there is a distinct difference between individuals and the sorts of things they prefer to draw. If you can identify that your little one is passionate about drawing and the arts, encourage this passion and take her to watch artists in action. There are many relatively inexpensive artistic activities for children.

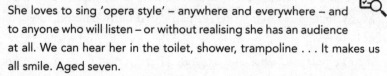
Craft activities can keep children busy for hours and, judging from my
survey, they are hugely popular with little girls. I have so many beautiful necklaces and bracelets that have been painstakingly created by
my granddaughters. Remember that gathering treasures in nature like
shells and nuts is a great way of creating natural jewellery and other
magnificent creations. Craft can also be incredibly messy, but I would
urge you to try to create a space for this activity in your home (maybe a
dedicated craft table on the deck?) where creativity can flow!

If your daughter is showing signs of enjoying drawing or craft,
then you may encourage her to watch some of the creative videos
or apps that are available. One of my granddaughters and I found a
video on how to draw a unicorn one day and she was beyond excited
and drew studiously for ages. Trips to art galleries and local markets
can also be excellent ways of stoking the creative artist within your
daughter. A small cautionary piece of advice when your daughter is
showing you her latest artwork is *to avoid telling her what you think
it is. Instead, ask her to tell you about it.* There has been many a
meltdown as a consequence of a loving grown-up getting it wrong!

Sometimes creativity can be nurtured by allowing our little girls
plenty of time to play without guidance from grown-ups. Resist the
urge to offer suggestions. Creativity needs a healthy imagination.

Physical strength and coordination

This would come under the bodily-kinesthetic intelligence in
Gardner's multiple intelligence model. You can often identify these

little girls because they would have climbed out of a cot very early, or climb very high even before they walk. One of my granddaughters was playing with a soccer ball with me and she threw the ball at me in a classic netball chest pass! As a former netballer and basketballer, I was totally chuffed. She was only three! This same little one can climb up poles and, at a gymnastics class, climbed almost to the top of the rope that hung from the ceiling quite effortlessly. Interestingly, she is more of a lamb and tends to be quite sensitive and shy in social situations. At her fourth birthday party, there was a traditional monkey bar set and, despite having many friends there and lots of yummy things to eat, she decided she wanted to conquer those monkey bars. Over and over again, she kept striving to get to the end and she continued even when she developed blisters. As she has grown, she has ridden her bike without training wheels from an early age, learned to ride a scooter confidently and took to skateboarding quickly. There is no question that practice improves performance, however, it's the speed with which she has mastered these challenges that is the real clue that this is going to be one of her gifts going forward in life.

One of my other granddaughters has a similar persistence when she wants to master something physically. For over six months she has persevered with practising to do a cartwheel and, finally, she nailed it. She, too, has a gift of physical competence, and heck can she run fast. That was definitely not something I could do, even though I was a passionate basketballer for more than 35 years.

For some girls with this natural ability, rather than being interested in sporting pursuits, they may pursue dance, martial arts, rock climbing or hiking. Sometimes little girls want to follow their friends into extra-curricular activities and there's nothing wrong with that. However, if they start to show a disinterest, it may be a sign that they have chosen it based on the friendships rather than their own passion, and it might be time to revise that choice.

Give your little girls a taste of as many physical activities as you can in those early years. Please ensure she learns to swim competently so she develops a life skill that will give her more options in the future, and decrease her chances of drowning.

Parents need to be mindful that they are not encouraging their daughters to pursue dreams that they were unable to achieve. Some little girls can thrive starting an organised physical activity quite early, while others can learn to dislike it intensely because they would rather spend that time playing with freedom and autonomy in the safety of their own home or backyard. There is no hurry. Ensure your daughter is consulted about what her preferences are rather than making decisions on her behalf.

Caring little protectors

Little girls who have natural interpersonal and intrapersonal attributes can easily become the carers not only of their friends, but also family members. One of my granddaughters is incredibly caring and empathetic and often notices the child who is being left out or if the family dog looks sick.

I have noticed over the years that little girls with these natural talents often also have a deep passion for nature and all her creatures. Spending as much time as possible in the natural environment will help these sensitive girls build a strong sense of belonging in the natural world, which can become a sanctuary for them later in life.

Choosing picture books and stories to read with these sensitive little carers can help them understand big feelings, social dynamics and develop courage. It can also be helpful to watch nature documentaries, provided no animals die or get killed by a crocodile or a shark. I have had many families tell me how the arrival of a puppy, kitten, guinea pig or other pet allowed their sensitive, caring little girl to shine. For many, it gave them something special to take care of while for others, they simply love having a pet.

If you have identified that your daughter is a caring little protector, please have conversations with her about *the importance of caring for herself*. Every little girl needs to know that she matters too and that creating healthy boundaries, and being able to say no when we really need to say no, are signs of strength not weakness.

One of the biggest challenges I have had to overcome in my life as a woman is acting on the knowledge that I do need to take care of myself. For so many years, I thought that to do so was a sign of selfishness and that by putting everybody else before me, I was being noble and responsible.

If we can teach our little girls to prioritise their own care, we will reduce the chances of them being in co-dependent relationships where they will feel valued only if they are needed.

PARENTS AND EDUCATORS' SURVEY

My seven-year-old daughter is incredibly social and will approach any child to play with her, without hesitation.

Time in nature

Creating spaces in your daughter's life to spend unhurried time in nature can be enough. Going for walks, afternoons at the beach or the river, or going for treks in natural parks will need to become a regular part of your daughter's life. It is not just about her physical health; it is very much about her emotional and mental health as well. Nature is her happy place where she doesn't have to 'do' anything – she simply needs to 'be'.

PARENTS AND EDUCATORS' SURVEY

My two-year-old loving puddles so much her gumboots would be overflowing and her clothes saturated. She'd be having so much fun she wouldn't even notice how freezing it was. We'd always have to carry a spare set of clothes and shoes whenever we were going outdoors.

Other ways to connect with nature can include creating and nurturing a vegetable garden, growing flowers, or helping a grandparent or neighbour with their gardens. Many nature-loving girls also like having a real treehouse.

For some animal-loving children, caring for one particular species that they are crazy about can be beneficial. She might be passionate about wombats (did you know they do square poos?), lions or koalas. Little girls can become passionate nature warriors especially where animals are threatened with extinction, so please encourage her to work out how she can help. As she gets older, she may be able to volunteer at an animal rescue centre, nearby farm, or for a vet. If animals are in her soul, please help her discover how she can spend valuable time in their company.

Finally, consider regular trips to the library to borrow books about animals and the environment, or consider subscribing to the kids' version of *National Geographic* magazine.

You can tell when a girl is feeling safe and fully alive because she seems to shine and her eyes have a glow. Something within her has triggered deep joy and delight.

The purpose of this chapter is to give you more clues to work out the unique, beautiful puzzle that is your daughter. Hopefully this will give you opportunities to make choices that will allow her to shine as naturally and spontaneously as possible by doing something she enjoys, loves or feels passionately about. Treasure these moments because as little girls leave childhood behind, they become less frequent and sometimes the light goes out completely.

I need to add a cautionary note here. Just because your little girl is naturally gifted in a certain area, please be careful of putting pressure on her to achieve. As I have already mentioned, our girls are very attuned to picking up parental pressure, and they can either push back by walking away from something they are naturally gifted at or becoming unhealthily obsessed.

Dr Leonard Sax, in his book *Girls on the Edge: Why So Many Girls are Anxious, Wired, and Obsessed – And What Parents Can Do*, shares a poignant and powerful story about a girl called Chloe, who had always enjoyed sports. Over the years, her passion for running became an obsession that created a serious imbalance in her life. Her dream of being successful saw her friendships wither and her body struggle with injuries due to the repetitive and consistent nature of her training. Dr Sax is concerned that many girls are driven to please their parents, especially if they already have an innate love of an activity. He believes it is like a form of 'anorexia of the soul' where the pursuit of their passion no longer brings them joy and delight. In a way, their dream has become a nightmare.

Another example is Australian champion tennis player Ash Barty, who lost her love of the tennis lifestyle, which kept her from her home and family, and went to play cricket for a few years. Fortunately for this dynamic passionate athlete, she re-found her drive and passion for competitive tennis at an international level and went out on a high.

Please remember, it is healthy to have dreams as little girls. However, be mindful of ensuring that your little girl continues to find light and joy in the things she loves.

Childhood is a time of wonder and awe as the world grabs our attention through our fresh eyes and ears. It is not hard to find a child absorbed in the blissful moment on a swing, or spinning just to feel the world move around them. Children are natural mystics. Sometimes the wonder opens all the way to ecstasy and unity.

– Tobin Hart, *The Secret Spiritual World of Children* (2003).

KEY POINTS

- The sooner we can identify our little girl's unique gifts, the sooner we can create opportunities and a positive environment for her growth.
- A strength-based approach to parenting is more effective than the deficit approach where parents identify what their little girls can't do and work out how to fix it.
- Some little girls have music in their souls from birth and we need to nurture and celebrate this as a gift.
- Nurturing creativity in our little girls is incredibly important and we need to be mindful that it is not outcome driven or overly directed by grown-ups.
- Some little girls are born with physical strength and agility as a natural ability and have very little interest in arts and crafts; each to their own.
- Mothers need to be mindful that they are not encouraging their daughters to realise dreams that they were unable to achieve.
- If your daughter is a natural caring protector please teach her that she also has to take care of herself, not just others.
- When little girls feel safe and fully alive they seem to shine and their eyes have a glow. Noticing this will help you make the decisions that may best support your little girl's healthy growth and development.

10

Sexualisation, body image and healthy self-esteem

PARENTS AND EDUCATORS' SURVEY
In my (early childhood) centre, some little girls are already focused on body image and body shaming.

The effects of competitive culture

Over the last 20 years, I have noticed a significant shift in the parenting landscape, particularly among mothers, and that is that there is a silent competition happening to be a perfect mother and to raise a perfect child. Many mums tell me how confused and overwhelmed they are with this silent pressure of being judged. Social media has not helped this, because the images shared are carefully curated (and often filtered) to show mainly the wonderful moments of being a parent. I remember seeing an Instagram post with image of sandwiches cut into star shapes for a child's lunchbox and I thought if I'd had time to do that with my boys' lunches, I would have probably preferred to finish my cup of tea or have a wee in peace. This pressure to create an image of perfection as a parent may also be contributing to a heightened sense of competition between our little girls.

> Girls learn from media, adults, and peers to please others in order to remain likeable. It's a phenomenon considered largely responsible for the loss of confidence that hits around middle school. Not surprisingly, many girls grow to fear failure. They think the more they succeed, the more liked they will be.
> – Rachel Simmons, 'How To Teach Your 3-Year-Old Daughter She Is "Enough"', romper.com (8 March 2018)

For any parent who is struggling with a lack of sleep, an image of an amazing, effortful lunchbox could leave them with a sense of being inadequate or, worse still, a failure. This same hidden drive for things to appear perfect could even flow onto things like whether to allow your daughter to choose her own clothes, knowing that she will most likely meet girls who are wearing clothes very carefully chosen by her mum to look fantastic. I celebrate the uncoordinated little girls who deliberately wear mismatched outfits, or clothes with rips and tears and the odd grass stain, because that's what they wanted to wear. Autonomy is an essential quality to nurture in our little girls.

Given that our little girls are so emotionally savvy and clever, I believe they can pick up on this subliminal pressure to please others, especially their parents. While this is quite natural and can be healthy to a degree, when our little girls feel they have let their parents down, or when they take time to master a new skill, it can be an entry to the slippery slope of competition.

MAGGIE'S MAIN IDEA
The key thing to remember with little children is that the process is often more important than the product.

This means that as they are learning to draw, to paint or to build Duplo, we need to let them know that it takes time for things to look really good. When well-meaning grown-ups take over the process to ensure the product looks really good, we are not only being disrespectful, we are sending a clear message to our little girls that they are not good enough. Please be careful not to put too much pressure on your little girl, especially in her creative pursuits. She is a little girl and it takes time and practice to improve performance.

The pervasive influence of a competitive academic environment, and the current tendency to give excessive awards to kids, are influencing our children's notions around their efforts and ability – and it can create negative mindsets if they don't 'win'.

I studied anthropology at university and I have continued my interest in early human civilisation over many years. I have been especially fascinated with First Nations cultures, and one of the things that was glaringly obvious was that both genders were respected and celebrated. There was a distinct difference between men's business and women's business, and this was reflected in ceremony, ritual, dance and many other cultural practices. Women were never in competition with each other as mothers – traditionally, they were a circle of rock-solid, unconditional support. Women of the community all shared the nurture and care, especially of the youngest and the eldest in their community, and they enjoyed creativity, music, song and preparing food collectively. Now, I'm sure they had their moments of conflict and annoyance with each other – I'm not idealising these communities because they are made up of human beings and there was never a perfect human. However, the further we have moved from traditional kinship communities and towards an individualistic, competitive, capitalistic model, the more unhealthy we have become both physically and mentally, and the notion of female competition has become a powerful overt reality.

We need to shift the pressure on our little girls to endlessly be competing against all other little girls. This pressure makes our little girls struggle to accept value and love themselves as they are. We must teach our girls that there is great power in cooperation, and that helping each other to shine – both giving and accepting help – is totally okay and acceptable. It is more than that, it is a pathway to a worthwhile life where she can find meaning and purpose, and be an original, authentic girl who has strengths, challenges and significant moments of happiness and joy.

> Girls learn early in life that everything is a competition. They are told that their worth, beauty and achievements are only relative to those of the other girls around them, encouraging them to see their allies and friends as competitors and foes.
>
> Whole industries are built on girls' fears of not living up to impossible expectations. With all this going on is it any wonder that many girls blame themselves for not meeting people's expectations and their own.
>
> – Kasey Edwards and Dr Christopher Scanlon, *Raising Girls Who Like Themselves* (2021)

Sexualisation

When little girls as young as four are asking their mummies, 'Am I sexy? Am I too fat?', it shows that something has shifted culturally to try to hurry our little girls up to become tweens and teens. Kevin Tutt, the former principal of Seymour College in Adelaide, told journalist Madonna King:

> Childhood is short and the societal pressure on young girls to be more teenage like, even more womanly is quite frightening.
> – Madonna King, *Ten-Ager: What your daughter needs you to know about the transition from child to teen* (2021)

Many of the girl experts who work with girls in our schools believe there has been a significant shift around girl maturation, and that age

10 now is more like age 13 was just a few years ago. While many tween girls may know more than their counterparts in previous generations, they also have more anxiety, face more expectations and seem less resilient.

PARENTS AND EDUCATORS' SURVEY

What worries me is the focus on how they look rather than who they are, and pressure to be people-pleasers. We aren't up to it quite yet it in our house, but I definitely fear early sexualisation, especially with products their friends are into e.g. L.O.L. Dolls.

The longitudinal Childhood to Adolescence Transitional Study being conducted by Murdoch Children's Research Institute is exploring some of the key concerns around this age. Significant hormonal changes, especially with the adrenal androgens, can be identified as early as eight. The research is showing that children with high levels of these androgens seem to be experiencing puberty earlier, and they are 50 per cent more likely to struggle with anxiety and mental health issues going forward. The research also shows that a high percentage of these students will struggle with their learning, and many are up to a year behind their peers by the age of 14.

This is a call to action for us as a society to help our little girls to stay little girls for as long as we possibly can, without feeling pressured or conditioned to act or behave in a way that is older than their years. When little girls play dress-ups to pretend being 'grown up', they need to be able to have to shove oranges or socks into mum's bras rather than wearing a bra that fits. They need to wobble on high-heeled shoes rather than wear high-heeled shoes made for little girls! One of my granddaughter's delights is wearing some of Nanny's dresses and shoes. Given that I have size 10 feet, she does struggle to walk very far in them!

How do we protect our little girls from sexualisation?

Everywhere I go, I hear stories. Of children using sexual language. Children touching other children inappropriately. Children playing 'sex games' in the school yard. Children requesting sexual favours. Children showing other children porn on their devices. Children distressed by explicit images they came across while googling an innocent term. Children exposed to porn 'pop-ups' on sites featuring their favourite cartoon characters or while playing online games.

Educators, child welfare groups, childcare workers, mental health bodies, medicos and parents are reeling. All are struggling to deal with the proliferation of hyper-sexualised imagery and its impacts on the most vulnerable – children whose sexuality is still under construction, children for whom pornography becomes a template for sexual activity, a 'how to' manual for future use.

– Melinda Tankard Reist, 'Early sexualisation and pornography exposure: the detrimental impacts on children', Australian Childhood Foundation (professionals.childhood.org.au) 6 July 2016

Sexualisation occurs when children are exposed to widespread sexualised advertising and popular culture that is mainly targeted at adults. Sexualised images are found everywhere – our social media feeds, on billboards, advertising on TV, in magazines both in print and online, advertising in all the major online platforms, on buses, and in train stations. Sadly, the influence of pornography means there is also *direct sexualisation* occurring, where children are photographed in suggestive ways too.

When women and girls are being objectified, or seen as objects rather than people, it is not only wrong, it is harmful to our children, especially to our little girls, who are being conditioned in this culture to think they need to be eye candy for boys and men in order to be accepted.

PARENTS AND EDUCATORS' SURVEY

My then five-year-old telling me she doesn't like her thighs as they are too fat. I cried on the spot as I am so careful about talking about weight, size and body issues. She has a friend at school who is constantly talking about it as that is what is modelled at home. The friend has also been talking about my size and commenting on how she thinks I must have been a fat kid, etc. How do I keep that kind of influence away?

I have been an advocate for changing school uniforms for girls in Australia because many of the rules are outdated, incredibly sexist and downright discriminatory. All girls need to be able to move freely without worrying about their underwear showing. The Girls Uniform Agenda list several compelling reasons why girls should have a choice, including:

- When girls wear dresses and skirts, it can discourage them from physical activity – they're less likely to do cartwheels and tackle those monkey bars, which are so important.
- Learning can be hindered if you're sitting on the floor in class and focusing on whether anyone can see your underwear rather than paying attention (or if your legs are cold!).
- Expecting girls to wear skirts and dresses sets up gender stereotypes and social expectations, which basically means that boys get to look and behave in a way that allows them more freedom.

It is fabulous to see that uniform policies are gradually changing around the world and our little girls and our older girls are being heard and respected. It has just been incredibly frustrating to see how hard-fought and lengthy the fight to make the change has been.

In July 2021, Talitha Stone, a self-declared 'sports-loving woman' from Australia living in Norway started a petition after learning the International Handball Federation's uniform rule insisted that the women's beach handball team must wear bikini bottoms instead of shorts. After the petition reached over 61,000 signatures, the Federation finally changed its mandate for female players to include new tank top and shorts, rather than the previously mandated crop tops and bikini bottoms. This is just one example of where women in sport are being pressured into wearing highly sexualised uniforms due to outdated mandates from patriarchal organisations.

Many businesses consistently plaster their display windows with pornified representations of women to an all-ages audience in shopping centres, and one of the most concerning is underwear brand Honey Birdette. They regularly feature full-size images of women in sexualised poses, with breasts, backsides and genitals emphasised. Not only are these images enormous to the eyes of children out shopping with their parents, they often also feature choking-themed images that eroticise violence against women. This business and many others are regularly called out in the media by the wonderful grassroots movement Collective Shout, which campaigns tirelessly against 'the objectification of women and the sexualisation of girls in media, advertising and popular culture'. Check them out at collectiveshout.org.

Because of the technological advances and the forces of globalisation, never before have television, film, magazines, advertising, music and other cultural influences such as food and fashion had the power to persuade, seduce, shape, control and manufacture imaginations and identities; not just of children but of adults as well.

– Dr Karen Brooks, *Consuming innocence: Popular culture and our children* (2008)

Dr Brooks wrote more than a decade ago about her concerns about how we are dressing children like adults instead of in fashions that acknowledge or celebrate childhood. She believed then that the weakening of boundaries around childhood and adolescence put enormous pressure on girls to dress to please. With sexual overtones present in many of the clothing lines for girls, our culture is suggesting that pleasing and appealing to men is an important part of being a girl. Add to that the airbrushed and digitally altered images that create a sense of perfect, and it is making it particularly hard for our girls as they step onto the bridge to womanhood.

PARENTS AND EDUCATORS' SURVEY
Awful stuff. A little girl (three years) being called fat by her peers and calling herself this. Telling me (her teacher) that she wasn't allowed to eat certain food at home as her mum told her it would make her fat.

The early sexualisation of our little girls is contributing to the higher levels of body dissatisfaction. I grew up on the farm, with no TV or access to magazines other than the *Australian Women's Weekly*, yet I struggled with enormous self-hatred and self-loathing about my body once puberty arrived. We can't solely blame the sexualisation that has increased incrementally over the last 20 years for our girls' body dissatisfaction. However, we need to see that it contributes nothing helpful in the shaping of our beautiful little girls' views about themselves, their worth and value and especially their relationship to their bodies.

PARENTS AND EDUCATORS' SURVEY
It upsets me to see young girls body shaming each other at such an early age. We no longer do gymnastics because of this.

In the last few years the light has been shone into the dark side of coaching for girls, especially in swimming and gymnastics in the UK, USA, Germany and Australia. Thanks to some brave young women who had been gymnasts as young girls, coaches have been called out for fat shaming, emotional and psychological abuse and sexual harassment and molestation. It has been happening for decades and this is why we must keep teaching our girls about protective behaviour and about speaking up. *They now must be heard, believed and action must be taken.*

There is no question your little girl will be exposed to sexualised images somewhere, and having conversations with her about women deserving to be treated with respect and not objectified will make a difference. You can't even avoid them at your local shopping centre; however, you are your daughter's most significant teacher around what she learns from seeing these images. Encourage the early feminist in your daughter.

Body image

Our body image is formed by the thoughts, feelings, attitudes and beliefs we have about our bodies and how we look. This includes our shape, size, weight, gender identity, and the way our body functions for us . . . . our body image can influence how we engage with the world.

– butterfly.org.au

To be honest, I might need to write a whole book to cover this one topic because for girls and women, it is huge. Body dissatisfaction is incredibly common. There is research around girls aged six to nine to show that exposure to sexualised media can be correlated with internalisation of sexualisation messages, and that then is correlated with negative body image.

Things didn't start like that.

Girls are not born hating their bodies. Watch young children play or look at themselves in the mirror and you will see them marvel at all their body can do. Body hatred is not innate; it is taught to girls in their homes, in their schools and peer groups, every time they switch on the TV, or get onto social media, or leave the house. From the time they open their eyes in the morning to the time they go to sleep at night, girls will learn that their body is flawed.

– Kasey Edwards and Dr Christopher Scanlon, *Raising Girls Who Like Themselves* (2021)

In my survey, in response to the question 'Which societal pressures on your little girls worry you the most?', 71.9 per cent of responses selected the option of 'focus on how they look rather than who they are'. On top of this anecdotal evidence of concern, there is some research that shows that increased TV and screen viewing can influence body image in a positive way as well as a negative way. One study aimed to examine the role of such viewing in the development of positive stereotypes towards thinness, self-esteem and body mass index standardised for child age and gender in very young girls. If the girls were exposed to positive messages about social stereotypes regarding body weight, they seemed to make better choices around food restraint and were less prone to the negative messaging. Common sense would suggest that parents be mindful of what their little girls are watching because they are easily influenced in the first years of life, and those messages become thoughts and belief systems that they can take forward.

PARENTS AND EDUCATORS' SURVEY

In pre-primary, so five years old, my daughter wouldn't eat her lunch at school for almost three weeks because another girl in her class called her fat and told her she shouldn't eat any more food – broke my heart! Took three weeks to get her to understand that she isn't fat and that she can always eat her lunch and not to listen to kids saying mean things and tell her teacher straight away.

The overriding message our girls are getting is 'thin is beautiful'. Media, advertisers, influencers, celebrities and your peers want you to believe that looking thin is the only way to find happiness and self-worth. The diet industry, the make-up industry and the clothing industry overall send very clear messages about the preferred way to be a girl or a woman.

The reality is that puberty brings with it an additional layer of body fat because it's a biological process to prepare the female body to start reproducing. This ancient wiring is like a trigger to begin menstruation and is entirely in opposition to the thin-is-best message. The various industries are selling expensive 'solutions' to a problem that they created. What a sad irony.

My nickname as a girl was penny stick, which was the name of a lolly like a musk stick. I was tall and thin, and when puberty got busy, I became much more solid and am very much genetically like other women in my ancestral line. This transformation took place much to my horror and despite me being active in sport and eating a normal diet.

'Being evaluated in terms of how you look, how you please others, how you are seen as a "product" has taken girls back fifty years.'
– Steve Biddulph as told to Melinda Tankard Reist,
'Stop selling-out our daughter's potential: Steve Biddulph on raising girls'. Collectiveshout.org (4 February 2013).

In an article written by Juliann Garey for The Child Mind Institute, Dr Douglas W. Bunnell, a specialist in treating eating disorders, emphasises that it's 'almost normal for adolescent girls to go through a period where they loathe their bodies'. That makes sense, especially given the adolescent drive to belong more with their friends than their families, and the hunger to be accepted and validated by others.

In the 2020 Annual Mission Australia Youth Survey of nearly 26,000 young people aged 15 to 19 the top three concerns for young people (56 per cent of whom were girls) were:

1. Coping with stress: 43 per cent
2. Mental health: 34 per cent
3. Body image: 33 per cent

However, body dissatisfaction is happening in our little girls as well. Our girls as young as seven are getting clear messages from toy and clothing companies that they should be 'sexy'.

Helping your little girl create a healthy body image

Create a clear intention to build healthy body confidence as early as possible. This may mean being mindful of not describing food as 'good' or 'bad', speaking respectfully about your own body – especially mums – and reminding our girls often that many of the photos they see in the media have been digitally altered and are false. Avoid criticising your own body and going on diets. Consciously embrace all body types and shapes. An excellent way to teach your little girls to not be overly consumed about how their body looks is to highlight brave and fearless girls who don't fit the mould. Watching the Paralympics is an excellent way of challenging the mindset that says only slim, 'perfect' girls have value. We need to also be mindful that we don't fat shame or skinny shame. I have worked with women who are naturally very thin, who have been abused and judged because others have believed that they must always be on a diet. Some of these women have told me they would do anything to be able to put on some weight!

Call out the fake and digitally altered images for what they are – unnatural and unrealistic – and start when your girls are under six. In adolescence, having conversations about unrealistic or fake images around the appearances of characters on television, in the hopes of educating your daughter, may actually have the opposite effect, and since early puberty starts as soon as eight, we need to get in early with these messages. Once girls are older, dietician and body image advocate Meg McClintock says that *even positive comments about someone's body or weight loss can lead to a destructive focus on body shape and size.* One study showed the impact of talking about disclaimer labels on altered images was also unhelpful. The children in the study (aged 11+) showed more negative emotion and greater concern about their own body image after having conversations about it! This suggests it is better to start educating your daughter as early as possible to create a healthy mindset around body image.

Avoid your daughter being consumed by cartoon programs and YouTube videos that are excessively about little girls doing their hair and nails or changing their clothes. If she watches some of these programs among others, like *Bluey* or *Playschool* or educational videos with dynamic females exploring science for example, then your daughter is getting lots of different messages about how she could be. If your daughter watches the glamour-focused programs it can be a valuable teachable moment to discuss and deconstruct the messages that she is getting.

Keep your daughter as physically active as possible, and engage her in sports, dance (choose that class carefully, as mentioned earlier!), gymnastics, athletics, surfing, skateboarding, football, tennis, karate or swimming. It needs to be something she enjoys and which she chooses to pursue. One of the blessings that came from the lockdowns during the pandemic was many daughters enjoying long walks, bike rides and treks with their parents and siblings.

Encourage your daughter to find ways she can express herself, stretch herself and enjoy herself. Avoid overly complimenting your daughter on how she looks, especially telling her she is beautiful. I know this sounds almost counterintuitive, however, as Sarah McMahon, a psychologist and eating disorder specialist, says in Edwards and Scanlon's book, 'beauty is, after all, a judgement that is bestowed upon us by other people – and it can be taken away just as quickly. If a girl's sense of identity is based on beauty, it is at the mercy of other people and not herself.'

There are so many other ways we can compliment our girls – her energy, her strength, her compassion, her problem-solving, her empathy, her humour, her memory, her thinking capacity and her creativity are just a few. Teach your daughter that almost everyone will have a part of their body that they like less – that's normal and not necessarily problematic. Maybe share with her your favourite and less favourite parts of your body with a light heart!

Surround your daughter with a tribe of healthy humans who see themselves as whole people with unique talents, strengths and attributes. A circle of aunties, biological or otherwise, can be a complete game-changer for our little girls.

Marinate your daughter with role models in the real world who display body confidence. It's been fabulous to see the recent, significant shift in status of women's sport. The women's football league of Australian Rules has been embraced by men and women alike. Watching women be fearless and physical is doing so much good by shifting social norms that say the only way to be a successful female is to be passively thin and beautiful.

As she becomes old enough, help your daughter choose her online communities so they promote body positivity and body satisfaction. There seems to be a gradual shift in the nature of online 'influencers' towards being more authentic and real. Models are showing that they get cellulite just like everybody else, and that being photographed without make-up is a sign of authenticity and courage. Let's hope this continues!

Choose advertisement-free content for your little girls. Thank goodness for ABC Kids and ABC ME channels in Australia, and high-quality streaming services which have appropriate children and tween/teen content with no advertisements! YouTube Kids has a lot of unhelpful advertising, especially junk food advertising, however, if you pay the premium, you will fix that problem instantly.

We need our girls to know they are enough exactly as they are because there is no perfect in humanity. Encourage your daughter to search for her own authentic sense of identity, the courage to speak her own truth and be heard, and explore the many ways of nurturing a healthy self-esteem.

Nurturing a healthy self-esteem and self-worth in our girls

> A poor body image can influence every aspect of your daughter's life; her mental health, physical health, her self-esteem, her relationships, professional ambition and even her finances.
> – Kasey Edwards and Dr Christopher Scanlon, *Raising Girls Who Like Themselves* (2021)

Self-esteem is something we want for our little girls and ourselves, yet it can be such a tricky thing, especially in the 21st century. Self-esteem is not a fixed thing; we can have it when our perception of ourselves and what's happening in the world around us feels good, then, just as quick, when something unexpectedly negative occurs or we stuff up, we can lose it. The other really frustrating thing about self-esteem is that we can't give it to someone else – every individual has to develop it themselves. As I wrote in my book *Real Kids in an Unreal World:*

> Self-esteem is the ability to choose to experience oneself as competent, to be able to cope with everyday life and particularly life's challenges, and also of being worthy of happiness and goodness.

Essentially, *self-esteem is how we evaluate our self, rather than how others see us.* Having a healthy self-esteem means that you have a good level of self-acceptance and self-love. Unhealthy self-esteem can exist at either end of a spectrum. If you have too much self-esteem, you can have tendencies to be narcissistic, and you might exaggerate your positive traits and completely ignore your negative traits. If you have low self-esteem, you will diminish or completely ignore your positive traits and overly focus on your negative traits. This can see you creating a negative mindset, which can feed your negative inner critic where you see yourself as stupid, worthless or useless.

PARENTS AND EDUCATORS' SURVEY

My ex-FIL frequently tells my four-year-old that she has a big/ chubby tummy. It pisses me off and I worry about it affecting her self-esteem.

Self-esteem is often used interchangeably with self-worth and while they do tend to overlap, self-worth is different. If you have self-worth, you will tend to have a belief that you are valuable and lovable, regardless of what happens with your self-esteem. This means you could fail something or be rejected out of a friendship group, and while you will feel awful, you still know that you are loved and valued, especially by those closest to you. This is why I keep repeating the need for parents to love their children fiercely and unconditionally because that is exactly what will build a strong self-worth. It is the foundation that our little girls will need as they grow towards puberty and womanhood. Self-worth can be built by consistently validating to your little girls that they are good enough and that they have an inner capacity to make our world a better place. We can model self-worth by respecting diversity in our families and communities, and by being mindful of teaching our little girls values and morals.

PARENTS AND EDUCATORS' SURVEY

When they lose (to someone else or a different class) the person who they considered their best friend, their whole world crumbles, their self-worth, their ability to make and be a good friend, their ability to make good decisions.

Another perspective says that your self-worth is based on your wants, which are common to everyone. Deep down, you desire peace of mind, contentment, relief from suffering, the realisation of your potential and, most importantly, a sense of belonging. These wants give you inherent value. Just as you respect others because of their wants, it's crucial to respect yourself in the same way. An excellent picture book that I recommend is called *A New Alphabet for Humanity* written by Leesa McGregor and illustrated by Daniela Sosa. It captures compassionately different cultures, special needs and is written with a profound sense of tenderness.

PARENTS AND EDUCATORS' SURVEY

I worry about the power of social media! It honestly scares me that we've created unrealistic expectations of life, appearance, etc. It creates this need for constant social approval and I feel that girls are relying on this far more than their own self-esteem!

The man considered to be the grandfather of self-esteem, Dr Nathaniel Branden, captures something really important for every parent and educator to know:

Self-esteem is an intimate experience; it resides in the core of one's being. It is what I think and feel about myself, not what someone else thinks or feels about me. I can be loved by my family, my mate, and my friends, and yet not love myself. I can be admired by my associates and yet regard myself as worthless. I can project an image of assurance and poise that fools almost everyone and yet secretly tremble with a sense of my inadequacy. I can fulfill the expectations of others, and yet fail my own; I can win every honor, and yet feel I have accomplished nothing; I can be adored by millions, and yet wake up each morning with a sickening sense of fraudulence and emptiness.

– Dr Nathaniel Branden, 'Our Urgent Need for Self-Esteem' (1991),
nathanielbranden.com

These words really resonated with me when I first read them. Despite my early childhood years experiencing physical punishment and being frequently shamed, I appeared to be a very capable student, leader and friend during my final years of high school with many sporting and academic successes. However, it was a mask covering a desperately low self-esteem. The difference between how others saw me and how I saw myself was enormous. When I failed a politics essay in my first semester at university – my first ever essay failure – I walked back to my lodgings and tried to take my own life by swallowing a bottle of pills, such was the fragile sense of self that I had been hiding. Retrospectively, I saw the experience very differently. In a way, it was a wonderful opportunity for me to learn about how fragile teenagers can be, and that experience allowed me to begin a lifelong quest on how to nurture self-esteem, self-worth and resilience in children and teenagers.

For me, I had built a belief that created a story that I only had value because of my academic success and my intelligence; with my essay failure, I had nothing else to give me any sense of value or worth. The second awareness I discovered, many years later, was that in response to living with a primary carer who struggled with her own low sense of self with distant mothering, I had built a wall of protection around myself that prevented anyone getting close to me. While I may have been everyone's friend and confidante, no-one was ever able to witness my vulnerability. This disconnectedness impacted deeply on my suicide attempt, as I felt I had no-one I could call upon to walk me through my moment of disaster. Connectedness is a key aspect of resilience and something I value enormously in my life today on many levels.

PARENTS AND EDUCATORS' SURVEY

I worry about the focus on how they look rather than who they are. Girls/early adults are looking so fake, I think it's incredible and hides low self-esteem.

The three fundamental building blocks in childhood that can definitely help to build a healthy self-esteem and self-worth and self-determination are:

- Connection
- Competence
- Control and autonomy.

If we keep these three Cs in mind as we are nurturing and growing our little girls, they will have the best chance of growing a healthy self-esteem.

Connection

It matters that girls have the three Cs, and when one or, worse, two are not strong, things can go wrong quickly, especially in the teen years. For me as a little girl, I had competence but very little control or enough connection. Going to boarding school in the last two years of my schooling meant that my safest connections with my dad and my sister were no longer nearby. Indeed, I can still remember that when I held that failed university essay result in my hand, I thought I had no-one to turn to – which of course was not true. The earlier chapters in this book explain the importance of healthy attachment and a strong sense of belonging with as many safe caregivers as possible. This is the very first foundation to build a healthy self-esteem for the tween and teen years especially. *Connection trumps almost everything when raising children* because without relational safety, the nervous system will have less energy to move into bravery and courage.

Competence

Competence is linked to self-efficacy. Essentially, that means we grow our little girls' capacity to do things for themselves and to stretch and grow to become more capable at anything they may choose. A key thing to remember here is that we must encourage our little girls to stretch and grow *for their own benefits,* not for parental approval or conditional love. Excelling at something, whether that be academics, music or skateboarding can definitely help build a healthy sense of self, but we need to be careful it does not become an obsession.

Competence also means learning many valuable life skills including how to manage setbacks and disappointments and failure, not just the celebration of achievement. Self-esteem influences our capacity to cope with life's challenges and in some ways, *it is the immune system of consciousness.* A healthy immune system doesn't guarantee you'll never become ill, but it does reduce your susceptibility to illness and can improve your odds for a speedy recovery if you do get sick.

Control and autonomy

As I have said before, little girls need choices and a sense of autonomy. We can do that in so many small ways – you want her to get her shoes on, so rather than commanding her to put her shoes on, ask, 'Do you think your gumboots or runners are a good choice for today?' It's hard with little ones when we want them to hurry up, but if you can possibly just weave in little opportunities to make decisions throughout the day, it can make a big difference. The most important message that can build this part of a little girl's self-esteem is having autonomy and a voice and being heard.

Another thing that's really useful is to help her to notice when she's struggling with something, whether it is within her locus of control or not (and you can do this by modelling yourself). This is so helpful to all of us, particularly in managing anxiety and stress. So often, trying to control things that we simply have no control over causes us to ruminate on negative thinking. This is hard for little ones to conceive, but our little girls are often very clever and it's such an important lesson for life. So look for opportunities to talk about moments where you literally have no control, like if you're stuck in traffic, or you're dealing with disappointment at missing out on something, or if it rains when you were supposed to go to the beach. 'Oh well!'

Unfortunately, becoming successful, powerful or well-liked does not automatically guarantee happiness or self-esteem. In fact, talented and powerful people who doubt their own core value are usually unable to find joy in their achievements no matter how great their external success. This can be seen today by the insatiable drive for some people for more – more work, bigger houses, better cars – striving for an unattainable marker they think will bring them peace. For our girls this can become the endless striving to be slim, have beautiful clothes and amazing eyebrows. What a horrible irony that it already lies hidden within us!

The power of joy and delight

Research, especially in the area of epigenetics, shows the impact of trauma on emotional and mental health outcomes later in life. In Chapters 3 and 4, I explored the importance of creating memories that matter in early childhood, especially those around joy and delight.

Over the years I have worked with many children and adults who struggle with chronic low self-esteem and many of them had few genuinely happy childhood memories. People with low self-esteem can really struggle to feel happiness. Have you ever noticed that there are some people who are just a delight to be around? They have a sense of fun, goodness, spontaneity and lightness? I believe that these people have experienced significant moments in their childhood that activated those positive brain neurochemicals and created neural pathways of predictability that allow them to feel happiness. Despite being raised in the 1950s and '60s, a time of tough-love parenting, I have found a pathway to healthy self-esteem and self-worth partly because of the other things that were happening in my childhood. As I wrote in my book, *Real Kids in an Unreal World*:

Outside of the house I was blessed to be able to run freely around a beautiful farm with 10,000 sheep, interesting bush and incredible freedom to explore the world unencumbered by adult supervision. My siblings and I had to help on the farm and be responsible for taking care of stock, driving farm vehicles and helping whenever needed. There were so many experiences of enormous joy – mulberry fights, endless hours in the local river or farm dams, riding bikes, and wild flower and mushroom picking. There were many bush barbeques and plenty of games of cricket, golf and football. My mum was a great cook who made many excellent meals and morning teas surrounded by family, farm workers and anyone who happened to be passing. These repeated happy experiences wired me to appreciate enjoying whatever life brought, and for that I am deeply grateful.

We need to ensure that children have opportunities to experience 'joy juice' for no reason other than to build a positive foundation for them to maintain or quickly regain a sense of hope, optimism and a 'yes I can' attitude to life.

The final messages around nurturing a healthy self-esteem and self-worth in your daughter are to avoid shaming, focus on her strengths more than her flaws and weaknesses, and connect her deeply to her very best friend – her higher self or her inner compass. Learning to trust her intuition and hear the quiet whisperings of her higher consciousness will definitely help her find a pathway to authentic self-acceptance, self-respect and self-love.

PARENTS AND EDUCATORS' SURVEY

As a teacher who has sought permanency, my daughter has been at four different day cares and now three different schools (as a now eight-year-old). At all her schools, she has shown empathy and understanding for all students, regardless of their ability or disability. At her most recent school, she has made a beautiful friendship with a student who is creative and has 'outside of the box thinking' like her. They are encouraging the other girls to play whimsically and to appreciate nature. 'What did you do at recess?' I ask.

'Today, my friends and I hugged our favourite trees,' she replies.

KEY POINTS

- The increased competition for women seems to have created a heightened sense of competition for our little girls as well.
- Given that our little girls are so emotionally savvy and clever, they can pick up on subliminal pressure to please others, especially their parents.
- We need to shift the pressure on our little girls to endlessly be competing against all other little girls.
- Sexualisation occurs when children are exposed to widespread sexualised advertising and popular culture that is mainly targeted at adults. We must protect our girls from this, especially our little girls who are busy forming belief systems and mindsets for life.
- Weakening the boundaries between childhood and adolescence puts enormous pressure on girls to dress to please.
- Sadly, you cannot prevent your little daughter being exposed to sexualised images. However, you can constantly be reminding her about the objectification of women. Please nurture the early feminist in your little girl.
- Body dissatisfaction is incredibly common around women, and it begins in childhood.
- Ensure that you compliment your little girl on things other than how she looks – her energy, her strength, her compassion, her problem-solving, her empathy, her humour, her memory and her thinking capacity.
- Marinate your little daughter with role models in the real world who display healthy body confidence.
- Choose advertisement-free content for your little girls.
- Self-worth can be built in our little girls by consistently validating to them that they are good enough and that they have an inner capacity to make our world a better place.
- The three fundamental building blocks in childhood that can build healthy self-esteem are connection, competence and control i.e. autonomy. Start your girls early in each!
- Avoid shaming your little girl and help her to find her own intuition and the quiet whisperings of her higher self.

11

The incredible importance of play

In the survey I conducted as part of researching this book, I invited parents to ask their little daughters when they were happiest. More than 50 per cent of replies mentioned it was when they were playing with friends, spending time with family, spending time in nature, and while on holidays. I will explore some of the interesting aspects of girl play and why it is so incredibly important for our little girls, but first let me talk about the incredible importance of play for all children.

One of the saddest realities of raising children in the 21st century has been the weakening and diminishing of the importance of play. As our education systems have become driven by competitiveness, academic testing and accountability to curriculum, play and the opportunities to play have become less important.

One of the sad things that research shows, as Dr Stuart Brown explains in his book *Play*, is that the impulse to play is internally generated, however, if a child is tired or hungry, the drive will be overridden by the need to survive. If a child is overly stressed, dys-regulated or frightened, the impulse to play is also crushed. That is certainly being seen in many children – both boys and girls – transitioning into big school.

Let's start with a really important statement of truth: play matters. Play is the way babies and children develop their sense of self, their sense of the world and the sense of where they fit in. When I ask a group of parents how they experienced play as children, they do not mention expensive toys or indoor games. The things they loved as kids were building cubbies, riding bikes (often without helmets, gears or brakes), catching tadpoles, building billycarts, climbing trees, and hours of playing chasey, hide-and-seek and spotlight. Many women remember elastics, skipping, clapping games and that game you play with string on your fingers. Many of these forms of play also took place well away from any parental gaze.

One parent shared with me her story of camping with her children at a beach campsite where there would be up to 30 children playing spotlight. Mind you, some of those children were in their 40s! Many of these play pursuits needed little direction from adults and cost very little money. These opportunities are still available – obviously we need to wear helmets now – if we prioritise play for our kids, no matter how much the world around us changes.

Babies, toddlers and children are biologically wired to play. Opportunities for play are essential because they help our little ones learn many of the emotional and social competencies they need to navigate their world. There is a condition called 'tactile defensiveness' which occurs when children who appear in our preschool settings lack the social and emotional skills to initiate play, or to interact with other children comfortably. Play is not something children do when they are not learning – play is learning!

The fun aspects of play also serve an important role in developing a child's psychology. The more pleasurable experiences that a child has the more chance they have of developing a pleasure-seeking response to unknown experiences. The opposite can also occur, where the more painful experiences the child has the more likely it is that they will seek pain rather than pleasure out of new experiences. This becomes an unconscious process that happens quite spontaneously. It is influenced by the core concepts that a child has come to believe.

– John Joseph, *Learning in the Emotional Rooms* (2006)

The consumer-driven world conditions our parents to believe that children need lots of toys to be able to play well. This pressure to buy toys and 'stuff' – often labelled 'educational' – implies that children will need these toys to be able to play well and grow well. The opposite is true.

Alice Zsembery, mother-of-two and author of *Real Kids, Real Play: The ultimate play guide for 0–5 year olds* found that her children became disinterested in some toys quickly and her house was filled with significant clutter. She began to reduce the number of toys and discovered ways of playing with 'non-toy' materials. Children are born with a strong 'seeking' mechanism that makes them incredibly curious about how things work and the different ways you can interact with them. Toys that only work one way – and there are many – can diminish your child's problem-solving capacity and creativity. A basket of clothes pegs, a bunch of keys, cellophane paper and empty boxes can be massively engaging for little ones, and children often use them over and over again without any adult interaction. Many store-bought toys with bright colours and loud noises can actually be problematic for many of our sensitive or neurodivergent children.

Hara Estroff Marano, in her book *A Nation of Wimps*, highlighted the importance of play this way:

Play is a much underrated but incredibly vital part of children's development. Put simply, 'play grows the brain.' Play fosters maturation of the very centres of the brain that allow kids to exert control over retention, emotions and to control behaviour. This is a very subtle trick that nature plays – it uses something that is not goal directed to create the mental machinery for being goal directed.

Why movement matters

Without plenty of natural movement, babies, toddlers and young children run the risk of experiencing developmental delays. Some of the setbacks that can occur if our children lack movement in the first two years of life are:

- Delayed motor development
- Poor coordination/balance
- Tendency to be easily distracted, lack concentration
- Language problems
- Emotional immaturity
- Motion sickness
- Reading problems
- Aggressive behaviour.

Australian children are not moving enough. A recent study showed that children today have experienced a significant drop in their capacity to hop, skip, catch, throw and run compared to previous generations.

> Sight combined with balance, movement, hearing, touch and proprioception (feedback from the muscles, tendons and joints, informing the brain about the body's status and actions at any moment in time) help to integrate sensory experience and can only take place as a result of action and practice. Movement is the medium through which this takes place.
>
> – Sally Goddard Blythe, *What Babies and Children Really Need* (2008)

Health professionals have told me about children who fall off their chairs in class and who need to touch desks as they walk around the room because their proprioceptive awareness is so underdeveloped. Yikes!

Proprioception is the thing that tells us where our body parts are without having to look at them. Children with poorly developed proprioception can waste energy pushing too hard being playful, fall out of their seat at dinner time or trip upstairs – lots! This is an example of how a child's 'body budget' works. See Chapter 3 for more details on how the brain works to balance the energy budget.

Vestibular sense helps us with balance – can you stand on one leg? A good friend who works as a primary literacy specialist and an educational kinesiologist told me she has noticed that less than a quarter of primary school children today can stand on one leg. In the past, almost all children could do this simple task. Poor vestibular development often leaves kids with no other option but to fidget, become frustrated when they are unable to sit for extended periods of time, and struggle to self-regulate when they are tired or fail.

For young kids (under six) to master the incredibly important abilities of being able to listen, focus, manage their energy and sit still, they must develop both proprioception and vestibular sense. This means they have to move a lot, and often.

A subtle conditioning that we must deconstruct is the notion that girls need to be less physically active and spend more time playing passively than boys. We need to prioritise keeping our girls physically active through play. This used to happen quite naturally with other children in the neighbourhood, but this trend has also diminished as working families spend less time at home. Passivity is a significant and often unidentified contributor to poor mental and physical health in the 21st century. As I have mentioned, many games girls used to enjoy like skipping, elastics and hopscotch simply don't happen anymore, especially in our school grounds. Some schools have banned cartwheels and handstands – activities girls enjoy – because of the risk of hurting themselves and others. All of these games and outdoor challenges help to build our little girls' physical, emotional and mental wellbeing, and we need to advocate for their return.

Movement is not just about how the physical body moves; it is a sophisticated necessity for developing healthy brains, healthy minds and nurturing the socio-cultural development of every human. Physical movement has been shown to increase the levels of positive neurochemicals in the brain, especially serotonin, norepinephrine and dopamine, and these neurotransmitters traffic thoughts and emotions throughout the whole body. Little girls may tend to have less desire for physicality and movement than little boys, but that does not mean they need to move any less than boys, and we need to ensure that this stereotype is not upheld.

PARENTS AND EDUCATORS' SURVEY

My little girl went go-karting with her family. She gave it a great go, ripping around the course quite quickly but every time she hit a wall, she said sorry to it before continuing on ☺

Interesting insights about girl play

In 2011, there was a fascinating story on the ABC TV program *Catalyst* called 'Mean Girls'. In the story, research experiments that had been carried out in the US were replicated to explore the differences in the way boys and girls play. The experiments were supervised by developmental psychologist Dr Marc de Rosnay from the University of Sydney.

The program showed footage of two different scenarios. In the first experiment, the children were sent to play with a large castle in the centre of the room. When the boys went in, they took up a position near the castle and began playing with it immediately, imagining that it was a zoo. When the girls went in, they began talking. After six minutes, they were still talking. After 12 minutes, they were still talking and finally, after 18 minutes, they had worked out the rules to the game that they were going to play with the castle. This fundamental need to sort out the rules is common in little girl play. Girls need to have a clear concept about how the play will unfold before they are ready to engage.

If you have a son and daughter, you may have experienced a situation where they run off to play and about 10 minutes later, you notice your son has become agitated with his sister. This could be because she is still working out the rules to the game that he just wants to start playing. This knowledge can help you understand their relationship and could help by giving them a few simple rules before they run off to play.

The second scenario was quite different. Researchers placed a large, attractive stuffed toy in the middle of the room and sent the three boys in to play. One boy picked up the stuffed toy and another boy tugged it out of his hands, as did the third boy. They then threw the stuffed toy away and began to play a game that had nothing to do with the toy.

With the girls, things went differently again. When one of the girls picked up the highly desirable toy, the other two girls turned their backs on the first girl, sat down and began playing their own game, ignoring the girl with the toy. Dr de Rosnay's observations on the girls' use of ostracism to get what they wanted reflected some evolutionary and biological explanations.

'[The girls' move] is sneaky and it depends on the power of social relationships, much more than the boys' strategy. Without a colleague, the girl who doesn't have the resource is a bit powerless. As soon as she can gang up on the girl who has the toy, then she's got power . . . The boys have a higher risk strategy. They have a lower chance of propagating and they need to take higher risks in order to assert their dominance in the group.'

– 'Mean Girls', *Catalyst*, ABC (7 April 2011)

Given that most boys use physicality to express their displeasure with other playmates, this moment of chosen social exclusion may be a sign that these four-year-old girls were capable of recognising how to manipulate a situation emotionally in their interactions with other children. When you add in the tendency for girls to have superior verbal skills in that same age bracket, it is no wonder that young girls from around the age of three-and-a-half can be quite skilful at emotionally manipulating their parents by using guilt.

Despite these tendencies, it is important to give our little girls opportunities to challenge the pink and blue haze by gifting them toys that are normally selected for boys, and the same goes for our boys. Whether they will want to play with them is up to them, but at least we are ensuring they have a choice. Advertising and packaging are two of the main ways our little girls and boys work out what toys they are meant to be playing with. In 2021, Danish toy manufacturer Lego decided to avoid gender bias by no longer marketing their toys towards boys or girls specifically. Lego made this move in response to a study that found gender stereotypes were harmful in holding back girls as they grow older. This seems like a pretty significant step from one of the world's most influential brands towards changing society's perceptions of what all genders can achieve.

I am a huge fan of Duplo, which is made by Lego, because of its ability to be used in a different way every time. My grandchildren are playing with the Duplo their fathers played with. I have been fascinated by how long it takes for little ones to be able to manage the fine-motor control of putting the blocks together, and how exciting it is when they can finally do it by themselves. My granddaughters are quite happy playing with the train set, the boat and the construction Duplo just as my grandson is happy playing with the Elsa set, the café and the animal farm. Technically, Duplo could be seen as a form of 'loose parts' play, because every time they tip out the box, it is a whole new experience. This is exactly what the 'seeking mechanism' in young children's brains is supposed to be doing.

Nature play

I have been a passionate nature play advocate for more than 20 years because we know that child-led playing in the unpredictable world of nature is one of the most powerful and positive ways of raising a healthy child. It is especially positive for girls, who have often been given messages that they are not as brave or capable physically as our boys.

Children are biologically wired to take themselves to the edge of their own fear each time they play in tricky environments without parental coaching. This is how bravery is built. Resilience researcher and clinical psychologist Andrew Fuller argues we should be actively teaching the type of courage that moves beyond taking a physical risk and instead requires young people to take social risks, because that matters as well.

Dannielle Miller, a former teacher and founder and CEO of Enlighten Education, has a great tool for this. She encourages parents to ask their child to tell them about a time when they were brave. Then she suggests that the parent share a story of their own courage. Given that Dannielle is recognised as a girl champion, I am sure she would encourage all parents to give their little girls permission to reach for their bravery and find their courage.

Around 30 years ago, there was a revolution in play where the dangerous risks in playgrounds – the big metal slides, wooden seesaws, the long monkey bars and any forms of spinning platform – were all removed. Interestingly, when Tim Gill, play researcher in the UK, did some research around the injuries that occurred in the more dangerous playgrounds compared to the ones that were built to be safe, he found that children were being injured at almost twice the rate in the 'safer' playgrounds. This is technically called 'risk compensation'. If parents and children perceive that playgrounds are safer, then children are likely to take less care when using them. In the playgrounds of old, our children were told that they needed to take care to manage risks because they could be hurt if they did not respect the equipment. This shift in consciousness around children needing to be 'overprotected', especially our girls, has seen a significant drop in the confidence and resilience of our girls later in life.

> . . . activities and experiences of previous generations enjoyed without a single thought have been labelled as troubling or dangerous, while adults who still permit them are branded as irresponsible . . . Society appears to have become unable to cope with any adverse outcomes whatsoever, no matter how trivial or improbable.
>
> – Tim Gill, *No Fear: Growing up in a risk averse society* (2007)

One of the best cultural shifts in the last 20 years is the acceptance and embracing of warm, connected fathering. Dads are stepping up and actively participating in a way that I call 'team parents'. This is fabulous because it means more little girls are spending more time with their dads in childhood, and dads are often a little better at allowing them to stretch themselves and take more risks. When children are allowed to play freely, they are biologically wired to take themselves to the edge of their own fear. For example, they will climb to a certain height in a tree. The next time, without any adult influence, they will tend to stretch themselves a little further.

Rough-and-tumble play is a form of play that is more common for boys than girls. This may be partly due to the stereotypical view that boys are tough and girls are not, and this needs to be challenged. Highly physical forms of play can be excellent for teaching consent, as well as to discharge excess energy and have lots of fun. When someone is too rough, there needs to be a clear message to stop. Often this is seen as a form of play that dads tend to do and I would love to see more mums having a go because that will help pull down yet another stereotype that may be preventing our girls from becoming stronger and braver.

The primal subcortical circuitry that prompts the young of all mammals to romp in rough-and-tumble play seems to have a vital part in the child's neural growth. In the emotional fuel for all that development seems to be delight itself.

– Daniel Goleman, *Social intelligence: The new science of human relationships* (2006)

One of the deficits that has been identified by teachers of five-year-olds who are transitioning into big school is their inability or weakness in gross- and fine-motor skills. Children who lack these skills can struggle in many ways. Paediatric physiotherapists have told me they are now seeing four-year-old children with significant posture problems as well as poor fine-motor skills, and there has been an increase in fractures of the wrist because they are not as strong as in previous generations. All of these issues can be prevented by allowing our children, especially our girls, to play freely and often in the natural environment where they can navigate uneven surfaces and climb over rocks, logs and trees, all incredibly important for strengthening the vestibular and the proprio-ception sensory receptors that influence the whole body and, at times, impact our capacity to learn in the classroom.

Hanging by your body weight is one way to strengthen your wrists and the full shoulder girdle, tendons and the muscles below the shoulder blades. It is fabulous to see that long monkey bars or tall climbing frames are making a return to playground environments, because they can help enhance all of these muscular and skeletal strengths.

Given that handheld devices and technology are now part of our children's lives, we need to prioritise time to play in nature, to hang by your body weight, to hang upside down, to do handstands and cartwheels, and to spend significant time tumbling and rolling. Yes, your daughters may get dirty and covered in grass stains, but we need to see that as a sign of healthy little girls with parents who are supporting their healthy growth and development.

PARENTS AND EDUCATORS' SURVEY

Recently my daughter had school swimming. She was in a higher grade then most of her friends and had to swim in the cold pool in winter. She wasn't happy with this. The first day, she pretended she had asthma, got out of the pool and got changed and just watched after 15 minutes. The following day, she managed to go down a grade and told me she would continue to swim badly until she was graded further down and back in the warm pool with her friends. No-one at the school or swimming were any the wiser!

I have been really proud to be a part of the return to nature play in my former home state of Western Australia. In schools and communities across the state, children now have engaging, unpredictable nature play spaces that are allowing them to spend more time playing, stretching themselves, engaging meaningfully with other children, getting wet, getting dirty and being incredibly physically active.

Across Australia, bush kindergartens are appearing in many communities and schools are embracing outside learning because the benefits are so worthwhile. Regular immersion in the natural world at a young age not only allows our children to grow healthy on all levels, it allows them to develop a more respectful consciousness around the environment and their place in it.

Richard Louv in his book *Last Child in the Woods* has explored the concept of 'nature deficit disorder'. He is concerned that this disorder of alienation from nature can create in our children diminished use of senses, attention difficulties, more physical illnesses, and more emotional disorders.

I would also suggest that separation from nature can impact the spiritual wellbeing of our children. There is something incredibly sacred about nature and unless our little ones are immersed in it in the early years of their life, they can miss a feeling of connecting to and being part of our physical world.

PARENTS AND EDUCATORS' SURVEY

On my little girl's birthday, when it was nearing night, she was playing outside and looked up into the sky and saw the moon. She came running to where we were all sitting with the biggest smile on her face and, with the most excitement, said, 'I can see the moon and it has a face on it.' We then all proceeded to go see the moon and this face. She talked about it for days with as much excitement and happiness. It reminded me to try and see the good in all the small things. Three years old.

Encourage your toddler to gather treasures like nuts, leaves and small sticks when she goes for a walk. Celebrate those significant natural events like full moons, starry nights, puddles from the rain, mud, stunning rainbows and spectacular clouds, and nature will always be a special part of her world. I know of many dads who have taken their daughters outside on a starry night to watch the stars and the moon together on a blanket. Rituals like these create memories that last forever.

Encourage your daughter to climb trees, sit among the branches and be still. I encourage you to teach her how to hug trees and to learn how to grow plants from seed. Creating vegetable or flower gardens are incredibly helpful ways of teaching young girls about life. Connect your daughter to the seasons of nature and, if you can, take her to see wildflowers, or canola crops in flower, or to pick her own fruit from a tree or her own strawberries.

Fortunately, in Australia there are now state nature play organisations that are helping to shift our collective consciousness and return our children to the natural world. There are also organisations running programs to help teach our children how to play in adventuresome ways in nature. Educated by Nature is one such organisation in Perth. The popularity of these programs has grown exponentially. Not only do they teach kids how to build cubbies, how to light and manage fires, how to whittle and carve and how to build rafts, they act as mentors and enable children to be the adventurers and explorers rather than always following directions from grown-ups.

The reconnection of children's minds, bodies and spirits to the natural world has been stunningly successful.

When a child is immersed in play so much that they do not notice time go by, they reach a place of incredible significance. First, it is a moment of transcendence from the ordinary world, and promoting natural, drug-free, chemical-free transcendence is very healthy for later life.

Second, that absorption can offer a clue in later life about life purpose, or what is important to them. For some children, the activity can be watching ants, playing nurses or maybe building in the sandpit. Whatever it is, it has a soul connection that needs to be honoured.

Finally, the silent search for meaning that gives such a deep and profound sense of joy and wellbeing is a totally normal human need. Unhurried time in nature allows an unforced and spontaneous connection between a person's inner and outer world to occur. This is pure magic. Allowing children these moments of profound transcendence can be deceptively powerful in helping your child find their own uniqueness, their own sense of self and maybe a glimpse into their own soul.

German pedagogue and creator of the kindergarten concept Friedrich Froebel saw play as the most spiritual activity in which a child can engage:

The child who has restricted opportunities for play is like a fruit tree which is planted in a small pot and therefore cannot bear good fruit.

– Friedrich Froebel

While play may be seen like the fun and easy part of being a child, it is vitally important for building human connectedness and healthy brain integration. These crucial processes assist with all other learning, such as literacy and numeracy, while enhancing emotional and social awareness and giving children opportunities to boost their competence in many areas. It can also improve the mental wellbeing of our children and helps them to create the essential building blocks for developing as loving, caring humans.

Please prioritise play in all its forms in your daughter's life. Find places where she can play with multi-age children, in natural environments where children have autonomy and freedom, and watch her thrive and fly.

KEY POINTS

- While play might seem like it's a fun and easy part of being a child, it's vitally important for building human connectedness and healthy brain integration.
- Play is the way babies and children develop their sense of self, their sense of the world and their sense of where they fit in.
- Babies, toddlers and children are biologically wired to play.
- Without plenty of natural movement, little ones run the risk of experiencing developmental delays.
- We need to deconstruct the notion that girls need to be less physically active than little boys.
- Little girls and little boys have some distinctly different patterns of play.

- Despite these tendencies it's important to give our little girls opportunities to challenge the pink and blue haze.
- We need to be mindful that the digital world does not steal vital time for real play, with other children, especially outdoors.
- Bravery can be encouraged and built, especially in nature play.
- Rough-and-tumble play is helpful for little girls as well as little boys.
- Encourage your daughter to find a safe connection to nature in the early years of her life.
- Unhurried time in nature allows an unforced and spontaneous connection between a person's inner and outer world to occur.
- Please prioritise play in your little girl's life is much as you can.

12

Why imagination matters

Children's imaginations, especially when a child is not yet seven, help them experience joy. They are totally unaware of the concerns of later life. More than that, a child's imagination can nurture, protect and insulate them from many of the harsh realities of the adult modern world that surrounds them. It can feed their growing spirits and build on emotional and social competencies that will help them in adolescence and adulthood. Imagination and the holistic growth of healthy, happy, resilient children have suffered greatly in the last couple of generations. Modernism, the rise of a popular culture that honours 'fast and quick' living, the 'must have' mentality and family and community disintegration have all taken their toll on children.

> I firmly believe that a rich imaginative childhood is essential for the evolving brain. It helps to create the neuronal templates that ensure emotional stability, social awareness and the spiritual strength to cope with life in this chaotic, constantly changing world.
>
> – Maggie Dent, *Nurturing Kids' Hearts and Souls* (2005)

In the survey of almost 5,000 people I conducted for this book, the thing that the majority of respondents (3,071 of them) said that fascinated them most about little girls was their amazing imaginations. So imagination is definitely a big thing! Delightful little moments of imaginary joy are incredibly important, particularly in the lives of our little girls. The first seven years of life are often seen as the magical window of childhood. Sadly, they are increasingly being stolen by the pressures of the consumer world, the screen world, the push-down of formalised learning and the fast pace of everyday family life.

We asked grown-ups to ask little girls when they were the happiest and pretend play, role-play and dress-ups and imaginative activities were among the top three responses. The top two were being with family or being with friends.

Imaginative play was the top thing that grown-ups observed little girls doing with their time. Given its obvious importance, we need to dive into imagination and discover how it can help support us to raise our girls to be happy, healthy and heard.

Many studies now show that the healthy pursuit of imagination can help stimulate the growth of neural pathways that subsequently develop as a child matures. However, we simply cannot analyse a child's imaginary world from the perspective of an educated, logical mind of an adult. As Dr Marjorie Taylor explains:

> Imaginative thought is an integral part of everyday cognition and human experience.
>
> – Dr Marjorie Taylor, *Imaginary Companions and the Children Who Create Them* (2001)

This means that imagination is woven into the threads of our lives without conscious thought or intention. It is so much more than a form of escape or a source of entertainment: imagination plays a very important part in the creation of a preferable future. Its role in modern thinking and consciousness, while undisputed, seems to now be undervalued.

More than child's play

Pretend play is also known as 'symbolic play' because it involves the use of symbols. Children do this beautifully. This might involve using a tea towel as a cape, shells and small stones as crystals and jewels, or sticks representing swords. Recently, one of my granddaughters has been using bars of soap as phones and she got very upset when I didn't answer my own phone-soap and use it appropriately! On another occasion playing doctors, one of my granddaughters shoved a teddy bear up her shirt because she was expecting a baby. It was really difficult not to laugh when she gave birth on the bed with much huffing and puffing! Again, this symbolic play is making sense of some of life's big experiences. Her little brother was only six weeks old at the time.

For our children, this is not just pretend. These props *feel real* and we need to be very mindful before we dispose of them, thinking they are unimportant. If your child has a special stone under her pillow, or she has kept a bar of soap in case somebody calls, please know that it is incredibly important to treat it with the respect it deserves.

> **PARENTS AND EDUCATORS' SURVEY**
>
> My five-year-old regularly puts on shows for us complete with colourful signage and a program. She has now started including a sign in form and is asking us to scan our phones. We now have COVID-safe home performances.

Pretend play or dramatic play, known technically as socio-dramatic play, is one of the best ways to consolidate oral language. Researchers have found that children who engage in pretend play often use higher forms of language than they would use in normal situations, often because they are pretending to be adults.

Imaginative play allows our little girls the opportunity to explore themselves and others in the world around them. This can enhance their social development because they can behave as themselves or pretend they are someone else, which allows the opportunity to explore the world from different perspectives and it requires them to be able to think about two ways of being at once. Pretending that she is a grown-up, using grown-up language and grown-up behaviour, is expanding her capacity to better understand the grown-ups in her world.

PARENTS AND EDUCATORS' SURVEY

Playing in her room with her dolls as a three-year-old, she was putting them to sleep and I hear her say very loudly, 'I've had enough. It's time to sleep and you WILL GO TO SLEEP!' Promptly walks out slams her door and plonks herself into the couch with a sigh. Looks over to me and says 'Kids!?', throwing her hands in the air!

I have seen many a little girl line up her teddy bears or dolls and then proceed to be the adult in the room. Sometimes they might teach them about the need to use their manners or to 'use your inside voice', or to scold one of the toys for being inattentive. It can be seriously a little confronting to hear how accurate their role-play is! Sometimes, something different happens after the girl has scolded her toy that may not have happened in her real-life experience that she is recreating. She may suddenly become tender and console the wounded doll, reassuring it with kind words and a hug – the consolation that she knew that she needed and wanted but never received. Her imagination is allowing her to explore her emotional world, and to make sense of how she felt about what happened. This exploration can help her soothe her own big feelings and set up a mindset that seeks to find meaning in upsetting situations.

MAGGIE'S MAIN IDEA

Little girls need opportunities to be in control and to have autonomy and pretend play allows for that beautifully.

The fascination and fun of joining in

One of the blessings of having grandchildren under six is that I get to witness them playing. Even better, I get invited into some of their pretend play.

During 2020 – the first year of the COVID-19 pandemic – my four-and-a-half-year-old granddaughter enjoyed playing doctors. Our front door leads into a small room, so it makes a perfect office. She has some toy medical equipment like a stethoscope, thermometer and the thing that looks in your ear. When it was my turn to see her, she walked out of her office and called loudly, 'Maggie Dent – next please!' When I took a seat, she asked me how I was and what seemed to be the problem. I had a sore knee and she examined it and put an Elsa bandaid on it. She then asked me had I had any coughing or a runny nose. When I answered no, she told me I was lucky because I didn't have the virus. She insisted on seeing my green (Medicare) card before I could pay my bill! At a second appointment, when I mentioned my knee was still sore, she suggested I go see another doctor. It was so hard not to laugh. Pretending to be a doctor or a shop assistant has been a part of traditional play for a very long time. As I've said, this is how our little ones make sense of the grown-up world.

Recent research has shown the value in early childhood education of using imaginary play that enhances the development of executive function in our children's brain architecture. This is also a wonderful opportunity for our girls to develop their authentic voice.

Imaginary friends and protectors

PARENTS AND EDUCATORS' SURVEY

'Mum, meet Jacob, Jaxon and Johnny.'

All her imaginary friends came for dinner with us that night and I had to serve up their plates too. (She is five.)

Many years ago, there was a perception that if your child had imaginary companions, it was a sign of a problem. Thankfully, the research has overwhelmingly dispelled such myths.

The girl who creates an imaginary friend has the opportunity to explore all the nuances of friendship without having to navigate the unpredictability of another person's behaviour, or risking the friendship ending. I have fond memories of a little girl who had created an imaginary friend called Claire when she was around the age of four. Her mum supported her imaginary reality and set a place for Claire at the table, and even made sure that Claire had her own toothbrush. The pretence even continued in the car, as Claire needed to have her seatbelt put on! One afternoon, the daughter became very distressed in the back seat and when the mum pulled up and went to see what was wrong, apparently Claire was the one who was distressed! This gorgeous mum still remembers standing on the side of the road, hugging and reassuring an invisible Claire until she stopped crying. What was really beautiful about this story was that when this girl grew up and turned 21, her mum and she were writing out invitations to her celebration. Her mum asked if they should write an invitation for Claire. Her daughter looked up with tears in her eyes and thanked her mum for letting her have her special imaginary friend all those years ago.

Children's imaginations can create new ways of seeing the world and of coping with things that challenge them. Dr Taylor explains that children who have imaginary friends appear to be mentally and emotionally more stable as adults. Rather than simply store, suppress or distort their experiences, they explored them with their imaginary friends. This allows the child the opportunity to diffuse any unexpressed emotion and to find a sense of meaning out of their experience.

Professor Susan Harter and Christine Chao from the University of Denver argue that children may fashion their imaginary companions in one of two ways: first, to create an imaginary friend who is helpless and incompetent, which makes the child feel strong or better by comparison. Second, they may create a friend who is extremely competent so that the child has a powerful ally, which boosts their sense of safety and their sense of self in the real world.

PARENTS AND EDUCATORS' SURVEY

My daughter (fourth child) has had an imaginary friend since she was three; she's now almost six. One day a few months ago, she asked me to keep a secret, that was her '(girl) friend Luke wasn't actually real'. But she still talks about her in her imaginary world, and in interactions with others, very creative and defends her reality to her siblings even now.

Dr Taylor believes the main reason that children create imaginary friends is simply to experience fun and companionship. Essentially, they can be great boredom beaters and for a lonely child, they can fill the need to have someone to play with. In our digital age, maybe little girls are finding this fundamental need for imaginary friends more in an online space. Sadly, the digital space is curating our children's experiences because their imaginary friends have been created by someone else.

MAGGIE'S MAIN IDEA

We need to ensure that our little girls are not discouraged from being in their own imaginary worlds rather than the real world or the digital world.

When I was a full-time counsellor, I worked with many little girls. The imagination was a pathway into their minds that could help me understand what was troubling them. I usually started with them drawing me a picture of how it was to be them, and they were always incredibly revealing. I believe girls intuitively know the power of colours and shapes to express fears and worries. Creating an imaginary, invisible protector that a little girl could take with her whenever she felt frightened was sometimes enough to transform significant anxiety. I created two creative visualisation audio tracks to support young children to create such a protector. Children get to choose whether they want a superhero or a guardian angel or any creature they can imagine. Often they draw this protector and give it a name, and this helps to anchor it into their mind. This has helped many children who have trouble falling asleep alone, feel they have no friends, experience school refusal or are frightened when their significant caregivers are not around. Both of these tracks, 'Safe 'N Sound' and 'Sleepytime', are available on my website for free.

PARENTS AND EDUCATORS' SURVEY

We bought her Elmo soft toy out to the park for a play. He was strapped into the extra seat on her bike very carefully and then taken around the playground as she explored. As we left the park and crossed the road, she suddenly remembered Elmo and we raced back to rescue him from the slide. 'I can see him, Mum!' He was lovingly snatched up and hugged as she said, 'I almost lost you!' (Four-and-a-half years old)

Superhero play

Normally, this is considered to be the domain of boys, and while there is a strong tendency for boys to use superhero play in response to their biological drives to be warriors and protectors, it can be incredibly helpful to give permission for our little girls to do the same. Sometimes known as 'the Batman effect', this play can give children opportunities to stretch and grow under the pretence of being a superhero. This is especially helpful for our more timid and sensitive lamb children.

This socio-dramatic play, when experienced within the safety of play, can allow our girls to be braver and more courageous than they may normally be. Such role-play can allow children to explore situations, experiences or emotions that they may be curious about because it is a risk-free platform. Giving our little girls access to capes, plastic or foam swords and other pretend weapons needs to be not only tolerated, but encouraged.

> **PARENTS AND EDUCATORS' SURVEY**
>
> Eight-year-old insisted on wearing a Wonder Woman costume to her doctor's appointment. It was worth every glare from judgemental old bat in the surgery to see her walk confidently into what for her is a scary situation.

As we have already explored earlier in the book social norms are deeply embedded into the human psyche. We need to seriously challenge that in some way our girls are weaker and less capable physically. They don't need to be rescued.

The little girl who impersonates a superhero can play out and achieve goals such as helping others and performing daring rescues. This kind of power is not easily found in a traditional girlhood. Thankfully, there are many images now of little girls being superheroes, sometimes still with a tiara on!

Lucky is the little girl who has brothers! She is simply included in all of the rough-and-tumble and adventurous antics of her siblings. Some of the most fiercely brave little girls I have ever met are the youngest in a family of boys. Having boy cousins or boys in the neighbourhood can also be helpful in allowing girls to play more vigorously or robustly.

What about the little girls who do not have brothers or boy cousins they see frequently? We need to have conversations in our early childhood settings and schools that encourage girls and boys to play together in whatever way they choose. This means that boys who want to do dress-ups in the home corner need to be welcomed as much as the girls wanting to play chasey and tag outside.

Gradually, more and more wonderful picture books are appearing that show our little girls as the hero instead of a supporting character or damsel in distress. I have a special fondness for an imaginary super heroine called Amber Dawn Princess Warrior. The story has a special sacredness to it because it was written by a lovely teacher about a beautiful little real-life girl called Amber Dawn Field, who was born with complex congenital heart disease. Even though she struggled with this illness, she never ceased to amaze everyone around her with her strong will, determination, bright spirit, big smile and zest for life.

Please marinate our little girls in stories where they are the superheroes.

Play and gender identity

Our belief systems and our filters are all formed in the first five years of life, and while they can be changed with intention, it would be so much better if our precious little girls were not observing the world around them so intently and forming the socially constructed, limiting beliefs that we know they form about their own uniqueness and competence.

There are so many negative messages that our little girls get from the grown-ups around them that can limit them later in life. If we want to raise our girls to find their inner courage and bravery we need to give them opportunities to stretch and grow.

Leslie Kendall Dye shares my concerns in an excellent article in *The Washington Post*. She describes her daughter as a cross between Spider-Man and The Flash because she has enormous agility and speed, and enormous energy. However, the voices of the strangers around her – men and women – having been causing her much angst. They are voices that a little boy in the same situation would not hear. Despite being fearless and highly active in ways that have been deemed not acceptable for little girls, her daughter has rarely skinned her knee or broken a bone.

One of the concerning messages in Kendall Dye's article was about the inferences from people that she must be an excessively permissive parent who doesn't discipline her child. She allows her to climb tall fences and trees – how permissive can you be? I share her frustration and annoyance that still as a society we tend to want to train girls to 'behave by undermining their confidence in their own body strength and ability'.

The article went on to explore yet another disturbing conditioning that well-meaning grown-ups are modelling. When strangers are surprised at the daughter's strength and agility, they seem to want to alleviate their own anxiety by reminding her and themselves that she is actually *just a girl*. They do this by making comments about how pretty she is or what a pretty dress she is wearing, in clear avoidance of the fact that she just leaped five feet through the air! We have so much to do to deconstruct these limiting influences, and imaginary play can play such a valuable role.

Gender identity is being influenced from the moment we are born. In my book *Mothering Our Boys,* I explore some research that shows that right from babyhood, boys are spoken to much more harshly than girls. As a grandmother who has gone searching for unique clothing for her granddaughters and grandsons, I still find it difficult to avoid the blue–pink dichotomy. It's the same (although it is getting better) with toys being labelled boys' toys and girls' toys.

It makes sense that gender identity can be influenced in the domain of imaginary play because of its importance in the psychosocial development of children. Role-playing may look like a simple activity, however, this is where our children can learn practical life skills like how to trust in themselves, how to cooperate and collaborate with others and how to share.

In a study called *Imaginary play, strengthening the gender identity and the gender role of children three to six years old*, it was quite obvious that young children had already clearly identified the roles that did not belong to particular genders. This means that if a little girl was playing the dad in a game, she would assume that dad went out to work, while mum stayed home and did the cooking. Presumably, she is basing that interpretation on what she has witnessed in her own home.

Sometimes, when children in the study were beginning their imaginary play, it was interesting to note that in the kindergarten room where the study took place, girls were often positioned in different places, such as near the home corner and dolls. This meant that the selection of the figures used by the children adapted to the rules of the play that they set up among themselves when they were playing in groups rather than by themselves. This suggests that we need to explore the placement of certain toys and figures that can be used in imaginary play. I do remember once visiting an early childhood setting that had dress-up clothes for the boys in one box and the dress-up clothes for girls in another!

Both the girls and the boys doing imaginary play in this study chose to play roles that fitted with gender stereotypes. The girls tended to play a mother, child, grandmother, educator or sister and boys were more likely to choose to play a role that was more stereotypically suited to the male gender. Interestingly, the children in the smallest group of three- to four-year-olds were able to correctly identify the roles and characteristics without the need to attach gender. It seemed that these children did not have a clear idea that a girl would not become a boy in the future or vice versa. This all suggests that there is still some flexibility in this window of under four, where some of the traditional social norms can be challenged through imaginary play.

MAGGIE'S MAIN IDEA

This magical window of under four is one where little girls can create a bigger sense of possibility for themselves in a world that is not limited by the social norms of the past.

As I've written, I was blessed in my childhood to have a wonderful dad who embraced my rooster qualities and who encouraged me to be me. My youngest brother was a gentler soul, and I feel that shaped my sense that boys didn't have to be tough and that being sensitive was still equally valid. The imaginative play that I remember most fondly took part in nature without any dolls, teddies, superhero characters or props. We made our own swords, potions and cubbies and pretended that trees could talk and lizards could be your friend. These opportunities of creativity are important as they build pathways to creative thinking and high-quality problem solving for later life.

You can't teach creativity; all you can do is let it blossom.

Little children, before they start school, are naturally creative. Our greatest innovators, the ones we call geniuses, are those who somehow retain that childhood capacity, and build on it, right through adulthood.

– Peter Gray, 'The Play Deficit', *AEON* (18 September 2013)

PARENTS AND EDUCATORS' SURVEY

She (age six) is desperate for a dog, to the extent she begged me to buy a harness and leash. She puts these on her little brother (age four) and we take him to the park for walks!

In 2001, a beautiful little five-year-old girl was brought to see me. She was very sad. Her mother told me how the little girl did not play with the other children at preschool. The doctor wanted to put her on antidepressant medication. This little one, who I will call Cindy, began to draw me an intensely black picture, even though I had given her a collection of brightly coloured pens with which to draw.

As she drew she asked, 'Maggie, how can you die if you want to?'

I gently asked Cindy what she meant. She responded that sometimes when she woke up in the morning, she closed her eyes really tightly and tried to die.

I wondered where this deep despair could be coming from – both her parents were concerned and loving. What had gone so wrong?

Cindy's parents were professional people. They had decided to give Cindy the 'best opportunity to be successful in life' by promoting the development of her intelligence. She had books full of facts about space, nature and science. Fantasy and the imaginary world were considered to be a distraction. She told me in a very despondent voice, 'Father Christmas doesn't come to our house.'

Cindy had grown up with no tooth fairy, no Santa, no picture books or fairytales and certainly no opportunities for imaginary play or dress-ups. Her parents were not aware of the protective role the imagination can play in a young child's life. Unknowingly, these caring parents had starved Cindy's emerging imagination and sucked the life out of her young spirit.

Recognising this, we were able to immediately bring wonder and creativity back into Cindy's life. Fortunately, Cindy had a wonderful early childhood educator who worked with the parents to restore her imagination. When I saw her a while later her eyes were shining, she had a beautiful smile and was accompanied by two very happy parents. She was wearing a pair of fairy wings and she told me that her daddy had told her a story about trolls on the bridge, and it had been really scary and Daddy had looked funny pretending to be a troll. Cindy was now full of life and energy with her mind, body, heart and spirit all well.

Interestingly, the week after I first saw Cindy, I met another pre-schooler who had a similar story. She too responded quickly to opportunities to expand her play, experience imaginary games and stories and have fun with her parents. These two little girls helped me understand the positive influences that play and imagination have in little girls' lives. I am deeply grateful to them for showing me this and the impact imagination can have on healthy mental, emotional and physical development in the lives of young girls.

Even though imagination may be difficult to measure, it really matters, especially for our preschool-aged girls. In fact, even though young children's imaginations are more fertile than those of adults, imagination can help people of any age with their emotional and mental wellbeing.

We must guard and protect the imaginary worlds of our little girls. Given how strong their imagination is so early on, we need to recognise this as a place where they can retreat from the real world if it becomes overwhelming or confusing. And in that place, they can explore, question and make meaning and sense through the wisdom of their childlike consciousness. Obviously having an exquisite imagination that is fertile and woven closely into the real world takes time to develop. We must prioritise it regardless of the busyness of family life.

PARENTS AND EDUCATORS' SURVEY

One night our little girl (who was no older than three years at the time) put her toy possum outside her bedroom door and put herself back to bed (with a variety of her usual cuddle toys in bed). We asked her the next morning why she did it and she said 'because he was talking too much'.

I know it can get tiring playing families, or hospitals or being construction workers in the sandpit! *Just know it is hugely valuable developmentally, emotionally, socially and cognitively.* Thankfully, the ABC's Emmy award–winning kids' show *Bluey* about a family of blue heeler dogs has given so many parents great insight into the importance of pretend play. Bluey's dad, Bandit, is a fabulous role model for parents everywhere on how fostering play can have so many benefits.

The gift of the imagination can be a powerful source of comfort, distraction and escape. However, it can be so much more than that for our little girls. It can help them to process life experiences, manage and balance their emotions, enrich their social understandings, explore their spiritual world, be incredibly creative, develop their communication skills and create wonderful possibilities for their lives. It is so valuable to have imaginary play, friends or explanations to help shield our girls from the often harsh, awful realities of the adult world.

We can all help our little girls build strong healthy imaginations by giving them the time and space and, most importantly, the willingness to value this as a gift in their early girlhood.

KEY POINTS

- Delightful little moments of imaginary joy are incredibly important, particularly in the lives of our little girls.
- Be careful not to steal girlhood – allow your little girls endless hours of autonomous imaginary play in the real world.
- There is a strong relationship between pretend play and the development of creativity, emotional literacy, empathy and social competence with other children.
- Children's imaginations can nurture, protect and insulate them from the concerns of the grown-up world.
- Pretend or dramatic play is one of the best ways to consolidate oral language.
- Please give our little girls access to capes, plastic swords and other pretend weapons so that they can participate in superhero play.
- We have much to do to deconstruct limiting influences in our little girls' lives and imaginary play can definitely help here.
- The gift of imagination can be a powerful source of comfort, distraction and escape and we need to value it right through life.
- From the age of around two, little girls use their imagination to process life experiences, achieve mastery of their emotions, enrich their social understandings, develop communication skills and create wonderful possibilities for their future life.

13

Raising girls in a digital age

PARENTS AND EDUCATORS' SURVEY

I worry about technology. She has grown up on a farm with minimal TV and no computer time. Schools seem heavily reliant on screens. Dreading sending her to school next year. Their values are much different to ours of nature, practical learning and building relationships. Sitting at a desk on a screen for the day seems toxic to me.

If this is the first chapter you turn to, you will not be alone. You were not raised with technology as children are today. Many of you will have been raised with the TV as being a part of your child-hood, so the main focus of this chapter is on the other screen world: handheld smartphones, devices, iPads and tablets. If we keep in mind that our little girls are very savvy and smart very early, and that they are modelling their initial connections to the small screen world on the behaviour of their key caregivers, especially mum, we do need to worry! I think every grown-up who has a smartphone is struggling to maintain healthy boundaries, and we can all get lost in scrolling when we were just looking for a recipe, or checking on the weather, or when making a doctor's appointment or ordering our daughter's lunch at school.

Technology is not all bad; indeed it has been positively life-changing in many areas of our modern world especially in the fields of medicine, science, and communication.

And now for the **but**: but it is definitely impacting our children in ways that we would prefer that it didn't.

But it is exposing our girls to more sexualised images than they are exposed to by the TV.

But it is increasing techno tantrums and conflict in our homes.

But it is contributing to, not necessarily causing, a significant increase in myopia in children.

But our children are experiencing a form of 'digital abandonment', with their parents experiencing *digital distraction*, which means less quality time with them because parents are engaging with their screens.

But our children are seeing violent and harmful content, even on apps made for little children!

But our children are not moving as much and that passivity is causing not just physical delays, but cognitive and brain processing delays as well.

But our young children are experiencing more developmental vulnerabilities and delays than in previous generations, especially around the development of oral language, gross- and fine-motor skills, self-regulation and an inability to play with other children or to sustain play with other children.

In her excellent book *Raising Your Child in a Digital World*, Dr Kristy Goodwin, who is a former early childhood educator, explores a thing called 'the displacement effect' and this is one of the most important things to keep in mind as you are raising your little girl in the first six to eight years of life. Screen use, especially small and interactive screens, can steal valuable moments of your daughter's life when she is supposed to be a curious, mobile, inquisitive child exploring the world around her using *all of her senses*. To discover more of this fascinating time of massive growth and development of the whole child, check out Chapter 2 on the first 1,000 days and Chapter 3 on the brain.

> **MAGGIE'S MAIN IDEA**
>
> The best advice I have been given from digital experts for our children under six is definitely as little small screen exposure as possible.

Screen time

When using a small screen with our little ones, the advice is not *how much time* should they spend on it, but rather – *what will they be doing* while using it. I am sure you have a question in the back of your mind about how much screen time is okay and healthy for your little girl, and Dr Kristy is mindful to say that there is no such thing. There is a huge difference between your daughter watching the ABC *Playschool* science program on the TV, or talking to Nanny via Skype or Zoom, and playing a violent video game or having access to TikTok, or watching videos that are highly sexualised and explicit. Not all screen time is equal.

Every parent needs to have some childfree time in the home, whether it is to do the grocery order, to do some cooking, to work, or simply for their own sanity. If you have tried engaging your daughter in a creative task, given her a construction task with blocks or Lego, encouraged her to play imaginatively with her toys, listened to music or an audiobook and they have all failed, then do not beat yourself up if you turn to a screen. My best recommendation is to put your child in front of the TV where there is a high-quality children's program that is the only thing available, with no advertisements. What tends to happen when children are watching a favourite program on the TV rather than on a small screen is that they tend to keep moving. Indeed, if you have boys, they will probably be doing somersaults off the couch while they watch TV. Many little girls continue with their craft or colouring while watching the TV. It is best to choose a well-loved program because it is familiar and can be quite calming, because the brain does not have to work very hard at prediction; in other words, what is going to happen in each story. For my granddaughters, they can narrate many *Bluey* episodes fluently because they have watched them so many times! Indeed, watching a well-loved, familiar program on TV can trigger the calming neurochemical serotonin, and it can restore your little girl's energy.

If you are seeking guidance, please choose a reputable, well-respected, credentialled website and avoid popularists, celebrities and bloggers. There is an Australian website called esafety.gov.au and they have excellent advice for parents of children under five. They also have a free booklet that can help parents around teaching your young children how to stay safe online.

PARENTS AND EDUCATORS' SURVEY

I am concerned about screen activities. Many of my daughter's friends spend too much time in front of screens, almost like the parents are using it as a 'playmate' instead of engaging with their children.

Appropriate content

Children under six are *highly susceptible* to being influenced by real experiences and virtual experiences, especially online. Keep this in mind as you review any content that you are about to offer your child. Many of the apps and games that are advertised as appropriate for preschoolers are the exact opposite. Before you choose any content that your child will have access to please check the appropriateness of it on childrenandmedia.org.au or esafety.gov.au/key-issues/esafety-guide.

One of the concerning realities in the space of technology for under sixes is that there are apps and programs that intentionally prey on little children's psychological vulnerabilities. Many of these apps are not appropriate for under sixes, even though they suggest that they are. One of the main reasons is that these apps use the emotional immaturity of children to encourage them to make in-app purchases or to watch pop-up advertisements. Some apps also contain buttons that use misleading symbols that little girls can be drawn to, like a teddy bear or a unicorn. If a child clicks those buttons, they see videos for more toys, junk food and, sadly, often sexualised images of children.

Not only are these advertisements conditioning our little girls, they can compromise any educational value that the app may have promised as they disrupt concentration and cause distraction. Be mindful of apps that promise to be educational, and avoid free apps because they will be using advertisements to fund their app. The best quality apps will need to be paid for and will not need in-app purchases or advertising. If you are looking for a guide to purchasing apps for your children, check out Commonsense Media app reviews.

The key message from digital educators is to avoid the digital world and the small screen world for as long as possible. The developmental needs in the first six years of life can definitely be displaced by screens. Be mindful of feeling pressured by what other parents are choosing to do for their daughters in the digital world. You need to be making choices in the best interests of your daughter, within your belief systems and values. At times, you may feel you are standing alone.

Avoid giving your daughter a smartphone for as long as possible, and remember that the minimum age for most apps is 13. Having the emotional maturity to make sound decisions and choices on what to share, what to comment on and what not to is very unlikely until the prefrontal cortex is much more mature, around 20 years of age. Some of the wisest voices to listen to around digital behaviour are girls aged between 18 and 24, because many of them have come to understand the positives, and the very dark side of being a digital citizen. Their regrets can be teachable moments for their younger sisters, cousins or friends because theirs is a lived experience.

PARENTS AND EDUCATORS' SURVEY

My daughter, totally unprompted, talking to Siri on the iPad: 'Can you clean my room?'

Sharing content

Given that consent is such an enormously important life skill that we need to teach our little girls as early as possible, please ask for her consent before you share her photo on your social pages. I have spoken with some teenage girls who are extremely angry with the number of images that their mother has shared on her Instagram page from their early childhood. Remember that our little girls are very switched on and want to be respected for their own points of view. To model this, we need to walk the talk.

Checking with her, especially from the age of around three, can make an enormous difference. Her digital footprint begins with you, and will continue with her, and there will be many conversations in her tween and teen years about the choices she may make.

KEY POINTS

- Before you give any child access to a digital device that has access to the world, learn everything you can about keeping them safe with parental controls, filtering devices and be careful to review carefully anything that your child wants to watch or interact with. Make sure you have control of the wi-fi.
- Establish clear boundaries before she is given the device, whether that is how many episodes, or how many games, and for young

children it can be helpful to put on a timer that lets them know that there are five minutes to go.

- For sensitive little girls who are prone to emotional meltdowns, be mindful that small screen use can create hyperarousal, where there's a sensory cup or energy that has been drained and they may need some help to refill it.
- Banning technology or using technology as a reward can become problematic in much the same way as promising lollies or desserts.
- Technology can be used for entertainment or education and deciding the intention of giving your little girl screen time needs to take this into consideration.
- Avoid any apps or games that reward your little girls because there are concerns it can create an over-active dopamine reward system or feedback loop that can increase the chances of addictions later in life or set our little girls up to be psychologically more vulnerable online later on.
- Have clear conversations about seeing disturbing content with your little girls and reassure them that they will not get into trouble if they tell you about the content. Suggest they immediately close their eyes or turn the device upside down. Sadly, they cannot unsee violent images or degrading pornography – prevention is essential.
- Keep devices in open areas and out of bedrooms and bathrooms from the get-go.
- Keep a healthy balance between screen and green, that is, between nature and the virtual world.
- Be mindful of digital boundaries when our children go to other houses, or they spend time with older siblings or older cousins who have different boundaries and preferences. Do not be uncomfortable checking the digital boundaries of other people if your child is going for a play.
- Prioritise play, human interaction, endless stories and conversations, the arts, crafts and music without a device as much as possible.

14

Little girls' friendships

PARENTS AND EDUCATORS' SURVEY

My biggest concern is the constant drama. Who's in? Who's out? Who's mean (they take turns with this one)? They do often play really nicely together, but it never seems to last long before there's a problem of some kind. Friendships for girls seem to be much more fraught than for boys. (I have one of each.)

There seems to be some confusion in the parenting world about what works best in building young children's socialisation skills. Some parents send their children to day care very early because they are worried about them having enough socialisation. Sadly many may not be developmentally ready at such an early age. Child psychologists agree that children are technically unable to master social skills until around three years of age, so we need to keep this in mind before we can explore little girls' friendships. It is a learning curve and just the same as resilience, parents will enjoy some of the delightful moments, and need to learn from some of the challenging ones. Friendship dynamics are more complex than most of us realise. When you blend in temperament differences, age differences, gender differences, cultural differences and neurodiversity, no wonder the friendships of our little girls can be tricky at times!

Dandelion girls will tend to navigate this journey with fewer upsets and tears than our sensitive orchids. Also our lambs and our introverted girls will tend to struggle more. It can be helpful to remember that our little girls have incredible memories and a capacity to ruminate on negative experiences when exploring friendship dramas. In the survey for girls aged four to eight, friendship dramas topped the list of most concerning challenges that parents and educators experience with little girls.

PARENTS AND EDUCATORS' SURVEY

I have been shocked at how young the mean streak in the friendships has appeared. My little girl turned five back in May. She was so excited as it was the first time she was having a big party at home with preschool friends. They are all horse-mad girls and I let them all ride Poco the pony. They had a blast and my daughter was on cloud nine. On the Monday when I picked her up from preschool, she was so downtrodden and forlorn. I asked her why and she told me none of her friends would play with her today. Her 'best friend' wouldn't even talk to her. I feel like it was the first moment her heart got broken at the hands of a friend. It's taken about two months for this group of girls to get back to a good place and the meanness towards my daughter to drop off.

Friendships are a lot about building alliances so that our little girls have support when they need it. Positive alliances offer opportunities for fun and empathy, and they feed our biological hunger to belong. These alliances are often threatened by some patterns of relational aggression like name-calling, put-downs, gossip and spreading rumours.

Having a fabulous, safe best friend is one of the most wonderful gifts you can experience as a human. However, negotiating the nuances of friendship can be confusing and really intense at times, especially for our little girls under six who have immature brain architecture and who aren't able to fully understand emotional and social influences and expectations.

'We'll be friends forever, won't we, Pooh?' asked Piglet.

'Even longer,' Pooh answered.

– A.A. Milne, *Winnie-the-Pooh* (1926)

The 'why' around girl friendship dramas

Humans are social beings, which means we are biologically wired to be in relationships in systems like families, neighbourhoods and communities. According to evolutionary biologist Robin Dunbar in his book *Friends: Understanding the Power of Our Most Important Relationships,* our capacity for having intimate friendships or relationships has an upper limit. He argues that for adults, our innermost layer is 1.5 people. I don't know about you, but I'm not sure how we can love half a person intimately! The second layer, which is the people whose shoulder you can cry on and who will absolutely be there for you no matter what, is five people. The next circle are your core social partners and that is around 15, including the five from the second layer. These are the people that can help out with our kids and who we call 'our village'. Dunbar argues that the next layer is around 50 people and they are your 'big weekend barbecue' people. The final layer includes around 150 and they are the people who come to your weddings and funerals, but who you don't necessarily have much to do with. His research also shows that introverts are unable to sustain the same number of relationships as extroverts. However, while the intimate and cry-on-your-shoulder friends may be fewer in numbers, they might be much deeper friendships.

Friendships are a critical part of a child's learning process. Through friends children learn about themselves and others, and model new skills and social behaviours. The very act of making friends is one of the major developmental tasks of early childhood, helping children to feel good about themselves, adapt more easily to new environments and build self-confidence.

– Claire Orange, parenting educator and founder of DiGii Social

There has been a lot of research on the origins and nature of same-sex friendships, the most renowned study of which was in 2009 by the National Institute of Mental Health (NIMH) and Georgia State University with the use of fMRIs (Functional Magnetic Resonance Imaging). This was the first time scientists looked at what actually happens inside the brains of children aged eight to 17 in response to potential friendship opportunities. The results showed a significant difference in the way boys and girls respond to the anticipation of making a friend. Various areas of girls' brains (areas associated with reward, hormone secretion, social learning, and subjective feelings) lit up with the prospect of a new friendship, while the boys' brains showed almost no activity and, in some cases, *even decreased activity*.

There are many ways to interpret this information, and scientists are reluctant to pinpoint causation, but it's safe to say that there's a lot going on for girls in the face of friendships. It may also suggest why many boys struggle in the friendship world. It also suggests that we need to support young boys on this journey as best we can and not just assume their friendships will form and progress in similar ways to girl friendships. I think that feel-good neurotransmitters are created in the brain more easily for girls, even before they connect with their friends and siblings.

Over the last six months, I have been observing my little grand-daughters and my great-nieces in their relationships with other little girls, and I am staggered by how quickly things change from happiness to upset. One minute they will be cheerfully playing and they are 'best friends forever' and then, in a nanosecond, they are never going to be friends again! Parents and early childhood educators have been noticing that friendship conflict and dramas are happening earlier in our little girls' lives. Katie Hurley explains in her book *No More Mean Girls* that she has found over and over again that young girls struggle with the art of friendship-making. Hurley agrees with me that we are stealing childhood from our children in the hurry to be ready for school, which means that the valuable time that all our children need to learn social skills and character development has been taken away from them. Our girls are being given very scripted lives, with lots of organised and structured activities, usually run by adults, and there has been a decline in neighbourhood play. Quite simply, our girls are losing the opportunities to learn important social skills independently and in the company of other children, particularly multi-age children, doing exactly what children are meant to be doing – playing in real time. Childhood nastiness, where children say things spontaneously in the heat at the moment or out of frustration, is normal childlike behaviour. When this occurs among hours of play, a little girl may have lots of opportunities to learn how it feels, and gradually how to manage it. It would be fabulous if the word 'mean' could be used less around girls' behaviour because it makes it sound like all girls have a tendency to be mean.

Friendship challenges – a part of life!

Let's be honest; as adults, and particularly as older women, we can still be incredibly hurt by some of the choices of friends or acquaintances who we thought were friends. We have most likely also made mistakes that caused others emotional pain too. There is no 'perfect' in human relationships. However, given the reality of friendship challenges for girls and the use of terms such as 'mean girl' behaviour, it could be helpful if we reframe how we describe this behaviour as 'unfair' or 'unkind'. The second perspective we can consider is whether exclusion behaviour intentionally causes harm or accidentally causes harm. The reality is, whether intentional or unintentional, relational aggression hurts.

Dr Matthew Lieberman and Naomi Eisenberger showed how powerful the impact of social exclusion is on individuals, including children. Using brain imaging, they found that when a person experiences rejection or social exclusion, they experience a form of physical pain. This body sensation is most likely going to trigger the primitive brain into fight-or-flight. We need to keep this in mind when a child has been hurt in a friendship dispute and care for them as though they have a physical wound. The researchers also discovered that being treated fairly activates the pleasure response, the same parts of the brain as having our basic needs met, like having a drink of water on a hot day, coming in from the cold or eating chocolate.

It is important to remember there is a science behind the emotional response that our little ones feel when they have been treated unfairly or excluded. Teaching emotional literacy and coaching them on how to navigate these challenges, especially for our little girls, needs to be a priority. We cannot simply leave it to chance and hope they figure it out themselves.

We also need to be mindful that the brain architecture of our little girls is still developing to enable them to identify and understand human behaviour. We need to see the world through their eyes rather than only through our mature, grown-up eyes. An excellent picture book that can help explain this tendency is *Rosie Leads the Way* by Renee Irving Lee. It shows how Rosie, who experiences rejection from a little girl called Penny, comes to understand that even though Penny looks perfect, Penny struggles with some things that Rosie doesn't.

A key message of mine is about three rules I feel are of utmost importance:

A key message to teach our little girls is the importance of

three rules

Please try to avoid hurting:
> Yourself
> Anyone else
> The world around you.

We do have to remind our little girls very early that words can hurt, and certain actions such as ignoring someone, avoiding someone or laughing at someone can also hurt. Another helpful tip to teach our little girls is that there are always two sides to every story and sometimes, we only have part of the truth.

> Being treated unfairly activates the social pain and disgust circuitry. In our evolutionary past, being accepted and valued by one's group is important because it means access to critical resources for survival and thriving.
>
> – Lieberman and Eisenberger, 'The pains and pleasures of social life', *Neuroleadership Journal* (2008)

A possible additional contributing factor to this increase in struggles for our little girls, besides a lack of play, can be the influence of relational aggression in children's programs, YouTube and online activities. Due to the mirror neurons in their brains, our children learn to copy the behaviour of others they see in our world. If they are watching the children and grown-ups in the world around them acting with compassion and consideration, that is what they will learn. However, even these children can learn how to behave quite differently because they are watching programs that include relational aggression like name-calling, exclusion and put-downs. For example, I have found some episodes of *Peppa Pig* have also used relational aggression.

> Some of the programs that were shown to negatively influence children's playground behaviour after being watched were *Clifford the Big Red Dog*, *Arthur* and *SpongeBob SquarePants* – all very popular children's programs. Children see TV programs as real life not as entertainment as adults do. This is brain plasticity in action.
> – Maggie Dent, *9 Things: A Back-to-Basics Guide to Calm, Common-sense, Connected Parenting Birth–8* (2014)

Heather Shumaker, in her book *It's OK to Go Up the Slide*, explains that there are two reasons why preschool-aged girls are more apt to use words that hurt rather than actions. As we have explored, most girls at this age are more verbal and express themselves and their feelings through words. The second reason, Shumaker argues, that girls are more likely to focus on relationships than boys are, is because they understand how powerful they are. This partially explains why girls are more likely to attack relationships and friendships when they get upset; hence the words, 'You are not my friend anymore!'

A final consideration in the background of exploring little girls' friendships is the evolutionary concept of 'tend and befriend', which we saw in Chapter 3. When faced with a significant threat, women have a greater tendency to reduce distress by tending – protecting and nurturing the young – and befriending – maintaining and strengthening social networks. Anecdotally, there seems to be some weight in this, however, cultural norms are shifting and it is now common for men to meet for coffee or go for walks and nurture deeper, more meaningful friendships. So, while this will not be all girls and some boys, it may be a contributing influence as to why girl dramas around friendships can be so complex and confusing. It can also explain why girls can focus on helping others rather than themselves, which can lead to people-pleasing, an inability to say no and being 'nice' when they really don't want to.

PARENTS AND EDUCATORS' SURVEY
My daughter doesn't have close friendships. She is friends with a lot of people in her class but does not buy into the 'best friend' ethos.

I have been surprised as to how early our little girls learn the game 'compare–despair'. I was at a birthday party for one of my granddaughters who was turning three when a massive emotional meltdown occurred because two girls were wearing the same shoes and they each wanted to be special by being the only one who wore the shoes! I have also witnessed little girls the same age at a birthday party celebrating the fact that they were wearing the same shoes! Yikes, it can be complicated, can't it? My granddaughters are constantly asking what the other granddaughters are able to do, like the monkey bars, riding a bike without training wheels or doing a cartwheel. They are very fond of their cousins, however, compare–despair is already a part of their psyche. If unchecked, it can lead to self-loathing and low self-worth.

Friendship coaching your little girl

Nothing tears at a parent's heart strings like hearing their child say the words, 'No-one wants to play with me!' or 'I have no friends!'. To our little girls, nothing is more heartbreaking than being told, 'I don't want to be your friend anymore!' or 'You are not my best friend anymore!' How can we help our children form good friendships that will not just be fun but will be supportive and long-lasting? Well, the main way that our girls learn the ups and downs of friendships is with the significant help of parents or other safe grown-ups – our little girls need a friendship coach who can help decode and deconstruct the complexities around social interactions and relationships.

PARENTS AND EDUCATORS' SURVEY

My five-year-old has connected strongly and made some beautiful friendships that have endured even long times apart. She gets very confused and upset when her best friend tells her, 'You're not my best friend anymore.' But we've been working on understanding that this is her friend's way of letting her know something is upsetting her, and she might not know how to say this yet.

Many girls can tend to be like butterflies, flitting around, being friends with lots of kids without necessarily being best friends with anyone. This is helpful because girls can also tend to be best friends today, worst enemies tomorrow, and then in a few days, they are back to being besties!

Child psychiatrist Dr Kaylene Henderson gave the following common-sense advice at a conference we were presenting at: she tells her three children that you don't have to be friends with everyone, you just need *to be friendly*. This is a fabulous reminder and quite a simple lesson that we can teach our girls early in life. It reinforces the significance of communication being so much more than words and the importance of smiling when greeting other children, waving hello, saying goodbye and making eye contact.

As parents, we need to recognise that there will be bumpy times and sometimes your daughter will be the victim of a drama, other times, the cause. We are all hungry to belong in healthy friendships and it can take a long time to work out the nuances of what this really means.

To find some clarity on this topic, I reached out to Michelle Mitchell, a serious girl champion of tween and teen girls and a former primary school teacher. In her experience, the big questions girls are seeking answers to are, 'Do I belong? What does it take for me to belong in this friendship?' Her thoughts on these questions often drive the difference between a girl seeking a best friend versus a good-enough friend. Securing a 'best friend' suggests a stronger sense of belonging and a degree of being more 'special'. It is a bit like a race, and having a best friend is like coming first and a good-enough friend is coming third. This approach can come at a price because a little girl may be overly invested in one friendship and has therefore put all her eggs in one basket. When there is conflict in this friendship, it can appear catastrophic.

Michelle's advice is to encourage your little girls – from as early in life as possible – to have good-enough friends rather than one best friend. Of course, friendship valuations are incredibly subjective, so you could remind your little girl that her very best friend is herself. Everyone else is good enough.

PARENTS AND EDUCATORS' SURVEY

My daughter and her friend were playing on the school oval briefly after school one day. There was clearly a disagreement of some kind as they both marched off in opposite directions, looking very unhappy. My little girl called to me for a hug but didn't explain what happened when I asked. Then she approached her friend and they sat on the ground together, facing each other, and had a deep discussion. (I couldn't hear what they were saying, I could only see them.) They were turn-taking, very thoughtfully listening to each other. After some time (at least five minutes), they got up and hugged, then came running back together, happy as Larry! It was amazing and I was so proud of both of them.

I have worked with a number of girls of all ages from primary school through to secondary school who wished they could have spoken to their mum about their friendship dramas, but their early experiences of sharing their stories – especially when mum wanted to fix everything – had made things worse, so they no longer sought her help. There were times when their mum's behaviour had embarrassed them so much, it had negatively impacted their connection to her.

Keep in mind that as your daughter's friendship coach, you can help her learn about the ups and the downs of human relationships but it is not your job to 'fix' things. Your daughter needs to develop the awareness and skills to navigate the evolving friendship world and your role is not so much to protect her as to empower and support her through the ups and downs. There is no guarantee that her heart won't be broken at some time when a friendship ends. If this is a dynamic that isn't working between you and your daughter, find another female ally who can be her friendship coach. My next favourite option is an auntie figure.

Some key skills for the friendship coach

PARENTS AND EDUCATORS' SURVEY

Miss 5: 'We don't say, "get lost", do we?'

Me: 'No, that's not a kind thing to say.'

Miss 5: 'We definitely don't say, "shut up" either.'

Me: 'No, that's not nice. We say, "please be quiet".'

Miss 5: 'Can I say, "bullshit"?'

Help her to learn to not overreact. If your little daughter comes to you really upset about something that has been said or done by another little girl, it can be useful to remind her about the glitter jar. This metaphor can help her realise that it is normal to feel upset when someone says hurtful things or excludes her. Just like a glitter jar that has been shaken, feelings can be quite intense, especially at the time. Teach her to take some steps to recognise that it can be difficult to resolve an issue in the heat of the moment and it is best to wait until the glitter has settled.

Friendship conflict can come in many shapes and sizes and it can take some serious listening to work out whether it is minor or serious. In the eyes of most little girls, even minor issues are serious. In one of their resources for children as part of their Best Programs 4 Kids social and emotional learning program, authors Helen Davidson and Claire Orange use an excellent easy-to-remember metaphor when exploring friendship challenges or 'flare-ups'. A small friendship flare-up is called a spark, and will probably settle quite easily. A medium-sized friendship flare-up is called a flame and this may need some help to manage or it may settle on its own. The big friendship flare-up that can be really hurtful is a bit like a fire, and it needs to be managed with the assistance of a friendship coach.

The key message is that we need to help our little girls **develop perspective** and, given that they have a very immature prefrontal cortex and an inability to use logic, be prepared for some irrational feelings around the stories that they are telling themselves.

Teach basic conversation skills. This is really easy for some children, but others can struggle without some coaching. Explain to your little girls that a conversation isn't just about the words we say, it's about how well we listen to what the other person is saying. You can practise this skill in imaginary play with your daughter by having conversations in the car or by intentionally creating opportunities to chat about topics that are interesting to her. I find I have great chats when cooking with my granddaughters, when we are going for walks or just before bed.

When it comes to social interaction, asking questions is a superpower. A single question has the power to break the ice, fill an awkward silence and convey to someone that you think they are interesting and important.

– Kasey Edwards and Dr Christopher Scanlon, *Raising Girls Who Like Themselves* (2021)

Teach her to trust her instincts. Remind your little girl about our early warning signs and body sensations, because sometimes her body will tell her that a friendship is not good for her. A handy question to ask your daughter is: 'Does it feel good playing with XXX . . . all of the time, some of the time or never?' Michelle Mitchell uses a lunchbox analogy to help girls understand friendships that tend to take rather than give. 'If you allow someone to take your lunch every day, at some point, you will get really hungry. Allowing someone to walk all over you is a strategy that is not good for you and possibly won't change unless you make the change.'

Talk about wishful thinking and recruiting tips. Mitchell says that one friendship pattern is that girls 'can get in the habit of projecting their wishful thinking onto someone else who they perceive as being more powerful than they are'. If our children focus their energy on recruiting support (usually in the form of gossiping, complaining, dobbing, begging, nagging, sulking or crying) rather than problem-solving, they don't have any need to listen to their own best friend – their higher self – because they are telling themselves a story that they can let someone else meet their needs. 'Bossy' behaviour is a sign that this could be happening. In my creative visualisation audio called 'I Am a Good Friend', I address bossiness. I have had a number of parents of girls who tend to dominate by being too bossy change their behaviour after listening to this audio.

Creating a friendship tribe. This means encouraging your daughter to see her friendships through a wider lens. She can call the girls in her gymnastics class, dance class, or neighbourhood friends, even if they only see each other once a week. The same can be applied with children in your adult circle of friends who your daughter might only holiday with from time to time. The same goes for cousins, who often develop friendships beyond blood connections. It can be helpful to draw a big map of this friendship tribe so that when she is rejected by one girl in her class, she is able to be reminded that there are so many more who are still her friends in that moment.

The quick comeback. Teaching your daughter what to do when a friend has said those dreaded words – 'I'm not your friend anymore' – can have an enormous influence on how she copes with that rejection, not just when she is a little girl but also later in life. Many parents and grandparents, including myself, have suggested walking away or ignoring the person who is being unkind. Dana Kerford, Friendship Expert and Founder of URSTRONG, believes it's more effective to teach girls skills to deal with poor behaviour in a productive way. Her name for this is the quick comeback. I would suggest starting with the clear message, 'NO' with a hand up, or 'STOP, I don't like it' then turning and walking away. Kerford suggests these:

- 'That's not okay'
- 'That was really mean'
- 'Excuse me!'
- 'Knock it off'

This works best when the quick comeback is assertive, non-blaming and non-inflammatory. That can be quite tricky for little girls who are still developing an understanding of what those things mean, but modelling and practising will definitely fine-tune the delivery.

Michelle Mitchell has a modified version of this approach that she calls, 'pushing back with truth'. This technique involves simply finding short, snappy statements to use in response to bullies' comments. These statements might include, 'No. I'm a really nice person' and 'I don't think you should be saying that, do you?' or 'That's okay – I have other friends.'

Another helpful part of this excellent resource for the friendship coach is a book created by Helen Davidson and Claire Orange called *Friends, Fitting In & All That Stuff*. A little girl can learn to manage various difficult situations, such as a refusal to be included in play. She can learn to use positive body language by standing tall with her shoulders back and her chin up. And then she could say:

> That's okay, I'll play tomorrow.
>
> That's no big deal.
>
> That's okay, I'll do something else.
>
> In response to a nasty, mean refusal to play, these are the suggestions;
>
> Don't be nasty.
>
> There is no need to speak to me like that.
>
> Saying no nicely would have been enough.
>
> Don't speak to me like that.
>
> I've changed my mind anyway.
>
> That's very rude.
>
> Ouch, that's mean.
>
> See you later.
>
> – Helen Davidson and Claire Orange, *Friends, Fitting In & All That Stuff*, 'What To Do About' Series, Best Programs 4 Kids (2017)

Don't overdo the kindness message. While encouraging our little girls to be thoughtful, considerate and kind is a good thing – and hopefully we are also modelling these attributes to her – we need to be careful not to overdo it. If we do, we run the risk of encouraging our girls to be nice and good all the time, and we feed into the mentality that girls need to be looking after others ahead of themselves. If you are having a conversation about a friendship conflict, you can remind your little girl how she could be kind to herself when things get a bit tricky.

Understanding boundaries. Developing and grasping a clear understanding of family values and expectations is really helpful for our little girls. In addition to the three rules, specific expectations around the use of inappropriate offensive language, telling lies, spreading hurtful gossip, any use of put-downs, name-callings and teasing, and having respect for elders will need to be clear and realistic. There may be times when, in order to belong to a certain friendship group, your daughter will cross boundaries she would not normally cross. Being excluded from a friendship group may be more terrifying than breaking a family rule! I have been staggered to notice the capacity little girls have in the art of persuasion and manipulation, and from such a young age!

Another key message around understanding boundaries for our little girls is *the ability to say no when they want to say no*, and to say yes when they really want to say yes. This is a skill for life! I was still struggling with saying no in my late 30s because as a little girl who had been shamed, I consciously and unconsciously never wanted to hurt anybody else. To be honest, I needed to work with a therapist to shift the stories I created around needing to please people, avoid disappointing people and avoid hurting people. Of course, what I was doing was disappointing and hurting myself!

Practising emotional attunement. So often we try to dismiss our little girls' emotions because, to be honest, they can be time-consuming. Creating a space and time to be present and to allow her to express all her big feelings is important, and it's okay to let her know when the space can be created. For example, if she gets upset at the playground, you could find some space for her away from the other children to explore what's happened, or you could whisper in her ear and let her know that when you get home, you will have a snack and some 'couch time'. Rather than dismissing her, acknowledge what's happening for her and reassure her that you are merely delaying the connection time that she is yearning.

By showing them that it is safe to express unpleasant emotions around you and in front of you and you respond with body language (e.g. leaning towards not away; offering touch) your words (i.e., I can see you're overwhelmed) and your empathy, you are helping them to reduce their defence mechanisms by teaching them that it is safe to express their emotions around you.

– Dr Renee Cachia, *Parenting Freedom: Transform stress and depletion to connectedness and meaning* (2021)

Dos and don'ts in the heat of the moment. These suggestions are for friendship dramas rather than intentional bullying which has been taking place over time.

Resist your desire to rescue your daughter and fix the problem! If you become the fixer for your daughter, she will never master the skills for later in her life to manage relationships that matter. In an episode of her podcast *Conversations with Lisa*, Australian transformational coach Lisa Corduff explores how women can learn to be overly responsible for others – or the fixer – and that technically, this is a form of co-dependence. Many women have an underlying programming that tells them that if a relationship is struggling, they need to work harder at fixing it. If their partner is struggling in some area of their life, we can often feel responsible for helping to fix that too. I certainly had a lightbulb moment in the personal growth workshop when the therapist said, 'The only person you can change is yourself.'

This is why it is so important that we help our little girls become their own problem-solvers. We can work with them to view these 'hot' moments as learning opportunities and we can start by:

- Breathing to keep yourself calm
- Empathising then really listening, without interrupting!
- Validating her feelings: 'You sound really mad!' or 'You sound really angry.'
- Checking whether she just needs to vent or needs your help to problem-solve
- Clarifying the facts calmly
- Exploring options to go forward

- Asking what she is learning from this experience
- Reminding her how much she is loved exactly as she is.

The more we help our little girls explore, problem-solve and understand the complexity of human relationships, the better equipped they will be in adolescence and adulthood.

> To parent right from the start means knowing and accepting that children must struggle in order for their brains to grow. The smooth ride with no upset, no invitation for strife, no need to accept that which cannot be, does not produce growth.
>
> – Dr Vanessa Lapointe, *Parenting Right From the Start* (2019)

This does not mean that we leave our little girls or our tween and teen girls to flounder alone. Sometimes, a girl's mother can be her friendship coach all the way through life, and other times they will need to lean on other significant adult allies, who I call lighthouses. This is definitely an area where the power of positive aunties can be life-changing for our girls. In adolescence there is a biological drive to push back and individuate from parents, so we need another safe, adult ally to assume the protective guiding role of the most connected parent.

PARENTS AND EDUCATORS' SURVEY

I have really enjoyed empowering my three girls with self-confidence and honesty to navigate friendships, meanness and their own bad choices by openly talking about other children and families in a non-judgemental way, encouraging my girls to accept the choices of others and to learn to navigate life based on their own choices and preferences. It has been a joy to watch them thrive and grow centred on their own abilities and choices, rather than being a slave to the opinions of others. They seem to have had far fewer 'friend' dramas than most of their peers, or at least that I know about!

When to worry?

Normal childhood nastiness can sometimes progress to something much more sinister and, indeed, can become bullying. Many of the issues connected to relational aggression that you will help your little daughter navigate will cause her much confusion and hurt. True friendship values trust and when that is broken, the consequences can be long-lasting and the healing process can require more than just a conversation with a trusted adult. Social manipulation with on-again / off-again friendships can be a sign that a little girl is learning how to use power over others. In the initial stages, it may be appropriate to dismiss this behaviour as not being too serious as you teach your daughter strategies to manage and navigate her interactions and responses.

Some little girls find it really difficult to share their stories of being rejected because they feel embarrassed. Sadly, a little girl who is being bullied will often believe that if she tries harder to please her bully friend, she may be able to rejoin the friendship group. However, this cycle can create a power differential, which technically defines bullying versus relational aggression. A response of 'trying harder' could give the little girl who is being the bully valued credibility because she gets what she wants, and her sense of power grows.

This is why it is so important that your daughter has a friendship coach who can help her identify some of the behaviours that need to be addressed in ways that she can manage while also protecting herself.

Cyberbullying

Sadly, this is happening at younger and younger ages for our little girls. Being able to use relational aggression from a distance does not reduce the amount of pain it can cause.

Girls and cyberbullying is a complex issue. While some level of friendship rupture and repair is necessary for learning how to manage difficult social situations, when cyberbullying happens it has its own distinct signature and level of lasting damage. So, call cyberbullying by its name. Try not to minimise it by using other stereotypical labels of girls' friendship issues. Believe the girl who reports and take immediate action. What we do know is that girls' cyberbullying is insidious and very damaging to long-term mental health, so education is an essential part of protection.

– Claire Orange, 'Girls and Cyberbullying', digiisocial.com
(12 February 2021)

If your daughter is being cyberbullied, keep photographic evidence in case it escalates and you need to work with the school or the police to have it addressed. The e-safety commissioner in Australia has excellent information to help you if this is happening.

One of my best friends is one of my sisters, Sue. I am not sure I would be here today if it was not for her. Even though I spent most of my childhood incredibly jealous of having a perfect sister, she was always there for me and still is today. If you have daughters, there will be moments when they fight and bicker because that is what siblings do. Keep reminding them that sisters can be best friends and that you hope that one day they definitely will be best friends.

Healthy girl friendships can be significant in so many ways. Not only are they an important protective factor in terms of resilience, they can enhance life experiences – the good, the bad, the horrendous and the spectacular! Even though you will have many moments with your little girls exploring hurt feelings, disappointment and rejection, keep coaching and affirming to her how wonderful your best friendships are. Model speaking positively about your best friends and remind her that with best friends, nothing is off the table. Women share everything with their besties, from embarrassing moments, treatment for thrush, dreams for the future, failed cooking, opinions on clothing, advice on in-laws, good books to read, children's disasters and yes, they talk about sex. Best friends can be trusted and do not repeat secrets or shared moments of intimacy, and we need to teach that early in life to our little girls, because gossip can be a toxic, destructive destroyer of friendships.

Be impeccable with your word.
Don't take anything personally.
Don't make assumptions.
Always do your best.

– Don Miguel Ruiz, *The Four Agreements: Practical Guide to Personal Freedom* (2011)

KEY POINTS

- Friendship dynamics are possibly more complex than most of us realise.
- When you blend in temperament differences, age differences, gender differences, cultural differences and neurodiversity, no wonder friendships between our little girls can be tricky at times.
- It is quite normal for our young girls to struggle with the art of friendship-making.
- Friendships are a lot about building alliances that ensure our little girls have support when they need it.
- Positive alliances offer opportunities for fun and empathy and they feed our biological hunger to belong.
- Relational aggression that threatens positive alliances is a learned behaviour. With emotional coaching, especially in the early years, a little girl may make different choices.
- We need to remind our little girls very early that words can and do hurt.
- Encourage your little daughter to have good-enough friends rather than aim for the best friend.
- Become your daughter's friendship coach, where you help her to learn about the ups and downs of friendship.

- Friendship conflict can come in many shapes and sizes, from a spark to a flame or a fire.
- Encourage your children with the message they don't have to be friends with everyone, however, they can be friendly to everyone.
- Teach basic conversation skills and welcoming and farewell strategies.
- Creating a friendship tribe can be helpful with friends from many different areas of her life.
- Be careful not to overdo the kindness message because it can give our little girls the belief that they need to look after others ahead of themselves.
- Teach your daughter about healthy boundaries and give her the ability to say no when she wants to say no.
- Cyberbullying is relational aggression from a distance and is becoming very problematic for all ages.
- See every friendship conflict as an opportunity to problem solve and explore the complexity of human relationships.
- If we can convince our little girls that the best friend they are ever going to have in their whole life is already hiding inside them, always with them, always loving them, imagine how safe their world may become.

15

Nurturing her voice

PARENTS AND EDUCATORS' SURVEY

Recently my daughter has been learning about kindness at school. I had just had my hair cut and she told me she really liked my hair. I said, 'Thank you' and she told me she was being kind and filling my 'bucket' with kindness. It was a beautiful moment. She is four years old.

There have been many hard-fought advances for girls and women over the last 20 years, even though pay equity still has a long way to go. There are female leaders of countries all around the world. Women are gradually speaking up about the injustices that unhealthy patriarchy still sees as acceptable and normal. However, there is still a lot to do, and we need to focus on this *before* our girls get to school.

I am a child of the 1950s and '60s, when traditional patriarchy was in full swing. Most mothers never had the opportunity to work or dream of a career, and women could not even take out a bank loan. In a 2020 post on social media, I shared that I clearly remember when I was about eight an elderly man telling me, 'Missy, you need to be careful not to get too big for your boots!' From the responses that I received, it seems that many women were given similar messages that were never challenged at the time. Even in the early '80s, I had to resign from my teaching position when I left to have my first son!

There is no question that the cultural messages and policies about keeping girls and women in their place, well below men, were pervasive. Little girls were often told to look pretty, stay quiet, be good and always have a smile.

Sadly, many girls and young women are still feeling silenced. I wrote a blog early in 2020 called 'Why we need much more than consent training in our schools to stop sexual assault' that explored the light currently being shone on the dark underbelly of inappropriate sexual behaviour, harassment and abuse, most specifically cases of rape by boys and men in Australian schools, communities, businesses and parliament. From the moment the courageous advocate for survivors of sexual assault Grace Tame became Australian of the Year, attitudes markedly shifted. After Grace Tame's award, the former Liberal staffer Brittany Higgins was inspired to disclose her alleged (I use that word for legal purposes) rape in the office of a federal minister. This disclosure from an eloquent young woman has been the catalyst for others to speak up about similar assaults. The months that followed have shown that there seem to be some serious cultural issues within the corridors of federal and state politics. I took part in a national women's summit to explore the issues in more depth, and I am hoping that rather than hearing more words, there may be some action that takes place to create both more equity and equality. Simply aiming to have an increase in respect for women in every level of our political systems should be the minimum expectation.

Next appeared a petition for earlier sex education in schools – which began as an Instagram poll – by former Kambala student Chanel Contos. At the time of writing, it had been signed by almost 45,000 people and more than 6,500 girls and young woman have shared their stories of sexual assault on the teachusconsent.com website. While the testimonies are harrowing and distressing, they allow us collectively to know more about the truth of this violent culture. There was also a massive nationwide rally called the March 4 Justice, where women were joined by men to show their anger and outrage at the lack of respect and action for injustices against women in Australia.

> **MAGGIE'S MAIN IDEA**
>
> These girls and women have been heard but have they been heeded? Is action and change in our homes, schools, universities and in the wider community going to take place?

What has happened to our girls' voices in a time of rising feminism that strongly advocates for respect and acceptance of the worth and value of individuals regardless of gender? In education, the impetus for breaking down gender expectations around mathematics and science has been largely dismantled. The world has witnessed young women being courageous and demonstrating leadership and passion to create positive change – think Swedish environmental activist Greta Thunberg and Pakistani activist for female education Malala Yousafzai. And yet we're still hearing about our girls being sexually harassed and demeaned at school. For all their empowerment, the situation seem to be worsening for our young women, especially in the area of their burgeoning sexuality and sense of authentic identity.

Women and girls advocate Melinda Tankard Reist has written extensively about the trend for many teenage girls in their early sexually intimate experiences with a boy to feel pressured to perform porn-inspired sex acts, such as being slapped, choked or coerced into painful anal sex. In her 2019 submission into the Inquiry into Age Verification for Online Wagering and Online Pornography, she writes of accounts of girls feeling they couldn't say no, and that such sexual behaviour was 'expected of them'. These statements were furthered by a GP, interviewed by writer Alison Pearson, who has in recent years had to treat a growing number of teenage girls – often under the age of consent – for incontinence, anal tearing and internal injuries.

This is beyond worrying. It is wrong, and it needs to stop.

I recently read a Facebook post quoting a teen girl saying that being forced to do oral sex on boys was just 'some of the stuff girls have to do nowadays'. How has that come to be seen as normal? Can we just blame the influence of pornography? Obviously there are some unhealthy influences coming from the digital world that are shaping the expectations of boys and girls, but they're starting a lot earlier than in adolescence.

After exploring the information shared by these brave young Australian women, the main message is that our girls and women are not being heard. We must ensure our little girls find their voices – voices they can keep without being crushed or silenced. We want all our girls to have a voice that allows them to be seen and respected from girlhood to their womanhood.

The survey I conducted for this book in 2021 enlightened me on many things, one of which was how worried parents and educators are about little girls finding their voice. I hope that throughout this book parents, grandparents, educators and community members may find ways of ensuring our girls keep their voices.

Margrét Pála Ólafsdóttir, founder and CEO of the Hjallastefnan schools, addressed her concerns about the lack of girls' voices in a simple and innovative way called the Hjalli method. She identified that girls are often kept in what she calls the 'pink haze', where they are conditioned to stay safe, not take as many risks as boys, and not be as loud as boys. So, in her nursery and primary schools, she sometimes separates the genders to help empower girls and break down long-held gender stereotypes and social conditionings. This method allows kindergarten girls to be given an opportunity to be brave and very loud. It promotes ideas such as stacking mattresses on the floor with a table beside them so the girls can jump from the table onto the mattresses, with an invitation to scream at the same time. Needless to say, it does not take long before the girls' room becomes as noisy as the boys' room and before too long, the girls want to have an extra mattress and then maybe another chair, as they gradually find their inner bravery. This invitation for these girls to be noisy, independent, brave, take initiative and to move around a lot are things that are so often conditioned out of our girls.

I have met many parents who have very fearless daughters who have arrived after a couple of sons. The lived experience for these girls has meant the pink haze is blended with the blue haze, and they are hopefully strong enough not to let social constructs diminish their voices or courage. This merging of the pink and blue hazes can also happen in extended families with lots of cousins that they see often and also in neighbourhoods, especially with mixed-age and gender-fluid children.

Modelling matters

We need to surround our girls with women and men who are positive role models, using our voices in respectful ways and encouraging them to use theirs. We are living in an age of outrage, particularly fuelled by social media, where people are able to not only express their opinions loudly, but there is a tendency for many to attack a person if they have a different opinion. This is not how we want our girls to use their voices.

PARENTS AND EDUCATORS' SURVEY

Funny, I had the most amazing father who always taught me to stand my ground and to have a voice. I remember standing in line at a store waiting to buy a drink. I had been waiting a while when an older man pushed in front of me. I turned to him politely and said, 'Excuse me sir, the back of the line is over there', pointing to the end. He turned to me and responded, 'Respect your elders, young lady.' With all the quick wit in the world, I remembered what my dad had taught me and replied, 'Respect does not come with age; it is earned. Now, the back of the line is over there.'

In their excellent book *Raising Girls Who Like Themselves*, co-parents and authors Kasey Edwards and Dr Christopher Scanlon argue that the most important thing a girl can do before adolescence and womanhood is to learn to like themselves. This can help girls have the courage to develop and use their voice. One of the main reasons that this is difficult is we often do not allow them authentic autonomy and choice.

> It's one thing to tell your daughters that their bodies are their own and that they have the right to make decisions about them. Our actions often teach girls the opposite, that they are not at all autonomous when it comes to their bodies.
>
> – Kasey Edwards and Dr Christopher Scanlon,
> *Raising Girls Who Like Themselves* (2021)

Do we really let our girls make choices about what they wear? Edwards and Scanlon argue that parents, particularly mothers, give our girls mixed messages about their appearance and if we want them to grow up to have an authentic voice, we need to allow little girls to make these choices – even if they sometimes challenge us by wearing, say, skimpy or masculine-looking clothes. If the choice is not harmful and it's not permanent – like wearing a pair of cropped shorts or a bra top when she is a preschooler – then they allow their daughter to get to decide. I am not sure everyone would agree with this, however being mindful of the choice they allow their daughter to make is what matters. They do have one excellent caveat about honouring your little girls' choices: sometimes, what is harmful may not be physical because harm can also be psychological or social. Given that our little girls do not have a fully developed executive brain to make sound decisions, they will need guidance to ensure their decision is based on what she wants, and not what she thinks others want her to wear. Also we need to explain the potential dangers of dressing older, and the gift of just being a young girl.

Empathy, kindness and fairness matter too

Our rooster girls, who are often stronger and feistier, need to learn the value of *having a voice that does not offend or hurt others*. Being intentionally or unintentionally mean is not a voice we want to encourage. Relational aggression – which includes name-calling, put-downs and exclusion – is hurtful and a powerful way of silencing little girls' voices. We must remember that these are learned behaviours and that with guidance and coaching, they can be unlearned.

PARENTS AND EDUCATORS' SURVEY

Generally, girls can be very mean to one another for no reason. Friendship groups don't seem to last long and they are all consistently looking for something better.

Having a voice is so much more than just being loud and opinionated. We need to teach our children that real empathy is important. There is a list of books on my website that can help with this – just search 'empathy' at maggiedent.com.

PARENTS AND EDUCATORS' SURVEY

Other girls always seem to hurt her feelings by betraying her. They are always jealous and end up being mean when they started out being her best friend.

Another attribute we can help instil in our rooster girls particularly is kindness. Kindness is technically the capacity of an individual to act from a place of genuine concern for oneself and others. Choosing to be kind is a choice that is made with an understanding that every action influences others and that being kind to ourself is not a sign of selfishness.

Dannielle Miller from Enlightened Education wrote an excellent blog post, 'Our girls are being killed with kindness'. There is so much messaging that if there was more kindness around, there would magically be less relational aggression, particularly girl 'meanness'. One of the strongest societal conditionings is that girls and women need to put others first or, in other words, we need to prioritise being 'kind'.

Author of *Odd Girl Out* Rachel Simmons told an interviewer for *ParentMap* in 2018:

> Girls are still raised with a psychology that is trained to think about other people before themselves. This ... is a real recipe for unhappiness.
>
> – in Hough, L., 'Girlhood', *Harvard Ed Magazine* (Winter 2019)

Simmons isn't against teaching thoughtfulness and kindness. However, she also believes we need to teach our girls to be kind to themselves and to value their own needs first.

Over the years as a counsellor and a coordinator of women's retreats, I have worked with so many women who struggle to take care of themselves or prioritise their own wellbeing. To help embed this mindset in our little girls, I developed a creative visualisation called 'I Am a Good Friend' to help children understand that being a good friend requires certain behaviours, including being kind and caring to ourselves as well as others.

PARENTS AND EDUCATORS' SURVEY

It gives me goosebumps when my little girl is always the friend that comforts and soothes her friends or siblings when they fall or are hurt in some way. She is just so nurturing and caring.

When we are kind, we don't take advantage of our own power or of other people's vulnerabilities. Instead, we seek to comfort, encourage and strengthen those around us. When our little ones are raised with a culture of care and compassion with a good dose of kindness, they will learn to treat others the same way and they will expect to be treated that way throughout their life.

PARENTS AND EDUCATORS' SURVEY

When she looks out for her little sister at day care, the three-year-old tells all of her friends about 'her' baby (one year) and tells them to be careful of her.

Being the best or the loudest can be a lonely place to be, and this often is a lesson our rooster girls need to learn early in life.

Practice improves confidence

For our less confident girls, it is important that we avoid the habit of speaking for them. Edwards and Scanlon suggest that when we speak for our girls, we can teach them that they are not capable of having an opinion or a voice of their own, which can be incredibly disempowering.

PARENTS AND EDUCATORS' SURVEY

A two-and-a-half-year-old little girl who was having a visit at her grandmother's was struggling to get out the side gate – a gate deliberately to keep her inside and safe. After pushing and shoving the gate she called out, 'Nanny, come and help me with the gate!' And when there was no response from her grandmother, she said the same thing again. With increasing frustration, she yelled next, 'Nanny, come and help me with the $%#%$#ing gate!'

It is important that our little girls practise having a voice in the real world while they are young. This may mean we can teach them how to go into a shop like the local bakery, order the bread, pay for it and show gratitude by saying thank you. Ask her to order her own ice cream, or if you are out at a restaurant, ask her to address the waiter herself with their order. This can often be quite easy for our rooster girls, with our little lambs perhaps needing some coaching. To do this I suggest a simple technique that goes like this: *I do: We do: You do.* For example, the first time you have explained to your daughter that you want her to get the bread from the bakery, ask her to watch how you do it. The next time, you might stand beside her, and encourage her do it. The final step is you stay outside the bakery and let her do it herself.

Conversation skills can also be learned from early in life. Encourage your daughter to be an active participant when you're with friends and family. She can ask how people are, or compliment the colour of someone's jumper, or she can simply sit beside a grown-up and have a chat. We need to keep in mind our young girls are listening to how we speak in our homes and, yes, that means they are often quick to use our expletives in completely appropriate ways!

PARENTS AND EDUCATORS' SURVEY

We were recently driving in traffic and I was running late to get Miss Five's older brother to footy training. I was calmly trying to explain to my seven-year-old son that the traffic was bad and we might be a bit late when Miss Five chimes in with a perfectly timed 'For fuck's sake . . . traffic!'

Our girls need to see and hear women using their voice in their homes, schools and communities. We can read stories and find inspiring videos of women from around the world that we can show our girls while they are still little so they can be influenced in a positive way. Over the page are some good resources for these inspiring stories.

Sometimes girls are silenced by other girls or they silence themselves because they compare themselves to other girls who have already developed a voice. Our society is very competitive and it's important we encourage healthy competition and cooperation in our girls. Girls together, watching out for each other and cheering each other on, is a great way to keep all their voices alive and strong. Again, we need to find teachable moments to show our girls such behaviour.

Beware of overapologising and 'hedging'

In my research, I came across several blogs and articles about the tendency for girls and women to overapologise and hedge, which was one of those lightbulb moments for me as a grown woman. I have been conditioned exactly this way! I have used these softeners so frequently – 'Sorry but I disagree' or 'Excuse me but I tend to disagree' or 'Sorry but I see this a bit differently!' What am I apologising for?

Author of *The Triple Bind*, psychology professor Dr Stephen Hinshaw argues that boys are more encouraged in the skills that lead to healthy individuation as an adolescent, while girls seem to be conditioned to seek individuation only under certain conditions.

- Be confident, but not conceited.
- Be smart, but no-one likes a know-it-all.
- Ambition is good, but trying too hard is bad.
- Be assertive, but only if it doesn't upset anyone else.

    – Hinshaw in Rae Jacobson, 'Why Girls Apologize Too Much',
    childmind.org

These messages are definitely confusing for our girls, as well as our parents and educators. It seems that our girls are more attuned to and responsible for how their behaviour affects others. Even though empathy is a noble trait, it can complicate the behaviours that encourage being successful, including winning, having a competitive drive and enjoying success without worrying how it impacts on others. When a boy wins, he's much less likely to consider how his victory may impact the other competitors, whereas for most girls, even though winning is great, she may downplay her success out of concern for the loser's feelings.

As Rae Jacobson writes, we need to keep an eye out for these habits in our girls and coach them to use more life-affirming language that helps them keep an authentic voice.

- Overapologising, like when ordering something, or apologising when she hasn't done anything that deserves an apology.
- Starting sentences with 'Sorry . . .'
- Hedging using terms like, 'Excuse me, can I ask . . .' or 'I might be wrong but . . .' or 'I am not sure but . . .'

Our sensitive girls who are more lamb than rooster can be taught to have a voice in a way that suits their temperament. Sometimes, our more sensitive girls use actions rather than words to express themselves. Teaching them to use their actions in ways that are fair, kind and respectful can be helpful, and can be used in the real and digital worlds.

A sense of humour can be an asset

Cultivating a healthy sense of humour can be a powerful way of empowering little girls to navigate the world. Humour can defuse conflict and can be deceptively valuable when a girl is being bullied. Having some quick, witty comebacks can definitely help our girls to be heard. We also need to help our girls understand there is a big difference between laughing at someone and laughing with someone.

Her inner voice

Part of our instinctual survival system means that our body will often display sensations of feeling alert before the conscious mind has registered a threat. Essentially, this can be what anxiety feels like, and we need to help our children learn how their body is trying to warn them of possible danger.

Talking to your young children about this 'imaginary wise voice' that hides within them can be very helpful. Some children can use the heart as a metaphor for where their wise voice lives. Remind them that this voice of inner guidance is the very best friend that they have and, like any friendship, we need to nurture it, encourage it and make time for it to be a regular part of our lives.

Some children and adults have an overzealous amygdala that can trigger warnings around situations that are not life-threatening. However, helping a child to know how their sensory processing system works to warn them of possible danger is incredibly important. Do they get butterflies in their tummy? Do they get goosebumps? Do they feel cold? It can be useful to discuss with children that these warning signs are how their inner ally is trying to communicate with them.

I suggest that when children feel these sensations, they ask themselves these three questions before acting:

- Am I in an unsafe place?

- Am I with an unsafe person?
- Am I about to do an unsafe thing?

If there is not a genuine threat to safety, then they may be feeling anxious rather than receiving a genuine warning message from their inner compass. It's good to know the difference.

Conversations around early warning systems need to continue from childhood into adolescence. This is how we empower the intuition to make it stronger and easier to find.

One of the biggest concerns for our little girls expressed in the survey was the worry about the pressure of their appearance defining their worth and value. The way she looks is not her voice. Valuing all body types and embracing genuine authenticity can help our girls to find their true voice.

PARENTS AND EDUCATORS' SURVEY

Trying to find my three-year-old daughter in the house, and there is she going through my handbag, putting lipstick on all around her mouth and also unwrapping tampons and placing them in her ears!

Consent matters

I can still vividly remember how it made my skin crawl when some of my parents' friends felt it was okay to give me a kiss to say hello. A key message coming from the brave young women who are speaking out in our world today is about consent. Teaching our girls to check if it's okay to give someone a hug, borrow one of their toys or wear someone's clothes needs to start in toddlerhood so it becomes a healthy habit for life. Waiting for consent can be hard for loving grandparents and close family, however, this is where true respect for boundaries starts. Even I had to pause and wait for one of our lamb granddaughters to be ready as she took until she was around three years old to warm up when we visited.

The next most important thing to teach our children is that if someone hurts them, either by the words they are using or their physical actions, they can say, 'NO. STOP. I DON'T LIKE THAT!' This clearly shows that we are not giving our consent and we want it to stop. Please teach your girls to do this, with both hands up in a clear non-verbal gesture and a clear loud voice. It can help to explain the difference between accidentally hurting someone and intentionally hurting someone and that saying sorry for unintentionally hurting someone is the right thing to do. Sometimes our girls can be the voice for a child who is not brave enough to say these words!

We need to keep reminding our girls as they grow older that they can say 'no' and 'stop' whenever something is happening that they don't like or that hurts them. This may be the most important message of this chapter.

MAGGIE'S MAIN IDEA

Building an awareness of healthy boundaries is a long game for both girls and women.

I recently saw a great example of the difference between healthy encouragement from a safe grown-up vs coercion in a post from blogger Christina of cmonmama.com titled 'Brave in the ways that matter':

> As my daughter watched her big brother hold an alligator, she declined the opportunity. The alligator's keeper remarked that usually girls are even braver than boys, and she must not be feeling very brave that day.
>
> He couldn't have been more wrong.
>
> I took my daughter aside, looked right into her eyes and told her how brave she actually was being in that exact moment. I pointed out the bravery it takes to stand up for what you do or don't want to do, especially when you feel pressured.
>
> I don't need my daughter to be brave enough to hold an alligator. I need her to be brave enough to stand her ground. Brave enough to trust the boundaries of what she does and doesn't feel comfortable with. Brave enough not to bend because the world says she should.
>
> – Christina, C'MON MAMA, cmonmama.com (12 October 2021), Instagram: @cmon.mama, Facebook: cmonmama

Now, for some sobering statistics.

According to the Australian Institute of Criminology:

- Up to **30 per cent** of children experience some form of childhood sexual abuse
- Between **5 and 10 per cent** of children experience severe abuse
- Children with disabilities are up to **seven times more likely** to be sexually abused than their non-disabled peers.

According to the National Center For Juvenile Justice in the US, with 14 per cent of all sexual assault victims reported to law enforcement agencies concerning children under the age of six years, it is imperative abuse prevention education starts for children as early as possible. Giving our daughters the knowledge and awareness about their personal safety needs to start as soon as possible. All families need to have some body awareness education or access to a protective behaviours program. On my website, I have a list of picture books that can help you teach your children about the importance of their private parts staying private.

With the increasing ease of access to pornography, there has been a disturbing increase in the number of child-to-child molestation cases and incest. Children behave in sexually inappropriate ways only if they have seen such behaviour or it has been done to them. We must teach them about protective behaviours.

We must remember that more than 90 per cent of perpetrators who sexually abuse children are known to the child – they are part of their world. This is why we talk to our children about their early warning systems because unless they know that it is wrong for others to touch their private parts, their early warning system may not alert them, especially for children under seven. Holly-ann Martin, CEO of Safe4Kids, believes children need to have five safe people who they can rely on when their early warning systems are telling them they could be unsafe.

It can also be helpful to chat to your little girls and boys about the ways that unsafe people lure children away. They often tell children their parent has asked them to come and collect them, or they promise them lollies or to show them a puppy or a kitten. They might tell a child that their mother is hurt and wants to see them. One way around this is to create a family password for use with people who would not normally be authorised to collect your children. This means if you as parents ever do need to ask anyone to collect your child/ren unexpectedly, then your kids know to ask that person, even if they are family or friends, for the password. If they can't give the password, then they need to very loudly say, 'No', and alert an adult, such as a teacher.

Practise different scenarios with your child as it's common to freeze when we feel threatened. Tell your child it's okay to yell and keep yelling until the unsafe person leaves, and then they must tell someone what has happened.

So often we tell children to look for a police officer, but quite often there is not one around. When my son was three-and-a-half years old and got lost, he kept looking for a police officer and when he couldn't see one on a Sunday afternoon in a metropolitan suburb, rather than asking any other person – he hid. It's best to make sure kids know that if they need to ask for help they should do so in a public place, and to preferably go to a store, library, café or friend's house.

Body safety education is incredibly important in developing the voice that our little girls will need in their tween and teen years and beyond, not just in the real world but in the digital world. I have been reading about a new practice that is known as 'capping', which is the recording of imagery or videos of others performing sexual acts without their knowledge or consent, and it is one of the fastest growing trends of online child abuse. The Australian Federal Police has issued a warning in a media release in late 2021 that children as young as eight are being coerced into performing live-streamed sexual acts by online predators, who often record and share the videos on the darknet and then go on to sexually extort victims into producing even more graphic content.

Queensland Police Service victim identification specialist Scott Anderson was quoted in an Australian Federal Police media release as saying:

These offenders are highly manipulative and, in extreme cases, they have tricked children into undressing and performing sexual acts on camera within 10 minutes of contacting them through a video streaming platform.

Please see this as a priority in parenting your precious little girls and boys. We can help empower our little girls to have a strong voice around their bodies that can keep them safe and hopefully help them to create and hold safe boundaries around their own emerging sexuality. If a girl discloses inappropriate touch or sexual molestation to you, please listen, believe them and seek help.

Making the time to listen

It can be difficult to find enough time to really be present and listen to a little girl as she shares the details of her day. I'm especially proud of my own adult sons and nephews who have learned the importance of simply chatting to their little girls. Many little girls need no prompting, however, having a grown-up who loves you and wants to check in with how you are feeling can be a supportive way to encourage conversation. Helpful questions can include: What was the best part of your day? When were you the happiest today?

It can also be valuable to tell your little girls that you missed them, you thought about them and you are so glad to see them. I have no memory of my dad telling me that he loved me, which was pretty common back in the 1950s and '60s, however, I have no doubt he did love me because there were many times when he would sit beside me and let me chatter away. I certainly was blessed to have been really heard when I was a little girl. As a grandmother, I am prioritising this for all my grandchildren because I remember how important it was.

Listening and letting your little girl develop their voice is essential practice for their adult lives. Author of *Enough As She Is*, Rachel Simmons captured the dilemma for many girls so accurately in a Facebook post when she explained that our girls who are still socialised by culture to obey, to please, to be compliant and to work very hard at school can struggle in workplaces where the rules and expectations of success change profoundly. Many workplaces value the 'muscles' – physically and metaphorically – that men have had years to flex as boys: self-promotion, risk-taking and assertiveness, just to name a few. The same behaviours that help girls do so well as young girls prior to joining the workforce actually hold them back later in life. Despite hearing the messages that girls can do anything, many find they can struggle to forge a path in their careers. It is so much more than just the glass ceiling that women need to smash. Simmons argues very strongly that rather than blame the institutions that are built around male norms, or the pervasive bias that exists – especially in the corporate world and government – women have a strong tendency to blame themselves for their inability to gain credibility and promotion. What many women do is turn their anger and frustration at the world inwards to themselves, endlessly questioning themselves, berating themselves and being angry at themselves.

> Let's teach women and girls to understand how gender and other identity markers (like race and national identity) shape leadership, how what we learned about gender in childhood informs how and whether we rise as professionals, and how the workplace was constructed to favor men. Barring this, we will consign our highest performing women to a lifetime of ruthless self-criticism – energy that they could spend changing the world, earning, and delivering results.
> – Rachel Simmons, facebook.com/rachel.simmons
> (21 November 2021)

This is just one of the reasons why we must encourage our girls to have a voice and the courage to take risks and be brave, and to know that they are capable and deserving of promotion and positions of leadership. Being ambitious and driven to grow personally and professionally are equally acceptable for all individuals.

Judy Daunt wrote a beautiful message for her granddaughter born in 2021, which was published in the *Illawarra Mercury* on Saturday 6 February:

> Message for my granddaughter
> My darling granddaughter, I promise to encourage you to speak out and assert yourself. I will always listen and value your thoughts and desires. You are strong, capable and as deserving as the next person. I will praise you for your intelligence, cleverness, creativeness, athleticism and so much more as you grow. I aim to guide and support you to be inclusive, respectful of others and to protest against injustice. I will model and demonstrate what it is to call out sexism

and harassment and challenge any stereotypical notions of gender. I'm determined to use language that breaks gender stereotypes, rejecting the binary currently restricting cultural perceptions of gender. I promise this and more as I love you unconditionally.

– Judy Daunt, chairwoman Illawarra Women's Health Centre

KEY POINTS

- What has happened to our girls' voices in a time of rising feminism that strongly advocates for respect and acceptance of the worth and value of individuals regardless of gender?
- Many teenage girls' early sexual experiences with a boy often include porn-inspired sex acts such as being slapped, choked or coerced into painful anal sex.
- We all want our girls to have a voice that allows them to be seen and respected from girlhood to womanhood.
- Having an authentic voice is much more than being loud and opinionated.
- We need to guide our little girls to be kind to themselves and to value their own needs as well as the needs of others.
- Be mindful of speaking for our less confident lamb girls as we can teach them they are not capable of having a voice of their own.
- Ensure your little girls see and hear women using their voice in homes, schools, communities, businesses, the media and in parliament.
- Encourage your daughter to use life-affirming language rather than overapologising and hedging.
- Teach our girls that positive actions, especially ones that are fair, kind and respectful, are also ways of showing their voice albeit silently.
- Cultivating a healthy sense of humour can be a positive asset for our girls today.
- Help our daughters understand their early warning systems is essential as early as possible.

- Teaching our little girls about consent and respecting their boundaries is really important.
- We need to teach our little girls that if someone hurts them, either by the words that they are using or their physical actions, they need to say, 'NO. STOP. I don't like that.'
- Body safety education is incredibly important in developing the voice that our little girls will need in their tween and teen years and beyond. Her body belongs to her.
- Frequently give your little girl permission to use her courage to strive to be ambitious and brave.

16

Building resilience, courage and 'glimmers'

A key finding of the Western Australian Commission for Children and Young People's inaugural Speaking Out Survey conducted in 2019 was that girls rated their wellbeing less favourably than boys.

> Indeed in this large-scale survey, female young people were twice as likely as male young people to report not feeling happy with themselves, feeling unable to achieve their goals or to deal with things that happen in life.
> – Commissioner for Children and Young People WA, *Exploring the decline in wellbeing for Australian girls* (2021)

Sadly, these findings are similar to those of other countries in the western world. Lisa Damour, author of *Under Pressure: Confronting the epidemic of anxiety and stress in girls*, believes figures have skyrocketed for girls. She reports that in the US, the number of girls who said they often felt nervous, worried or fearful jumped 55 per cent between 2009 and 2014, while the comparable figure for adolescent boys remained unchanged.

I believe we can build resilience, courage and 'glimmers' (more on that soon) in our little girls' lives so they can take these positive traits forward into adolescence and womanhood. Unhelpful stereotypes and social norms that encourage our little girls to believe they lack the strength and courage of little boys are gradually being challenged, but there are still many fairytales and archetypal stories that suggest our little girls are waiting for a prince to help them live happily ever after. We must deconstruct these myths because they aren't helpful for little girls or little boys.

In the first five years of life, all our children are developing belief systems and a sense of their own identity. In psychological terms, this is called the time when we develop a 'theory of mind'. We can help positively shape a child's belief systems and sense of identity and, in so many ways for our little girls, I believe this is the foundation we need to address to help them thrive. Please be mindful of marinating your little girls in stories of exceptional women who have often gone unnoticed. An excellent website for books, biographies, films and articles is amightygirl.com.

What is resilience and why does it matter?

First, it is important not to interpret building resilience in your children as 'toughening them up'. Resilience refers to the ability to successfully manage your life and adapt to change and stressful events in healthy and constructive ways. Two other helpful definitions of resilience are:

An individual's ability to thrive and fulfil potential despite or perhaps because of stressors or risk factors.

– Dr James Neill, The University of Canberra

A universal capacity which allows a person, group or community to prevent, minimize or overcome the damaging effects of adversity.

– The International Resilience Project (2005)

Lyn Worsley, creator of The Resilience Doughnut model for building resilience in children and young people, prefers the definition that resilience is a process with no endpoint. By this, she means no-one is born resilient and someone doesn't necessarily end up being resilient – we are only ever in the process of becoming more resilient.

One of the most important factors for resilience is human connectedness and a feeling of belonging. In 2015, I attended an international resilience conference in Halifax, Canada, and the researchers who had been exploring resilience around the world reached a consensus that it is difficult to be resilient on your own. We are social beings and we live in systems – families, neighbourhoods, communities – and when adversity arrives, or we experience a major trauma such as a natural disaster or global pandemic, individuals recover with the support of the resources available within those systems and through help-seeking behaviour. Interestingly, many of our tween and teens today are more connected virtually than they are in real time, and that may be coming at a cost to their emotional and mental wellbeing.

As parents, we need to recognise that there are things we can do to help nurture and build resilience in our children from birth. It is a sad irony that the shift from punitive parenting to connected responsive parenting may have had a part to play in lower resilience. Today, I still hear of whole classes of children being invited to birthday parties so no child feels left out. Also, traditional birthday party games like musical chairs and pass-the-parcel no longer have just one winner – they are often organised so everyone is a winner. Out of a deep place of love, parents overprotect their children rather than let them feel disappointed or left out. But there is one way to learn emotional buoyancy and how to recover from being left out, excluded and failing, and that is through experience.

A wonderful woman called Bonnie Benard is considered as the mother of the concept of building resilience. In 1996, she co-founded Resiliency in Action, a publishing and training company, and she worked for many years with children who were deemed at risk until she had the insight to focus on what things were working for the children rather than the things that weren't. We have become fond of pathologising normal development and seeing it through a deficit lens. Parents focus on what their children can't do and what they are struggling with, often missing opportunities for significant growth. Benard, with her shift of focus, may have given birth to the strength-based modelling of raising children that is very common today.

MAGGIE'S MAIN IDEA

If you want to raise a resilient and capable little girl so she can navigate the bumps and bruises, and the joys and delights of life, the first reality for you is to avoid doing things that she can do for herself. Feeling competent and capable, especially as a little girl, builds an authentic self-esteem and is a sound grounding for a secure sense of identity.

Given that every child is different, the focus for parents may need to be different. With our confident rooster children, parents might need to focus on building life skills around empathy and cooperation. For the sensitive lamb, parents may need to focus on building self-mastery so they can build a sense of confidence within a child who may lack the get-up-and-go of rooster children.

I created the 10 Resilience Building Blocks model to help parents recognise the different areas in which they can build strengths in their children that sits beautifully on the well-known Maslow's hierarchy of needs, which is a reminder that we need to focus on our basic needs first, before we can build other competencies. Given that I devoted a whole book (*Real Kids in an Unreal World* and later a pocket guide called *Building Children's Resilience*) to exploring these building blocks, I am choosing here to explore some of the key areas that can help build resilience for your little girls.

10 Resilience Building Blocks
for children aged 0–12 years

10 Strengthen the spirit

8 Absence of stress

9 Self mastery

5 Build life skills

6 Meaningful involvement with positive adults

7 Clear boundaries

1 Positive healthy pregnancy

2 Good nutrition

3 Safe nurturing care within the circle of family

4 Plenty of play

In a strength-based exploration of resilience, I use another simple visual because I am a visual-kinesthetic learner and I know it can be a helpful way to remember the concepts I will be exploring. Adversity and challenge create stress in our lives that triggers our amygdala to fight to survive. I want to explore the concept of balancing the things that cause us stress – the stressors – against the things that nurture us – the protective factors. When you focus on these, you can see that you can be proactive in building resilience in your little girls. Protective factors can also be called 'glimmers', which I think is a magical term, especially for little girls. This term was coined by Deb Dana in her book *The Polyvagal Theory in Therapy: Engaging the Rhythm of Regulation*, describing glimmers as the opposite of triggers. Put simply, just as triggers might cause our brain and nervous system to enter a survival state, *glimmers help us to feel safe*. The more glimmers we give our girls when they are little, the better they can cope with the stressors of life.

RESILIENCE MODEL

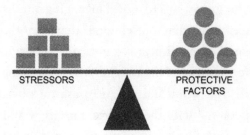

STRESSORS   PROTECTIVE FACTORS

Key protective factors for our little girls

Learning to lose

Let's be honest: we all continue to make mistakes, to lose and to fail right through life. If you are unable to experience the moments of failure or discomfort and learn how to manage them, then you may become someone who learns to avoid things, procrastinate about things, cheat or blame others for your lack of achievement. Ouch!

Children are playing less with other children, so they may be lacking enough experience to get really good at failing. No-one likes to fail. No-one likes to lose. And yes, it does suck when we don't win or we don't get what we want, or others behave in ways that we would prefer they didn't. That is called disappointment and it is a normal human response. The sooner our little girls learn what it is, how to acknowledge it and what to do with it afterwards, the better.

If you remember the way that we create our emotions from the work of Dr Lisa Feldman Barrett from Chapter 5, it is all happening in the early years. It means that if we are able to allow our children to experience as many authentic moments of disappointment as possible with support, they will create neural pathways that will help them manage and cope. Yes, this includes not being allowed a biscuit before dinner, not being able to get a pink unicorn at the shop, not having yet another story before bed, not being able to use rude words . . . the list goes on from toddlerhood to teenagehood. So many wonderful opportunities to practise understanding and navigating disappointment. It is also helpful for grown-ups to model managing our disappointment. We need to keep reminding our children that even though it isn't a pleasant feeling, disappointment is a normal response.

Consider for a moment the toddler who is learning to walk. We know they fall over a lot and yet there are no obvious signs that they are disappointed with their efforts. Barrett would argue that is because they haven't formed a constructed emotion around failure – that will come later, and largely in response to us big people. When they drop their dinner on the floor or they throw their food or fail to fall asleep when we want them to, they are forming those pathways that will trigger emotions particularly around disappointment. The traditional understanding is that humans are largely reactive creatures responding to things that happen around them. Barrett's theory is that we, *together with our children, can help them become the architects of their own experience.*

Katty Kay and Claire Shipman, authors of *The Confidence Code: The Science and Art of Self-Assurance – What Women Should Know*, argue that one of the reasons girls' confidence plummets after the age of eight is because of a lack of openness to taking risks and stretching themselves. There are so many of those unhelpful social norms that have been conditioning our little girls to be careful, to strive for perfection and to avoid risk. As puberty begins and their bodies are flooded with oestrogen, which can heighten emotional intelligence, most girls become even more cautious, more careful and less likely to trust the courage that lies within them.

Boys risk and fail more easily, so they build confidence. Yet for girls, we unwittingly encourage their perfectionistic, people-pleasing tendencies.
They need to increase healthy risks and failure in their daily diets. Risk and failure and then the process of recovery and mastery are the things that actually create confidence, build more of it.
– Katty Kay and Claire Shipman quoted in 'Girls' Confidence Plummets Starting at Age 8: Here's How to Keep Her Confidence Strong'. amightygirl.com/blog (12 September 2021)

The difference between feeling ashamed and disappointed

Children who have been shamed when they experience quite normal toddler and infant experiences will tend to create the brain architecture and beliefs that will make disappointment a reason to feel ashamed rather than just feeling disappointed. How we were parented has an enormous influence on how we parent. If we experienced shame-based parenting, the same or similar approaches can come out of our mouths spontaneously at times, despite the fact we might have read good parenting books or attended parenting seminars. If we are able to acknowledge and accept that some developmentally normal behaviours are exactly that, rather than assign a meaning to the behaviour – such as that our little ones are intentionally being destructive – then we are already helping them create more resilience and capacity for overcoming failure and disappointment. It does mean we have to reframe our own inner voices that tell us that some of our children's behaviour is bad or naughty, instead of a consequence of the curious 'seeking' mechanism in their inquisitive minds. They don't feel any disappointment when they draw a lipstick picture on the wall; they may be really proud of it because they wanted to draw a big, happy picture to make mummy smile! It is our reaction in these moments that sets up the unconscious emotional pathways that can cause problems, especially during the adolescent years.

We can begin with a simple responses like, 'Oh dear' or 'Whoopsie doopsie!', then in a gentle voice, we can explore how we are going to clean up the mess together – or, as they grow older, by themselves.

I have a four-step process to nurturing toddler genius that may be helpful.

4 steps to nurturing toddler genius

1. Pause and become present.
2. Ask 'Did you do that all by yourself?'
3. Explain why you would prefer they didn't make that choice again.
4. Have them clean up the mess.

www.maggiedent.com

These same steps can be applied with our little ones as they get older, with the addition that we start the process by validating how disappointment feels. It sucks! This shows that we understand how they feel and that it is normal and healthy to have that response when things don't go the way we want.

Disappointment creates a flood of sensations throughout the body, depending on our prior experiences and our own unique temperament. There is no question that optimistic individuals can navigate disappointment more effectively than more pessimistic individuals. Some of that tendency may be imprinted on our DNA, but the more pessimistic child will need to work harder at being able to master the hidden gifts that disappointment can bring into their lives.

It is important to teach your children – early and often – about disappointment, as even though it feels yucky or unpleasant, it is a normal human response. There are two ways we can be disappointed. One is through situations that are out of our control, such as when changes have been made by others – for example, decisions that have been made during COVID-19 lockdowns which have impacted us. Disappointment can also arise when an event is cancelled, or when we have not been invited to a birthday party, wedding or celebration.

Disappointments can also come from situations we do have control over, like forgetting our lunchbox, losing a much-loved jacket, causing a friendship conflict, or failing a test we didn't study for.

> **MAGGIE'S MAIN IDEA**
> When learning about disappointment, children must learn that there are some things we can fix and some things we just have to learn to accept and adapt to.

The gift of grit

Dr Angela Duckworth, in her excellent book, *Grit: Why passion and resilience are the secrets to success*, argues strongly that talent alone is not enough to reach a high level of success in life. Sustained practice and effort when combined with an interest that has a sense of purpose, which Duckworth calls grit, are the keys to genuine success. The more our little girls practise overcoming setbacks in moments of disappointment, the better they get at it. *Rather than avoiding moments of disappointment, we need embrace them as a form of training for life.*

If our little daughter is struggling to achieve something – like riding her bike without training wheels – remember the magic of the word 'yet'. 'Sweetheart, you can't ride it *yet* but with more practice you will be able to.'

As parents, we can be enthusiastic and encouraging about recovering from life's challenging moments. I always found it helpful to look for the learning experience that was often hidden under each moment of disappointment. The failed test was often a chance to explore gaps in one of my sons' learning or lack of preparation.

Setting a new goal following a moment of failure can also be helpful, as it refocuses a child towards a future possibility of success. The old metaphor about getting back on the horse when you fall off seriously has some merit, and it was one that my dad used often (even though we didn't have any horses on the farm). It is helpful when parents display a strong 'have a go' mentality, even when you have no chance of winning. Persistence and grit are qualities that we can cultivate in childhood, especially through play experiences.

My dad was a very wise man. When I was around eight, he identified that I couldn't run fast and often came last in races. He kneeled down beside me and told me that it can feel really yucky if you're always coming last, and he suggested that I could wave at the crowds and that would help me feel more cheerful. He was right. Every running race after that, I would wave at the crowd – I even fell over once because I was waving so enthusiastically. I also noticed

I wasn't the only little girl who couldn't run fast, and there were times that I would hook my arm with another little girl and we would run together.

PARENTS AND EDUCATORS' SURVEY

My daughter loves to jump and climb and has more courage than her brothers at the same age. She's a go-getter!

There was another thing my dad taught me, which is possibly the biggest takeaway for this chapter. He said there would be many times in life when I might feel reluctant to participate in something because I didn't feel I was good enough or that I had no chance of winning. He told me that the most important thing to him was that I always had a go.

Encouraging little girls to step up and have a go, regardless of possible outcomes, is teaching her about resilience and grit.

In Michele Borba's latest book, *Thrivers*, she reviewed studies on resilience and surveyed widely and came to the conclusion that being resilient has very little to do with grades or test scores. She determined there were seven character traits that set capable, confident individuals apart from the rest – the thrivers.

> These traits – confidence, empathy, self-control, integrity, curiosity, perseverance, and optimism – will allow kids to roll with the punches and succeed in life.
>
> – Michele Borba, *Thrivers* (2021)

Our little girls need to experience moments of autonomy where they stretch and grow themselves in their own way, and in their own time, to develop authentic competence and confidence.

Play, in all its wonderful and varied forms, is still the very best way to cultivate a strength around managing disappointment. Emotional buoyancy is only learned through experience and by learning and adapting. We don't have to force them to climb a tree if they are not ready, as that is likely to do the opposite to building capacity, but we are meant to fall out of trees and we are meant to graze our knees when we run too fast. We can certainly lose our minds when we lose a game or miss a goal or target. However, recovering from these moments is what matters. Every one of those moments has a gift of grit.

Playing endless games in real time with real humans is another good way to learn how to lose and recover. No digital device will ever give you an authentic experience of disappointment and recovery. Indeed, in the virtual world, you are often encouraged when you fail to have another go quickly rather than feel the emotions that disappointment can bring. This can mean children simply choose avoidance and distraction rather than learn authentic coping mechanisms.

Here are some tips to help build disappointment 'smarts' in your little girls:

- Always validate how disappointment 'sucks' and feels unpleasant.
- Don't avoid or minimise the emotions that arise – remember the three As – allow, acknowledge and accept the emotions.
- Teach strategies to shift emotional energy – deep breaths, walking, patting the dog, playing music, tapping on her K27 acupressure point.
- How can you make it right? Celebrate effort and persistence.
- Do you need my help?
- Remind your child of previous moments of disappointment that they have overcome.
- Remind them about learning to be stronger and grittier.
- Choose an affirmation that works: 'I have got this'; 'I am, I can, I will.'; 'I am more than this . . .'
- Reassure them of your unconditional love for them which does not change when things go badly – you love them always and forever, no matter what.

- Accepting, understanding and even appreciating the role disappointment can play in raising a competent, confident, resilient little girl or boy might not be something you have pondered before.

We cannot leave it to chance to raise our children to believe that this rollercoaster ride we call life will ever be a peaceful field of daisies without any prickles.

Feeling disappointed in ourselves or in our lives, or in the world around us is normal because we are human. The more that we can armour up our children with helpful information, strategies and a 'get back on the horse' mentality, the more we increase their chances of living meaningful, successful lives.

When I worked as a teacher, I would encourage my students to explore the learning experience that may present itself after a disappointment over a low grade or a failed test. That experience could be an opportunity to explore the gaps in not only these students' learning, but my teaching!

> **MAGGIE'S MAIN IDEA**
> Failure can give us an opportunity to reflect and possibly to set a new goal or a new intention that can give children a focus towards a future possibility of success rather than leave them being stuck in a pile of disappointment.

Remember, persistence and practice can improve performance, and failure is just a part of life, not a sign that we are lousy parents.

Building life skills

The early years are when children begin to build a toolkit of life skills. The more tools in the toolkit, the more resilient the child will be. Building the life skills toolkit starts from birth, and sometimes it is the little things, like getting a drink of water for themselves when they need to, getting themselves a snack or dressing themselves, that help us build towards the big things. These small milestones build a child's belief in their competence to accomplish tasks, which in turn helps build self-esteem.

As they grow older, encourage your girls to continue to build their competency and abilities. If you are carrying your daughter's bag to the classroom when she is in Year 3, question why you might be doing that. If it is because you love her, of course, that is a good motivation. However, through the eyes of your daughter, you may be sending her a message that she is not capable of carrying her own bag and finding her way to the classroom. Are you choosing what your daughter has to wear every day? While your motivation may come from love, the message she may be receiving could be compromising her sense of self-determination, confidence and autonomy. Sometimes fathers can struggle with this more than mothers as they have been conditioned to see girls as weaker and in need of a male protector.

Toni Christie is the Director of Childspace Early Childhood Institute in Wellington, New Zealand, and a passionate advocate for the respectful honouring and nurturing of our little children. She once ran a seminar that I attended where she said that in her centres, babies around the age of one could go from a breast or a bottle to a cup without a lid just by being taught how to do it. All they needed was guidance and practice, and once they had mastered it, they rarely spilled it. She argued that our children are hungry to learn skills that their parents are doing for them. When they want to dress themselves, it can take ages and if we get frustrated because it is taking too long, we are the problem, not our little ones! Young children, especially under three, have absolutely no concept of time and that is why mornings can be so tricky. Despite your best intentions of keeping everything moving, your little daughter might become fascinated by a bracelet that she just found in her room. Our little ones are naturally mindful, they are only in the present moment.

The list of life skills can be quite long:

- Communication skills
- Thinking skills
- Social skills
- Practical skills – wiping bottom, snot, sneezes
- Personal hygiene
- Calmness skills
- Protective behaviours
- Manners
- Fairness and kindness
- Feeding themselves
- Family rituals
- Chores
- Life understanding around family, school and life challenges like loss, death and transitions
- Sense of humour.

– Maggie Dent, *Real Kids in an Unreal World* (2016)

Avoid doing things that your little girl can do for herself. The more competent your little girl can be and will be, the more capable and confident she will feel and you may have more time for a quiet cuppa or two.

Nurturing a sense of humour

Resilience research shows that having a sense of humour is a protective factor, and it is something we can nurture and cultivate in our little girls. I have shared elsewhere in the book how I tend to sing badly to my granddaughters, and I distort common nursery rhymes to make them laugh. We need to make it as easy as possible for our little girls to be able to find laughter as a substitute for tears. Laughter:

- Transforms emotional states
- Stimulates endorphins and creates wellbeing

- Increases levels of serotonin
- Is a key coping skill
- Is an anti-bullying strategy
- Encourages lightening up for serious moments
- Is a bonding experience when shared in groups
- Builds inclusivity and connectedness
- Releases tension and stress
- Is a key element in effective communication, especially in close relationships
- Is an antidote to violence.

Laughter can transform negative emotional states faster than almost any other strategy or technique. It is unfortunate that a sense of humour does not arrive in a box underneath the Christmas tree; it would be so much easier than cultivating it as a child has to do, along with so many life skills.

Sharing simple riddles and jokes with young children is an excellent way to nurture a sense of humour. There will be times when children share a joke that is a little inappropriate and it's important to avoid shaming or overtly sanctioning their attempts. Parents can model making light of embarrassing moments or failures.

Problem-solving and creative thinking

An important life skill involves the art of finding solutions. This involves helping children to discover other choices that they could make in response to a challenge, whether it's a disagreement with a friend or a toy that has broken. I have loved doing this with my granddaughters by simply asking, 'How do you reckon we could fix this?' As parents we are automatically wired to want to fix things for our children to shift their discomfort. If you want to raise a resilient child, we need to flip this so our children have opportunities to solve challenges themselves.

There is a great temptation for parents to rescue their children, especially girls, from struggles and challenges, however, this denies them vital opportunities to learn life management skills. The free-range childhood that many older parents and grandparents experienced was full of opportunities where children, including girls, had to stretch themselves and often problem-solve themselves because there was no adult around.

Here are some questions and statements that may help you . . . and be prepared to be surprised when you ask them of your little girls!

- 'How might we resolve this?'
- 'How can we make this better?'
- 'What do you think needs to happen now?'
- 'What can I do to help you complete this task?'
- 'Sounds like you/we have a problem.'
- 'Whose problem is this?'
- 'There is a conflict here. How can I help you to sort it out?'
- 'Please consider making a different choice.'
- 'Act as if you have already done this . . .'
- 'Check it out inside. Does it feel right?'
- 'What's your goal? What's your intention?'
- 'I'm willing to help you complete this task.'
- 'I know you can handle it!'
- 'What do you think we can do now?'
- 'It won't be long before you will be able to do this.'
- 'Every problem has a solution.'
- 'I noticed that . . .'
- 'Inch by inch we can achieve things . . .'
- 'Now, that's interesting!'

As educators, rather than simply encouraging children to say sorry, encourage them to try and resolve their conflicts in a way that is meaningful to them. Children often come up with wonderful ideas of how they could feel comforted by their peer after an argument.

Children who are surrounded by optimistic language which encourages thinking and decision-making have the opportunities to become resilient when managing setbacks and challenges. They are much less likely to succumb to 'learned helplessness', where they expect an adult to always be there and do things for them. There is a line between doing too much for your children and having expectations that are too high, and possibly inappropriate, for your children. This needs to be a priority when raising our little girls, because there is a thought conditioning that little girls are more likely to be victims and incapable of coping with big things, quite simply because they are girls.

Mastering anxiety

Anxiety is a consequence of our amygdala constantly scanning our environment to ensure we are safe, as we explored in Chapter 3.

> **MAGGIE'S MAIN IDEA**
>
> Parents can help educate our little girls by normalising anxiety in their life or feeling stressed by owning it and by taking proactive steps to manage it. Step outside, use a calming chair, take some deep breaths or make yourself a cuppa!

Statistically and anecdotally, our children are struggling with high levels of anxiety, however, that may have more to do with how the world has changed around our children rather than something problematic in parent land.

When our little girls experience heightened levels of cortisol, commonly called the stress hormone, because they feel threatened, unsafe, uncomfortable, frightened, worried or unable to cope, anxiety is doing its job. It is making our little girls pay attention and respond to their environment by seeking out safe grown-ups. This sometimes means they will crawl into bed with you in the middle of the night, cry when you drop them off at school or possibly have an after-school meltdown once they return to their safe base.

Anxiety is normal because we are human and our amygdala is doing its job. We are meant to feel anxious when we experience change like starting big school, when there is a marriage breakdown, when there is a massive storm or when there is a significant adverse event that impacts the whole family. Anxiety becomes problematic when it stops our little girls from enjoying their life and doing things they might like to do if they were a little braver.

Interestingly, the anxiety we feel before a test or starting school can be helpful, because the increased cortisol can give us more energy so we can be more focused. It is important to teach your little girls that a little anxiety can be their friend. It can be helpful to explain that anxiety feels very much like excitement in the body, and sometimes, instead of saying, 'I'm feeling anxious', we can encourage them to say, 'I'm feeling excited!'

Psychologist and author Karen Young, who created Hey Sigmund – a popular online resource – works in the space around anxiety has written an excellent picture book *Hey Warrior*. The book explains that the amygdala can sometimes be a little too enthusiastic or it can be working too hard to keep a child safe. It includes a call for bravery within a child once they are able to identify their early warning signs. In an episode of the ABC's *Parental As Anything* podcast called 'Do you have an anxious child?', Karen suggests that we validate how our children are feeling with words like, 'I can see this is really big for you and I can see this feels scary for you and yet I know you can do this.'

Helping our little girls to tune in to the early warning signs in their body is incredibly important. This is how they work out the difference between feeling safe and unsafe. The key message is that when little girls experience uncomfortable feelings in their body, they need to pause and ask themselves these three questions that I shared earlier in the book:

1. Am I in an unsafe place?
2. Am I with an unsafe person? or
3. Am I about to do an unsafe thing?

If they answer yes to any of these questions, we need to teach them how to speak up very loudly and find a safe person. Our first reaction to a worried child is often to minimalise their experience with words like 'it's okay'; 'everything is going to be fine' or 'there is nothing to worry about'. Sadly, that is really unhelpful for the person experiencing the anxiety. The key behaviours as a parent to avoid are:

- Excessively reassuring the child
- Being too involved and directive
- Allowing avoidance
- Becoming impatient with your child.

One example might be working with your anxious daughter who has decided she can't go into the dance class today. Firstly, we allow, acknowledge and accept her feelings and remind her that she can be brave and have courage. Next, we suggest that all she has to do is to go in for five minutes and that you will either go with her or be waiting for her, and you will take her home. My daughter-in-law, the dance teacher, has said that it is helpful to know before class if there is an anxious little girl who is struggling to come in the door so the teacher can come out and offer a welcoming space.

Here is a problem-solving strategy that may be helpful if your daughter is struggling with unhelpful anxiety. To start with, correct her language from 'I am anxious' to *'I am feeling anxious'*. Then:

1. Listen really carefully.
2. Validate her feelings.
3. Encourage her bravery.
4. Explore and clarify the problem clearly.
5. Explore some possible solutions.
6. Empower your little daughter to choose which she would like to try first.
7. Practise or do 'let's pretend' with the strategy she chooses.

8. Come back after the experience, and if that was unsuccessful, explore another solution.
9. Repeat the process.
10. Celebrate success.

A key message that can be really helpful when our little girls are feeling really anxious is rather than saying 'Everything is going to be OK' or 'There's nothing to worry about', get in the habit of saying 'Together, we are going to get through this'. We can help our little ones maintain calm nervous systems so they have more energy and less tension to navigate life.

Ways to create serotonin

Serotonin is the neurochemical that gives us that calming effect. There are ways that you can help your little girl create her own serotonin.

- Take three breaths often
- Take big sighs
- Hum her favourite songs to herself
- Give herself a hug
- Request a hug from people she loves
- Do the 'Round and Round the Garden' nursery rhyme in the palm of her hand
- Spend time with a comforter like a teddy bear or a special doll
- Stroke or cuddle her favourite pet
- Be close to her safest grown-ups.

Building courage and bravery

One of the myths that the patriarchy has perpetuated is that women need the protection of men. This conditioning can lead our girls to feeling powerless and fearful. Sadly, so many of the concerns and limits that we establish around our little girls are totally unconscious. All little children have the same biological drives to explore the world, often fearlessly, and we need to celebrate that. I have a photograph of one of my granddaughters just before her second birthday climbing over a fence with a hose over her shoulder! Both her parents were worried that she was going to hurt herself. When they asked her what she was doing, she replied indignantly that she was simply being a fire person going to put out a fire. Obviously, she wasn't going to be held back as a little girl.

Thankfully, we see fiercely brave girls everywhere today and it is making it much easier for girls to stretch themselves and become stronger and braver. In the 2021 Olympics, it was incredibly heartening to see how young some of the girls were who were competing in the skateboarding competition, and how incredibly fearless they were.

Play research suggests that children are biologically wired to take themselves to the edge of their own fear each time they play, provided grown-ups allow them to do this. As soon as well-meaning parents step in with 'be careful' or 'that's too high', we challenge their inner warning system and they start to doubt themselves.

Heather Shumaker is a passionate advocate for encouraging children to be allowed to stretch themselves and take healthy risks. She argues:

> A child who grows up taking healthy risks is more apt to be cautious about dangerous risks. She will also gain confidence, independence and a sense of joy in the world.
>
> – Heather Shumaker, *It's OK to Go Up the Slide: Renegade Rules for Raising Confident and Creative Kids* (2016)

One of the reasons that children want to go up the slide is because they are seeking risk and challenge in their play and it helps them feel powerful. I am pretty happy that my granddaughters have all enjoyed going up the slide many times!

In the survey for this book, around 7 per cent of girls responded (via their parents) that they are happiest when they're participating in physical pursuits, like horse riding or having fun going down steep waterslides or tracks on a bike. Other little girls said they were happiest putting on shows, dancing, playing with their siblings or having fun at school. The growth of courage is gradual, and we need to be mindful of nurturing it and encouraging it so that we can temper the social norms that suggest girls are incapable of being strong and brave.

Australian soccer superstar Sam Kerr and Australian tennis champion Ash Barty are two sporting role models that I point out to my granddaughters. Both of these young women are ferocious competitors and women of character who are respectful and authentic. There are lots of women like this featured in the book *Good Night Stories for Rebel Girls*.

Physical risk is one thing, however, taking social risks and learning risks in the classroom is equally important. If your little girl approaches others in the playground, hoping to be included in the play, she runs the risk of being excluded. Even though that can be painful, the benefits of being included far outweigh that disappointment. The key to helping your little girl grow in confidence in this area is to encourage her and give her the freedom to take these social risks. Avoid forcing or coercing her to take a risk, even if you are confident she will succeed.

One thing you can encourage with little girls is that they can also play superhero games with little boys. By not encouraging or allowing a girl to play these roles, we are sending her clear messages that being brave is just for boys and not something girls do! Indeed, the latest Wonder Woman movies show just how powerful women can be. And there have been a number of films over the last 10 years with women as powerful heroes and warriors. Obviously, you won't be showing your little girls these movies, however, you can tell them about them if they come across other children or other grown-ups who tell them that it's not okay for little girls to be superheroes. Correct the myth right there!

Being their own best friend

I found that one of the biggest challenges when working with a troubled child or teenager was weakening the inner critic that was yelling loudly in their head. The endless voice that told them they were too fat, too ugly, too dumb, too useless or that nobody liked them, and to convince them that those voices were incorrect.

One of the reasons I really like the book *Raising Girls Who Like Themselves* by Kasey Edwards and Dr Christopher Scanlon is that the basic premise is so accurate. The biggest challenge is to raise a girl who likes herself because, quite simply, that is the best way we can steer our girls away from the self-loathing, self-hatred and self-doubt.

The reason I use mindfulness and creative visualisation in all my therapy is because once the ego chatter in the mind has quietened, one can find the quiet voice of our higher self or our inner compass. It is always there whispering to us, letting us know that we are okay, that we do deserve to be loved, and we are perfect exactly as we are. In my 'Safe 'N Sound' audio visualisation, I use the metaphor of an external imaginary protector that is always beside a child, especially when they feel frightened or alone. If we can convince our little girls that the best friend that they are ever going to have in their whole life is already hiding inside them, always with them, always loving them, imagine how safe their world may become. This inner guidance helps to build a moral courage that can help them make fewer risky choices.

Interestingly, it was a six-year-old girl who shared this insight with me, many years ago. Her grandmother had given her this wisdom – she had told her granddaughter that her best friend was hiding in her heart. This little girl had experienced significant trauma, yet she had a glow of iridescence about her. She was thoughtful and kind towards others, and fiercely protective of her little brother and her mother.

It took me a long time to find that my higher self had been my best friend all along. When I was a little girl, I knew this quiet voice within me really well, however, I lost touch with it in my tween and teen years. The punishment and shaming that I experienced in my childhood gradually silenced that quiet voice within me. I told myself stories about being unlovable, worthless, and that I was too loud and too much. To compensate for these beliefs, I became aloof and never trusted anyone with any vulnerabilities. I was a people-pleaser, or the helper who helped everyone but myself. Just as the research shows, I coped with the shame I felt in my late teen years by developing an addiction to a legal prescription drug. I reconnected with my higher self quite accidentally when I did my first meditation with the wonderful Petrea King, author, counsellor, creator of meditation and relaxation resources and CEO and founder of the Quest for Life Foundation. This reconnection with my higher self was like finding a long-lost friend, and it gave me the impetus to start my healing journey. The more I changed the stories I told myself, the easier it was to hear the quiet voice of wisdom within me and then I began to consciously seek it out. Now, I can choose to breathe deeply and be still so I can hear the whisperings of my invisible best friend. Sometimes, I need to sleep on things to make sure that I can hear a message of guidance. Other times, I need to find a quiet place in nature to truly ground myself.

There are times when my best friend urges me to be fiercely brave, to stand up for others less fortunate or to reach out and be a human who genuinely matters. Mostly it urges me to be kind and true to myself.

PARENTS AND EDUCATORS' SURVEY

My daughter just has an awareness about others' feelings, especially those with troubled families. She gravitates to other children with little friends and makes them feel special. Her kindness and generosity towards others fills my heart and heals my soul.

There is no question in my mind that we – as parents, grandparents and significant caregivers – can build resilience, grit and courage in our little girls. We can challenge the unhelpful social norms. We can help to identify their glimmers and we can keep on building those right throughout life. This strange dance called life will bring us moments of exquisite joy and immense suffering, and being able to adapt and cope with all it brings is what real resilience is about.

KEY POINTS

- Unhelpful stereotypes and social norms that encourage our little girls to believe they lack the strength and courage of little boys are gradually being challenged.
- We can cultivate and nurture resilience in our little girls without needing to toughen them up.
- Protective factors that help nurture us in times of stress can be called 'glimmers'.
- The more glimmers we give our girls when they are little the better they can cope with the stressors of life.
- Our little girls need to learn the art of losing or failing and recovering.
- We need to remind our little girls that even though disappointment isn't a pleasant feeling, it is a normal human response.
- The more our little girls practise overcoming setbacks in moments of disappointment, the better they get at it.
- Encouraging little girls to step up and have a go, regardless of possible outcomes, is teaching her about resilience and grit.
- Reassure your little girls of your unconditional love for them which does not change when things go badly.
- The more life skills in a little girl's toolkit in the first six years of life, the more resilient she will become.
- Avoid doing things for your little girl that she can do for herself most of the time.
- An important life skill involves the art of finding solutions by encouraging creative thinking and problem solving.
- When our little girls experience high levels of cortisol because they feel threatened, unsafe, uncomfortable, frightened, worried or unable to cope, anxiety is doing its job.

- Teach your daughters simple ways to create calming neurochemicals like serotonin.
- To build resilience, grit and courage in our little girls we need to challenge the unhelpful social norms that teach our girls that they are weaker, less capable and less brave than little boys.

17

Embracing neurodivergence – girls who see the world differently

We are all neurodiverse. This means that we all have different brains as a consequence of our DNA, the environment we were raised in, the humans who have cared for us, and the experiences we have had. Technically, a group of people are neurodiverse, but an individual is not. Being neurodivergent means that an individual has a brain that thinks, behaves and learns differently from what is most common – in other words, neurotypical. Founder of Tilt Parenting Deborah Reber in her book *Differently Wired* prefers to use the term 'differently wired' when talking about being neurodivergent. Having a less typical cognitive variation in responding to the world can include, however, is not always, ADHD, autism, sensory processing disorder, dyslexia, dyspraxia and dysgraphia. Thankfully, with advances in research and lived experience, we are now able to see that these conditions are not pathological but rather just a sign of difference. Indeed, the focus is now on what unique strengths and superpowers exist with being neurodivergent.

In this chapter I don't plan to explore the many ways the neuro-divergent brain can impact our little girls in the first years of life as I am not an expert in the mechanics of such things. Rather, I want to bust some myths, build more understanding and give parents some practical suggestions from those who experience the world a little differently from many others.

PARENTS AND EDUCATORS' SURVEY

My daughter has a girl at her day care who has non-verbal autism. My daughter is extremely verbal in her communication, and she has developed a lovely relationship with this child, understanding what this child needs even without speech.

ADHD

In Australia, roughly one in 20 individuals has ADHD, and in other parts of the world it is one in 10. In reality, it is most likely under-diagnosed, especially in girls and women. ADHD is a neurological condition that cannot be cured through diet or mindfulness or anything else, however, some of its symptoms can be helped and supported by many techniques and strategies, including medication. Having a child with ADHD is not a sign of poor parenting, and it is highly hereditary. Also, several of the people I have spoken to who live with or work closely with this reality want me to remind others that when you have met a person with ADHD, you have only met one person with ADHD.

Over time, ADHD has been stigmatised through a problematic lens and it's time to explore the gifts that it can bring into individuals' lives. Every single human is a unique being, and the same goes with being neurodivergent. Every single human yearns to be seen, heard, loved, valued and accepted exactly as they are.

When I was teaching many, many years ago, ADHD was something that only came up with male students. Our girls can slip through the cracks, and struggle silently with a neurodivergent brain without understanding or support. Over the last five years, I have had a number of female friends who have been diagnosed with ADHD or autism, and all of them have expressed their sense of incredible relief to finally discover the reasons why they were sometimes seen as lazy, unreliable, forgetful or 'too intense'.

In an episode on my podcast *Parental As Anything*, I spoke to Christina Keeble, a special education teacher who has ADHD and is autistic, and who is also a mother of two children with the same diagnoses. One of the reasons that Christina suggests little girls with ADHD are harder to diagnose is that they do tend to be more socially aware and acceptable. Boys tend to display behaviours more externally and are more obviously disruptive. Girls can be identified as spacey or disorganised, with a lack of focus and a tendency to daydream. This is quite a worry given that *girls and boys, and women and men, tend to be equally likely to have ADHD.*

Other characteristics can include being highly energetic, having difficulty sitting still and being seemingly always raring to go. Impulsivity and distractibility are another couple of possible characteristics. There are also emotional mood swings when having challenges and they can also struggle dealing with big emotions. ADHD girls and boys can have trouble with transitions when they are hyper-focused on something they are enjoying. These behaviours can cause problems in social settings and in classrooms, and many children with ADHD are viewed as problematic, naughty or bad because they can't behave better. Interestingly, for some ADHD children, moving around a classroom is how they improve focus. I was a very high-energy little girl, and there are some in my team who would argue that I am still a high-energy woman! My brain works most effectively when I am moving, and if you have been to any of my seminars, you will be aware that I pace the entire time. If I don't move constantly, I can't remember the research that is under much of my work and I lose focus. My husband is constantly annoyed when I start tapping my leg or jiggling my feet when we go out for a meal. Maybe this is one of the reasons why, as a classroom teacher, I ensured there was plenty of movement and lots of brain breaks for my students and myself.

The work of Dr Lisa Feldman Barrett and Dr Mona Delahooke has shown how important interoception is – the brain constantly working with the body, to ensure there is enough energy to not only allow the body to thrive, but to manage the sensory input and requirements that surround the body. Many years ago (well before talking about neuroscience was popular), a paediatrician explained to me how he thought the ADHD brain worked. He said there is a reticular activating system at the base of the brain, which acts like a gateway to all the stimuli coming in through the sensory receptors placed all over the body. Because there are thousands of stimuli every second, this gateway narrows down the number of stimuli coming into the brain, for example, to 200. For children with ADHD, he believed the gateway was held much wider open, so that around 2000 stimuli were flooding their brain at any one time. This flooding of stimuli made it difficult for these children to focus and to regulate themselves and their emotions. Put simply, he was explaining the concept of neuroception and interoception. While this massive flooding can seem problematic, especially when you have an underdeveloped executive brain, learning to master such a flooding of stimuli can become an advantage later in life. The capacity to hyper-focus on a task, whether in technology or creatively, can be a superpower. We only have to look at some of the successful people with ADHD like Michael Phelps, Jamie Oliver, Bill Gates, Richard Branson, Justin Timberlake, Michael Jordan, Emma

Watson, Simone Biles, Solange Knowles and Lisa Ling – and some experts even believe Albert Einstein had ADHD tendencies too.

PARENTS AND EDUCATORS' SURVEY

To be honest, life with a high-octane inattentive ADHD daughter is an extreme sport: I am finding it difficult to remember a recent light moment! But she makes me smile often – she still fiercely loves her Mum and Dad and tells us effusively every day. She loves to burrow in and cuddle us and still loves being touched – back scratching, cuddles etc. I see others at this age becoming more independent and she's not quite reached this stage yet, which is nice.

One of the key things to keep in mind if you notice some of the tendencies of ADHD in your daughter is to avoid seeing it as a disability or a disorder. First, it would be prudent to speak with your GP or paediatrician, as early diagnosis can be hugely helpful, and it may be that your daughter doesn't have ADHD despite displaying characteristics. Either way, if you view it through the lens of potential giftedness while helping her to build strategies that help her with self-regulation, she will see herself differently as well.

Overstimulation can definitely create problems for children with sensory processing issues and ADHD. Taking steps to create predictability in the home, creating a calm environment without too much noise and visual stimulation, helps all our children, especially those who are neurodivergent. The important thing is to work with your daughter to help her to identify the things that overwhelm her, cause her distress and what can trigger spontaneous meltdowns. This also means that you give her opportunities to shine in the areas where she does have strengths.

Dr Gaylene Clews, a former sports psychologist at the Australian Institute of Sport and an elite athlete herself, argues in her book *Wired to Play* that a significant proportion of our finest sportspeople, both male and female, have ADHD. Training and competing at a high level requires intense focus and high energy, both things that ADHD can gift.

Helping our girls to understand their unique brains, and how they can get it to work most efficiently, is especially important in the early years as she creates her own sense of self. Every child will have unique challenges because there is no perfection in humanity. We are all learning all the time how to navigate this strange dance called life.

Reber believes that this is the consistent message our neurodivergent kids need to hear:

> There is nothing wrong with you. We are all working on things. The great thing is once we know how our brains operate, we can support ourselves in making things easier for ourselves.
>
> – Deborah Reber, *Differently Wired* (2020)

Christina Keeble had similar messages in the *Parental As Anything* podcast, and she also stressed the importance of parents being strong advocates for their children. Constantly educating yourself and being a part of supportive groups are important ways to be the positive advocate your daughter needs.

Working collaboratively with your daughter on building confidence and competence is important and it will be gradual. There is so much negativity expressed towards children who struggle with impulsive behaviour, often driven by stress. Much of this comes from an ignorance about how our brain and body work in every moment. Educating your family, your neighbours and those in your school communities about ADHD will not only help your daughter, it will help many other children as well.

Autism

Autism is a developmental condition that typically finds people experiencing challenges with communication, social interaction, and repetition or restriction in interests and behaviours. Sensory issues are common. While it is often not until children start school that autism becomes noticeable, parents and professionals may pick up signs as early as 12 months, but more commonly by the time a child is two or three.

According to Autism Awareness Australia, some of the social and communication challenges may include:

- Conversational issues, dominating conversations about a favourite topic or perhaps struggling with turn taking
- Issues interpreting others' non-verbal communication cues
- Unusual speech patterns/delayed speech/repeating words and phrases
- Being very literal in interpreting things
- Preferring solitude, feeling stressed and exhausted by social interaction
- Being a stickler for following rules
- Challenges with friendships, especially through misunderstanding social cues
- Unusual or quite obsessive interests
- Possibly unusual physical movements, such as touching, rocking, flapping, spinning objects or flicking fingers
- Very attached to routine in order to feel safe and struggling to cope when routines change
- May find loud noises distressing
- Heightened (or dampened) sensory issues
- Anxiety is also common in autistic children and teens.

– Summarised from autismawareness.com.au

I need to state again that if you have met a child or person with autism, you have only met one autistic person. Next, you may have been advised to describe an autistic person as a person first, for example, Sandra is a person with autism. For some in the autism community, this can be problematic because it implies that autism is something separate to who the person is or it's something they don't like, or something they can get over. For this reason, many people in the autism community like to be referred to as autistic rather than a person with autism. The correct way to address someone is with their preferred terminology, which means you need to check in with them.

My friend and colleague Allison Davies is an autistic person with attention, sensory processing and executive functioning difficulties. She runs seminars and workshops educating people about brain care and regulation, especially for children and grown-ups within a neurodiversity framework. Not only is Allison autistic, her daughter is, too. I chatted to Allison for an episode of my podcast because of her lived experience, as well as her extensive work using music therapy to help lower children's stress levels.

One of her most significant messages is that autism is not pathological or a 'disorder'; it is a neurotype that just describes who someone is, a bit like gender does. It is not something that is lesser than or something that needs to be fixed or changed. It quite simply needs to be understood.

Autism has a strong tendency to be genetic and it is definitely not linked to vaccination. Many advocates in the autism world are passionate about changing the dialogue around autism from being under the social model of disability. Autistic people can feel disabled because society isn't able to cater for their needs. If we are able to cater better for their needs in schools, in the community and in workplaces, the world would be a much better place for us all. Quite simply we need to drop the D in ASD, the same as we need to drop the final D in ADHD!

There is a tendency to see autism as a linear spectrum from high-functioning to low-functioning and indeed Asperger's – a term that is no longer used in diagnosis – was considered to be a classification for 'high-functioning' autism. This is a problematic and potentially debilitating way of describing autism because, as Davies would describe, some children or adults perceived to be 'high-functioning' can still struggle in certain areas, while some who are considered 'low-functioning' can lead incredibly effective lives. Labels are seldom helpful, and it is something we need to be mindful of around our neurodivergent little girls so that we don't put them in a box.

Diagnostically, autism can be described as mild, moderate or severe, however, much of those diagnoses are made subjectively rather than objectively.

In an episode of *Grey Matter*, the Queensland Brain Institute's neuroscience podcast, international autism expert Professor Elliott Sherr gave a great summary of some key characteristics that are considered autistic:

- Difficulty with oral communication, from no words at all to just being unable to understand the subtleties around communication, especially facial expressions
- Having a low threshold for sensory input in certain areas
- 'Stimming' (repetitive movements or sounds) or 'flapping' (flapping the hands) which are forms of self-stimulation and interestingly are an attempt by an autistic child to self-regulate
- Rocking, squeezing their muscles and chewing on things like their shirt collars or fingers are other ways some autistic people try to regulate themselves in a world that is not designed to meet their needs
- Spontaneous meltdowns when their nervous system becomes overloaded
- Hyper-focus on things that interest the child and difficulty getting them interested in anything else.

One of the key myths that Allison is passionate to dispel is that autistic children and adults don't feel empathy or can't show it. She argues it's almost the opposite; that they can be highly empathetic and that can make it really hard at times because they can be overwhelmed by empathy. Often, autistic people have a really strong sense of social justice and they can pick up and absorb the energies of people around them, even if they then find it impossible to express in words or actions. This can create enormous tension in the nervous system, which can lead to spontaneous meltdowns. How challenging must that be for our little girls, who already have a tendency to be more emotional than boys, being unable to express big feelings of caring concern for others and themselves?

PARENTS AND EDUCATORS' SURVEY

We have one little girl who always helps a boy who has autism. She helps him to put his belongings away and supports him to join in with the other children. Sometimes she hugs him and kisses him. She doesn't see him as different yet it's interesting how she has taken on this supportive role with him.

Many autistic girls, especially little girls, can miss being diagnosed early because they don't necessarily display the same overt behaviours as boys. This is similar to what happens with ADHD. Another reason is that girls are generally more socially adept than boys, so if you start with a higher skill level and the autism brings it down a little, it may be harder to identify. Allison shares her experience as a little girl, which demonstrates this beautifully. She tells me that she noticed girls look in each other's eyes when they talked and they looked at each other's faces. Even though this was really difficult for her to do, she created a technique where she imagined a triangle over a person's eye and she would count '1, 2, 3' and focus on each point of that imaginary triangle while she was speaking or listening to someone. She learned to make eye contact – in her own way – based on modelling how other children behaved. How absolutely fascinating!

Allison was finally diagnosed with autism when she was in her late 30s, and she says the day she realised it was 'the best day of her life'. Finally, everything that she had struggled with made sense. All the stories she had made up around feeling shame about how she was lazy, disorganised and 'bad' dissolved instantly. She said it felt like veils dropping off her and all of a sudden *she made sense to herself*.

In the podcast, Allison explores the difference between her own experience and her daughter's experience, being diagnosed at five. She can talk openly with her daughter about autism and know that it is part of her identity. This helps her to work out her boundaries and her daughter is happy to tell other people she is autistic and that if she can't do something she can ask for support. She won't have the need to create all those shame-based stories that Allison formed because she did not know that there was an underlying reason for some of her difficulties. We can now take the deficit lens off and start looking at autism as potential for strength and 'superpowers'. Every child still yearns to be seen, heard, valued and loved and it is exactly the same for autistic children of all genders.

We need to question our expectations around how we want our little girls to behave in social settings, especially expecting all girls to be quieter, to sit more patiently and generally be nicer! Autistic kids can enjoy playing with other children, even if they're not looking at them or talking to them; they are still participating socially in play. To help your autistic little girl participate in other activities like dance or gymnastics, ensure that you communicate with the coach around her needs. Flexibility is really important, and that may mean she is only able to do half the class or she may need to have a week or two off. Sometimes, a child may choose not to compete and just do the training. Having them participate to a level they are comfortable with is really important.

Parenting a little girl who is neurodivergent can definitely be really difficult at times. Many parents struggle with a sense of isolation, guilt, fear or judgement, and endless worry and anxiety around how to best support a little girl's healthy growth and development. 'Find your people' is the message I hear from those raising differently wired children. For many, the village is a virtual one and often, that virtual village really has been a lifesaver. I have two links on my website that were gathered by my extensive virtual community to help those of you who have a neurodivergent child. They not only share the best authors, educators and groups for support but they list many wonderful books for both grown-ups and children that can help you on your journey of parenting your exceptional child. To find them, just type 'ADHD' and 'autism' into the search at maggiedent.com and you'll find our best resources.

PARENTS AND EDUCATORS' SURVEY

My son, Ollie, was talking about his frustration at school and his autism. He asked me whether I would prefer if he didn't have autism. I replied that if he didn't have autism, he wouldn't be the boy he is, and that I love him so much for who he is. From the back seat, my five-year-old daughter said, 'I want autism! If Ollie has it, I want it! Mummy, can I have autism?'. Both Ollie and I chuckled conspiratorially about that comment, knowing that she does.

- Being neurodivergent means that an individual has a brain that thinks, behaves and learns differently from what is most common – in other words neurotypical. This can include – however, not always – ADHD, autism, sensory processing disorder, dyslexia, dyspraxia and dysgraphia.
- If you have met a person with ADHD, you have only met one person with ADHD. Every individual is unique and different.
- Little girls can be harder to diagnose with ADHD and autism because they do not display the same overt behaviours as boys and are more socially aware and adept.
- Please avoid seeing ADHD in your daughter as a disability or a disorder. Often it can be a pathway to a superpower or a significant gift.
- Be a strong advocate for your ADHD daughter by educating your family, your neighbours and those in your school communities about how they can better understand how to support her and other children who have ADHD.
- Autism is also not pathological or a disorder, rather it is a neuro type.
- It is not something that is lesser or something that needs to be fixed or changed – it simply needs to be understood.
- Autism is not a linear spectrum from high functioning to low functioning – it is far more complex than that.
- It is a myth that autistic children and adults don't feel empathy or can't show it; often it's the opposite.
- If you have a little girl who is neurodivergent find a virtual village with understanding people who have lived your journey.
- Every child is yearning to be seen, heard, valued and loved and it is exactly the same for all neurodivergent children and adults too.

18

Transitioning to big school

Things have changed in the expectations of our little children around the ages of four to six. In the western world, there has been a pushdown of formalised learning, which means our little girls and our little boys are somehow magically all ready to do things that are developmentally challenging for a number of them.

In 2021, I was nanny-teacher to one of my granddaughters during lockdown. I am a former high school English teacher and I was gobsmacked that my little granddaughter, who had not yet completed her letter formation of the alphabet, was expected to be able to write a story with a beginning, middle and end, while using adjectives!

According to the Australian Early Development Census, the national average of children with developmental vulnerabilities is 21.7 per cent, however, it is much higher in communities of lower socio-economic status and much lower in wealthier communities.

As I explored earlier in the book, long-term early childhood educators have been telling me for a while that today's five-year-olds are arriving in our school systems with these four challenges:

- Less oral vocabulary
- Poorer fine and gross motor skills
- Poorer self-regulation
- An inability to initiate and sustain play with other children.

These challenges are appearing across the board, not just in our more vulnerable communities. There are many complex reasons why, but one of the most glaring likelihoods is that our children are not playing enough in the physical world with other children. Also, they are not being spoken to and read to at the same levels of previous generations and, yes, the digital distraction for parents does appear to be an issue. Our children are turning up as five-year-olds less capable and less resilient than in previous generations. How can our politicians, education experts and bureaucrats think that less capable children can cope with more formalised learning at the age of five?

It must be noted this change has been mandated from both state and federal governments in most western countries without true consultation from key stakeholders, and many early years educators are struggling with stress, burnout or are leaving their jobs in despair.

It is important to emphasise that changes in curriculum expectations have not been created by teachers, and they have set up an unrealistic and unhealthy competitive perception that the earlier children start formal learning (especially around reading), the better for all children. In short, there is little or no evidence that pressuring children to read at five rather than seven improves their later reading; in fact, there is much concern that it is damaging. There is no hurry. Essentially, the current school system in the western world caters for those who have strengths that suit that system. Those with learning challenges and the gifted can often fall by the wayside.

The reason I began with that explanation is that the experience you had when you transitioned to big school may have been quite different from what your little girl experiences. We must keep in mind that every single child is a unique miracle, a one-off, and the expectation of our current education system is that one size will fit all; that is absolute rubbish. Children who have experienced trauma, who are neurodivergent, who are Indigenous, who have English as a second language, or who are living with a serious illness will obviously have additional challenges.

Thankfully, we are gradually shifting from shame-based methods of behaviour management in our schools. I clearly remember being smacked with rulers for fidgeting, having to sit under the teacher's desk when I had been naughty, or having to stand in the naughty corner for hours on end. Unfortunately, some of the strategies are still inducing shame in our sensitive children, including the traffic light system of behaviour modification and the writing of names on the blackboard (especially in red), or earning points for being good versus losing points for being bad. Excessive praise and rewards through handing out stickers and stamps are also still being used to manage classroom behaviour, despite the value of this method being disproved quite strongly. Hopefully the shift that is now taking place is with a better understanding of stress-informed or trauma-informed behaviour.

Stress of change

Changes of environment, people and routines – especially outside the home – can all cause spikes in cortisol. This is the hormone that creates the stress symptoms you may see – crying, clinging, tummy aches, refusal to leave your side, poor appetite, restless sleep, outbursts and tantrums. Remember this means the 'downstairs brain' is registering threat, and is acting accordingly. We need to reassure our little ones that their response is real and valid. Please avoid minimalising in these moments by telling them, 'Everything will be all right', 'You have nothing to worry about' because sadly, and counterintuitively, that is actually unhelpful. Instead, maybe try 'Hey, you look like you are having a hard time' or 'You seem to be feeling stressed or worried'. Remember the three As for big emotions – allow, acknowledge and accept while offering a safe base to be.

This transition to big school will be stressful because change is stressful. It can take four to six weeks for children to really settle, and sometimes they have regressions. Some may return to bedwetting, thumb-sucking or needing to sleep beside their safest grown-up. Allow them to settle with as much tenderness as possible, because the calmer their nervous system is each day they go to school, the better they will be able to cope. You do not need to 'toughen them up'; they will gradually become more confident.

PARENTS AND EDUCATORS' SURVEY

What worries me the most about my daughter – meltdowns/tantrums, sensitivities, leaving at school drop-off. Lots of hanging off my arms.

The good news

Little girls tend to transition better than little boys and have fewer learning and behaviour challenges. If your little daughter has older siblings, this can be really helpful when she transitions to big school. If your little daughter has spent time in a high-quality early childhood setting – especially between the ages of three and four before she starts big school – research shows she will be better prepared. Even better still if some of her friends are starting big school at the same time.

The Australian Early Development Census (AEDC) collects data every few years from five-year-olds in Australia, and this information can act as an excellent guide as you raise your little girl towards school-starting age. These measures show that while your little girl might be able to count to 1,000, her preparedness to manage full-time schooling needs to consider other factors as well.

The AEDC measures five important areas of early childhood development:

1. **Physical health and wellbeing**: fine and gross motor skills, good health, being well fed, and well rested, capable of sitting, listening skills, able to grip a pencil, turn pages in a book, build with blocks, can toilet themselves, feed themselves, dress themselves, blow their nose, wipe their bottoms and wash their hands.
2. **Social competence**: their primary need is to be able to get along with other children, cope with the different social setting, be able to take learning risks, have healthy assertiveness, ability to play by themselves and with other children, and have pro-social behaviours.
3. **Emotional maturity**: some ability to self-manage their emotions, be able to cope with minimal adult contact in group settings, develop friendships, and able to separate from parents even if gradually and with many tears.
4. **Language and cognitive skills (school-based)**: basic counting, following basic instructions and basic thinking skills.
5. **Communication skills and general knowledge**: basic conversation skills, some manners, ability to communicate needs and ask for help, some understanding of the wider world, and some degree of independence when needed.

Dr Kaylene Henderson, a child psychiatrist and parenting educator, believes that a successful transition has a lot to do with a child's social and emotional skills. In an interview for my podcast with the ABC, *Parental As Anything*, she asked a series of questions for parents to consider – these are equally important for little girls as for little boys.

1. Is your child able to get along with others, including members of your family, teachers, friends and peers of the same age?
2. Is your child able to join in with a group and cooperate with others

in play? They don't have to get it right all the time, just most of the time.

3. Are they able to make sense of other people's behaviours and feelings? Or does your child find these things confusing or jump to the wrong conclusions?

4. Can your child think of appropriate solutions when conflict happens? If your child has a tendency to lash out physically or maybe even hide meekly, and struggles to stand up for themselves, these can be red flags to consider.

5. Can your child understand and follow directions, again most of the time? This is as much about your child's ability to comprehend language as it is about their listening skills.

6. Does your child have any significant expressive language difficulties or significant speech delays or any other sort of problem that affects their ability to articulate words that will make it harder for them to communicate at school, to participate with show-and-tell moments and even to join in with their classmates?

7. Does your child have special needs that have been identified (such as autism, or other neurodivergent conditions)? If so, the key is to identify them early so you can explore and access the supports your child will need. Some schools specialise in in-house support for neurodivergent children and it may pay to seek one of those out.

– Maggie Dent, *Parental As Anything* (2021)

As the big day approaches, consider how you can ease the transition by building familiarity and confidence in your child. You might like to try the following:

• Reduce stress and anxiety as the big day approaches by building predictability and familiarity. Of course, this needs to start at home, by teaching a little girl where her school clothes will be, where she will hang her school bag, and where she will put her school shoes. It can be helpful if your daughter creates some visual cues for what needs to happen every morning before school. Even though they have fabulous memories, sometimes anxiety or excitement can mean they can forget things and become easily distressed.

- For your more sensitive little girls, please don't overdo talking about school. Do not oversell it because not every moment will be fun. Remember, it is not a field of daisies that we are preparing our little girls to experience in life; there will always be prickles.

- Orientation opportunities are excellent for building familiarity. If your daughter is unable to attend an orientation day, check with the school so you can arrange an opportunity for her to have a walk around before big school starts. The most important things for your little girl to know are where the toilets are, where the classrooms are and where she will find you after school!

- Have your little girl practise dressing herself in her new uniform, packing her bag, using her water bottle and opening her lunchbox. 'Let's pretend' is a great way to do it without getting too serious and putting too much pressure on her.

- Nurture a relationship with her teacher. This is the key to a smooth transition because your little girl is going to be leaving the safety of her home and safe grown-up, and having a new grown-up be her big safe person. If you can take a photograph on the first day, please do so. Print the photograph and put it on the refrigerator in full view. This way it is easier for your little girl to become more familiar with her new big person.

- If your little one is not transitioning with some little people she knows, help her create new friends. If you can collect her in the afternoons, it's a good opportunity to chat to other mums or dads. It doesn't take long before groups of classroom parents form an online place to connect. It's helpful joining these groups because parents remind each other of upcoming events . . . and every parent needs that sometimes! It is easy to organise a group play date this way, which will also help build friendship opportunities for your daughter.

- Your little girl's imagination is how she explores the world, so encourage imaginative play that may also build capacity, confidence and resilience. Let you be her in a 'classroom setting' where you can ask for help or ask the teacher to help with a conflict scenario that could occur.
- Read picture books about starting school, and don't forget your local library has plenty of books available for free.
- Separation distress is not a sign that your daughter is weak or that you have done something wrong as a parent. They are biologically wired to fear being separated from their safest grown-ups.
- Practise drop-offs and goodbyes so she is able to access some bravery when you leave her at the beginning of the day. It can be helpful to remind her when you leave about something fun you are going to do when you pick her up again. If she is sensitive, please leave her at school with a person rather than an activity.
- You can build positive neurochemicals in your little daughter's brain before she steps into a school environment, which may reduce cortisol. Some ideas include singing fun songs loudly in the car and sharing funny jokes or riddles. If you sense she is feeling anxious, you can also activate some serotonin by stroking your hand on her tickle spot which is high up on her back.
- It can be helpful to write loving notes and put them in your daughter's lunchbox, or you can write a message on a banana or put an unexpected Smartie in the bottom of her lunchbox! These unexpected treats can provide a little zap of an endorphin of love in the middle of her day.

PARENTS AND EDUCATORS' SURVEY

I am happiest when I am reading a book or with my friends at school. Reading is like an adventure and then you can re-enact that adventure. Daughter, six.

When I was counselling full-time, I worked with a lot of little ones, mainly girls, who were suffering separation distress in the first term of starting big school, or when starting at a new school. Given that I knew how wonderful the imagination could be for little girls, I found some of the following ideas helped shift their anxiety quite quickly, until a new habit formed.

- Help them create an imaginary protector. Ask them to imagine having their huge protector with them while they are away from you. I have two free audios available on my website which could help with this: 'Safe 'N Sound' and 'Sleepytime'.
- Fill a small, empty container with a lid with kisses from everyone they are fond of, and tuck it in the bottom of their backpack (don't forget the family pet!).
- As they leave home, form a habit of placing a kiss from one parent in the right hand and the other parent in the left (if you're a sole parent, you might place a kiss in each hand) . . . these kisses are magic and stay there all day.
- Draw a heart on your daughter's hand that matches one that you, or she, draws on your hand.
- Practise imagining you are sending your daughter rainbows of love from your heart to theirs at recess and lunch and ask them to send one to you when they miss you.
- Put a really small stuffed toy in the bottom of the backpack. Again, this helps your child not to feel so separate and alone.
- Draw funny pictures to put into her lunchbox.
- Give them a lanyard or locket to wear with a photo of a parent/s or their key caregivers – they tend to look at the photo often and even talk to it.
- Teach them how to take three big breaths and breathe out the butterflies hiding in their tummy. Or they can gently rub their tummy and tell the butterflies they are safe.
- Teach them how to calm themselves by singing 'Round and Round

the Garden' while making circles in their hand, just as you would do – music and touch trigger feel-good hormones.

Feeling brave enough to manage being away from your safest grown-up can be prolonged for around 4 per cent of our children. The good news is this is nothing new for experienced early years educators, and you'll be able to work with them to facilitate this transition. It can take lots of patience, kindness, compassion and a good dose of fun – but we know that, over time, children can get through this scary time.

PARENTS AND EDUCATORS' SURVEY

Our daughter (says she) is happy . . . 'When I see Mummy after school.'

After-school meltdowns

The biggest thing with handling the actual 'blah' at the end of the day is to remember where it is coming from. It is coming from a place of, 'I missed you, I needed you, and I am so glad you are here.'

– Dr Vanessa Lapointe in a TV interview with Laurel Gregory for *Global News, Canada* (6 October 2020)

It takes a lot of energy for our little ones to cope for a long period of time in an environment that is busy and full of people. By the time they re-unite with their safest big people, they often have an enormous meltdown. This is definitely not a sign that they've had a bad day. This meltdown is a sign that they are exhausted and experiencing displacement attachment. That means they have suddenly realised they have been away from you all day, and this intense emotion can trigger a cortisol response. At the end of the day, some of our children have an overloaded nervous system that does need to discharge the 'yuck', and the safest place is with you.

Remember that you can help your little girl generate positive neurochemicals by the choices you make in those first moments after school. Some little girls love it when you ask them lots of questions. Their love language may be quality time. Others can get distressed because they feel they are being interrogated – ouch, that's a bit unkind! Some just want to be held and helped. Some are ready to have some ridiculous fun in order to be very physically active. I explore love languages a bit more in Chapter 4.

Some of our little girls will already be going over everything that happened in the day, especially the bits that caused them emotional pain. Because they are so little, a tiny conflict can appear to be enormous when they are physically and mentally exhausted. Remember just to listen, validate their feelings and ask how you can help. You do not need to fix anything and remember, you only get part of the story. Please avoid speaking negatively about any other child in your daughter's class, the teacher, the education assistant or even the canteen. Anything negative that your little girl hears will contaminate her experience.

PARENTS AND EDUCATORS' SURVEY

My daughter has become best friends with one of her friends we met through mothers' group. They are chalk and cheese, but somehow they play lovely together most of the time 😊 They do fight like sisters, having big disagreements but over the last two years going to school together (seeing or video-calling each other pretty much every day) they have learned so much about life. They have learned that not everyone likes everything the same, sometimes you need alone time, sometimes it's fun to do/try different things, good friends can even say mean things sometimes but they don't really intend to hurt your feelings – they are just sad themselves and still learning at age five.

Be a positive parent. Student educational outcomes are influenced positively if parental involvement is affirming, co-operative and positive. Participate to the level that works for your family, and be mindful of avoiding drop-off or carpark dramas. Model to your daughter the adult you hope for her to become, and remember she is always watching, listening and forgets nothing!

KEY POINTS

- Transitioning to big school is a change experience and feeling anxious or worried is normal.
- Little girls tend to transition better than little boys and have fewer learning and behaviour challenges.
- A successful transition depends more on your daughter's social and emotional skills then her cognitive skills.
- The best way to reduce stress and anxiety is by building predictability and familiarity.
- Practising simple tasks like dressing themselves, packing their backpack, opening the lunchbox, and farewelling parents can be really helpful.
- Be as organised as possible the night before so that there are fewer tasks to do in the morning.
- Be prepared for after-school meltdowns as they will be physically and emotionally exhausted.
- The less stress on our little girls' plates as they begin the transition to big school the better for her and definitely the better for her parents.
- Be a positive parent and nurture a healthy optimistic relationship with your daughter's teacher and other parents as well.

19

Daddies and aunties and little girls

PARENTS AND EDUCATORS' SURVEY

What makes you feel sad?

When my dad yells at me.

In a perfect world, it would be fabulous for all little girls and little boys to have two loving, safe biological parents. I have met many same-sex parents who are conscious, committed, loving parents. This chapter about the importance of father figures is in no way disrespecting either solo mums or two-mum households. However, given that more than 90 per cent of children have mums and dads, or started off having a mum and dad, the importance of father–daughter relationships still needs to be explored. Father figures such as grandfathers, uncles, stepfathers or other significant males who are a regular part of our children's lives are all included.

I was definitely one of the lucky ones – my dad was a true kind gentleman. Modelling is one of the most influential ways little ones learn about themselves and life and as preschoolers, my siblings and I were able to spend lots of quality time in Dad's company. Not only did he have a fabulous sense of humour and an excellent wit, he was a passionate, just humanitarian and a huge lover of nature. Little did I realise at the time, but all these qualities were being embedded into my mind and heart.

While I have no memory of Dad ever telling me he loved me, I have a very clear memory of one significant time when I realised he did. I was in my first year of school and after school one day, Dad and I were in the farm ute, driving around checking on sheep. I was telling him absolutely everything that had happened in my day from the time I had left in the morning, and I could talk really fast. At one point, he stopped the ute, put it in gear and turned the engine off. Then he turned to me and listened for a number of minutes until I had finished updating him. That moment of complete presence with my dad was the moment I felt not just seen, heard and understood – I felt loved.

In a way, a little girl's first love is her daddy, if he is a safe man. He's the man who models how to be a partner and a protector. In many of the personal growth workshops and seminars I have attended, this core relationship comes up either positively or negatively. In a way, we unconsciously look to find our father in our male partner. If we have had a toxic relationship with our father as a little girl, we may consciously think we're looking for a very different man in an intimate relationship, however, we often attract a man with some similar traits, even if his form or looks are different.

PARENTS AND EDUCATORS' SURVEY

My daughter, seeing a champagne cork pop and her reiterating the action by saying, 'Dad pop, daddy pop'. She was about 18 months old.

Many years ago, I came across the work of Dr Bruce Robinson, who has worked closely with men at the end of their lives, and he noted over time how many expressed regret about the relationship they had with their daughters. So he set out to interview more than 400 men from 15 countries to explore the importance of this relationship.

Fathers who love their daughters unconditionally give girls a sense of security about themselves and a stronger sense of self-worth. Not only that, Dr Robinson argues that girls who have a strong, warm relationship with their father tend to menstruate later, become sexually active later, and develop a stronger sense of self-confidence. As teens, girls who feel loved by their fathers don't need to look for love elsewhere. Even though his book *Daughters and their Dads* was written in 2008, it is just as relevant today.

PARENTS AND EDUCATORS' SURVEY

My girl's friend at school was being verbally tormented by an older girl. My girl told the older girl to stop picking on her friend and to stop being mean, to which the older girl walked away. The friend's dad approached me several days later to tell me the story and say how proud and thankful he was of my girl for being so brave and such a great friend to his daughter.

Connecting with our little girls when they're young is essential if you want to stay connected as they grow older, especially in the teen years. Given that our little girls have such fantastic memories, creating memories that matter and last can be easy. They will remember the night when you helped them up onto the roof of your house to watch the stars or the full moon. They will remember the day you went swimming and pretended you were a dolphin splashing around. They will remember you reading them bedtime stories and the time you farted in the bath. They will remember you crying when you watched a sad movie together.

After a seminar one night, a dad came up to me with tears in his eyes. During the seminar, I had talked about the importance of family rituals as well as the significance of singing to your children. The dad said he didn't know the words to nursery rhymes or kids' songs when his daughter was little, but he was a big ACDC fan, so when they were together in his car, they would sing ACDC songs. Then he paused, and said that the week before he and his daughter had been on a dad date, and they had flown across the country and gone to an ACDC concert. How special is that story?

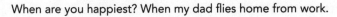

PARENTS AND EDUCATORS' SURVEY

When are you happiest? When my dad flies home from work.

How dads speak to their girls

Steve Biddulph's bestselling book *Raising Girls in the 21st Century* offers dads key message about the loudness of their voices. Men do generally have louder and deeper voices, and when our little ones are very young – especially girls, who also tend to have more acute hearing than boys – they might be easily frightened by Daddy's big voice.

I have had the privilege of working with Steve Biddulph in conferences that we have run together, and as part of the ABC's *Parental As Anything* podcast, and we've also presented an online masterclass together. And there is a story he tells that brings tears to my eyes every time. He tells me that he often talks to the dads in the audience about the importance of making time to spend with their daughters because if dads are always too busy, he believes many girls choose to believe this is because they are boring or not worth it. Steve says he notices that many women in the audience start shedding tears, and they are either happy tears because their dad did make time for them, or they are sad tears because they missed out and are grieving.

It's an intense and life-changing relationship – a dad and his daughter.
– Steve Biddulph, *Raising Girls in the 21st Century* (2019)

One of the cautionary messages that dads and father figures need to be mindful of in today's highly sexualised world is the 'princess' message. It sounds so sweet to call your little daughter a princess, especially if you read traditional fairytales where the princess was always beautiful, often with long blonde hair, and waiting for a prince to rescue her so she can live happily ever after. However, these messages are giving your little girls a sense of not having their own strength and power to look after themselves, and that they will always need a male figure to support them. It may seem benign, but this is setting up our girls to have expectations of neediness.

Thankfully there are lots of picture books now for young girls that give very different messages, including: *The ABC: What Can She Be?*; *Chapati Moon*; *My Body Belongs to Me*; *No Means No*; and *It Feels Good to be Yourself*. There are also now kids' movies celebrating strong, capable girls such as *Moana*, *Encanto* and *Frozen*. Please cheer along beside your daughter when she chooses her own unique expression of herself, and she doesn't rely on others to define who she is.

I have loved meeting dads who have fingernail polish thanks to having a spa treatment with their little daughters.

PARENTS AND EDUCATORS' SURVEY

Her dad told her that he was 'off fast food and ice cream'. I asked her if she was going to do the same, knowing full well that she loves ice cream.

She said, 'Oh no, I'm off onion.' Six months later, we still haven't had any onion.

Beware teasing and shaming

One of the things I have come to understand about boys of all ages, is that one of the ways they develop perfection and connectedness with other boys is through physicality and humour. When little boys really like other little boys, they will jump on them, wrestle them, tease them and be ridiculous to make them laugh. Sometimes our dads think this is how little girls like to feel loved and connected! Teasing from a dad to his daughter has no intention to cause long-term harm, however, due to the sensitivity of little girls' feelings and their long-term memories, teasing can do exactly that. Rather than being a source of connection, teasing can be a very early source of shame that can break a little girl's heart.

Shame is a name we give to the overwhelming feeling that we get telling us that we are wrong, bad and flawed. The follow-on feeling from that is that we are unlovable, especially from the person who has shamed us, even unintentionally. Deep shame is distressing, and can begin so early in life. Shaming makes it difficult for children and adults to come to a healthy place of self-love and acceptance, and instead leaves a person feeling unworthy of happiness.

Shaming can come from mums and dads, and often is created through either overt words said in frustration or quite innocent, seemingly innocuous comments from grown-ups and even loving parents. The impossible pressures being placed on today's parents are contributing significantly to more shaming in our children. Do any of these sound familiar:

- Stop crying or I will give you something to cry about!
- Do you want a smack?
- Stop being a sook.
- Get out of my face.
- What is wrong with you?
- You ought to be ashamed of yourself!
- You've been a bad little girl.
- You're acting like a selfish brat.
- Stop acting like a baby.
- What are people going to think?
- Don't be such a sissy!
- Don't be so overdramatic!

Sometimes our gestures are shaming and as our girls are super tuned in to being rejected, judged or excluded, they can feel shamed when this happens as well.

- Deliberately being ignored
- Being sarcastic
- Walking away as though a child does not exist
- Rolling one's eyes
- Glaring at a child with disgust
- Shouting, yelling and swearing at a child
- Hitting or shoving.

Teasing from dads, which we have already mentioned, is another source. There is an excellent episode of the ABC kids' cartoon *Bluey* that explores how Bandit, the father of two girls, was upsetting Bingo, Bluey's little sister. It is an excellent episode because the dad's actions could have been seen as playful, but the key is in observing our little girls' physiology, as well as their words when we are playing a tickling or other playful game, including teasing. And we must stop immediately if we can sense they are not enjoying themselves.

Some dads have said to me that they are trying to toughen up their little girls; unfortunately, this is seen through the lens of the male gaze. More often than not, they can be really upset by it and start to distrust the big, safe father figure. Often some of the things we say we believe are harmless because we know we are using a teasing tone, irony or sarcasm, but the capacity to understand this type of communication does not develop until much later in childhood. This is not exclusive to dads – some mums use the same shaming patterns.

PARENTS AND EDUCATORS' SURVEY

I always tell Hazel's dad to stop snacking before dinner. Hazel, when she was two, was watching her dad in the kitchen looking in the cabinets.

Next thing, she's standing in the kitchen next to him. Then we hear the voice, 'Get out of the kitchen, hun, no snacking', or 'It's tea time, you cheeky bugger'.

Dr Brené Brown has devoted years to exploring shame and vulnerability and she argues that the shame and guilt our children experience when they are little can influence the negative self-talk that appears in adolescence. This is why I believe it's so important to focus on what our little girls experience in the first six years of life – it can impact them later quite significantly. I can speak from experience, as I was significantly shamed in my early years of life. While I looked like a capable, competent teenage girl who achieved academically, played sport, participated in school activities and was a school leader, I secretly loathed and hated myself.

Experiences of shaming can debilitate us, especially during adolescence, when brain changes create more confusion and vulnerability. Our girls who have been shamed will simply shame themselves, and most adolescents struggle with crippling self-doubt and self-criticism that will be fuelled by shaming from early childhood. This shaming can come from other figures as well as father figures, however, often accidental shaming comes from dads and father figures.

In her audiobook *The Gifts of Imperfect Parenting*, Brown talks about a longitudinal research study of a large group of fifth-grade students which measured whether these kids were using more shame self-talk ('I'm an idiot'; 'I'm a failure') or guilt self-talk ('Heck, I made a bad choice there, I didn't do well at this'). Her research followed the children into their final years of school and found that:

> the kids who were shame-prone were more likely to commit suicide, drop out of high school and engage in high-risk drug, alcohol and sexual behaviours. The guilt-prone kids were more likely to finish high school, apply for college, engage in community activities and engage in lower risk sexual, drug and alcohol behaviours.
> – Brené Brown, *The Gifts of Imperfect Parenting* (2013)

A way to compensate for feelings of worthlessness can be through comfort eating, anger, perfectionism, or an empty yearning for fame, fortune and celebrity status. Striving for validation and acceptance from the digital world and a hunger for some sense of rewards, which increase compliance and obedience, are other ways girls can choose to compensate.

When little girls experience intentional or unintentional shaming and guilt, they also often seek validation through praise or over-achievement. Perfectionism and obsessions can form during the adolescent years and while a girl may appear successful and healthy, she may be experiencing an incredibly fragile sense of self. Sometimes girls can feel they need external validation or they are driven to gratify others in order to find any sense of value and worth. This can be where people-pleasing and being good and kind to everyone except themselves can become problematic.

I am sorry that I have dived down such a dark hole simply to explain that it's important not to tease your daughter using sarcasm and irony, especially when she is a little girl and does not have the capacity to understand either. If you are tickling and teasing, please stop when she says stop, apologise quickly and make amends. It is not your job to 'toughen up' your little girl by doing these things that are often accepted in the male world. The best way to allow her to find her own sense of strength and courage is to show her that she is seen, loved, and heard always, not just when she behaves well. Be her safe base – knowing that you have her back no matter what is the most important thing she needs to learn when she is a little girl.

If you, or whoever you are coparenting with, need more guidance in this area please look up an article written by Ruhi Lee for SBS called, 'I'm teaching my daughter to take up space in the world'. She explains that when she reads her daughter's picture book that has girls relegated to the background, or worse still omitted completely, she takes to the book with a black marker and 'corrects' it. She is passionate that her daughter will develop a strong sense of belonging and confidence so she can take up space in her world in a way that Lee wasn't able to.

Rough-and-tumble is still okay

Even though I have given a strong caution around teasing, the research is very strong around the importance of rough-and-tumble play for all children, not just little boys. Dads tend to be the ones who throw their kids into the air higher, who give them bigger frights and who tackle more strongly, and our girls need to experience this because it helps them develop emotional and social competence and courage. If that sort of behaviour is only reserved for boys, what are we unintentionally teaching our girls?

I'm incredibly happy that my sons have their little daughters climbing trees, riding bikes without training wheels quite early, riding skateboards and scooters, and have them in swimming lessons so they can join their dads surfing.

Warm, connected dads and father figures who allow our girls to be seen, heard and respected, teach our daughters self-respect and acceptance. That key relationship can help our daughters learn how to negotiate fairly with boys and men. Having that relationship as a tween or a teen can help show a girl how to relax and be affectionate around men without being sexual.

A warm father–daughter relationship does not just help a little girl feel loved, it helps her to feel that she matters not because of her appearance or her sports or academic prowess – she matters because of who she is.

PARENTS AND EDUCATORS' SURVEY

At seven years of age, my daughter was asked by her school principal to do an Anzac speech in front of her school as her dad is in the Navy. I have never been prouder of her standing up there next to her dad and telling the whole school about her own experiences surrounding her dad being away and her feelings surrounding Anzac Day. They were her own words spoken from the heart with such feeling and pride. There was not a dry eye in the school. Very proud mum here.

I was once asked to work with a little four-year-old girl who had become quite sad and withdrawn in her life, both at school and outside of school. When I asked her to draw a picture of how it felt to be her, her image was dark and gloomy. After we had done some emotional cleansing with colours, she seemed a little brighter and yet I felt there was something else troubling her. I have a sparkly wand that I often use, even with grown-ups. I handed it to the little girl and said that if she could use this magic wand, and say abracadabra, what would she do to fix her sadness? She sat still for a moment or two, then picked up the wand and said, 'Abracadabra. I just wish my daddy would play with me sometimes.' She had a loving dad, however, he was busy. Once he realised she was feeling disconnected from him, he was able to spend some time more regularly with her, and her sadness went way.

'Who Knew?' From Bouncing and Barbells to Ballet and Braids, is a fabulous book by Michael Ray, who became a solo dad around the age of 50. He embraces the role with passion and gusto despite many of the challenging misconceptions and social conditionings about being a father, and especially being a solo father. It's a warm, honest and real book that will have you laughing, and possibly crying.

In her book Fathers and Daughters, Madonna King asked thousands of girls what they wanted from their dads, and the answers were overwhelmingly that they wanted their father to be home more and to be present in their lives. One of the most positive shifts that has happened around parenting in the last generation has been around fathering. I get a lump in my throat sometimes when I see one of my sons brush their daughter's hair or help them put their hair in pigtails or plaits, because the little girl inside me would have loved that to have happened to me with my dad.

Obviously, daughters want their dads to show they care and to be prepared to really listen to them, even if they disagree with what their daughter is saying. This is a key way of ensuring your daughter's voice is not silenced and she learns the art of conversation and communication. We can disagree with others' views and still love them!

Father figures who show their love and affection through safe connection are significant for solo mothers and re-partnered mothers. Some solo mums have told me that their girlfriends' male partners have become non-biological fathers for their girls and they are beyond grateful.

The hunger for a strong warm connection to a dad came up so often in my counselling, from little girls right through to elderly women. The good news is that to be your daughter's hero, you don't have to be perfect. Indeed, if you're able to make mistakes and show her how to overcome them and make things right, you're teaching her a valuable life lesson and maybe building her resilience, especially if laughter and lightness are involved.

The power of aunties

> **PARENTS AND EDUCATORS' SURVEY**
>
> My gorgeous daughter, aged seven, was curious as to why her aunt was a vegan. I answered that it was because Auntie Tay thinks that it's mean to kill animals to eat them. After a reflective pause, Miss Seven responded, 'Well, I don't think that's mean. It would be way meaner to eat them while they were still alive!'

When I was growing up in a rural community, it was common to call our parents' friends auntie and uncle. I was lucky to have a warm, generous auntie who lived not far from us and as the years have gone by, I realise how much I became like her. I was drawn to her happiness, her cheekiness and her absolute loud authenticity. Some of my non-biological aunties and uncles are still alive today and when I see them, I still call them auntie and uncle and, even though I am in my 60s, I view them with the same reverence that I learned as a child.

They keep telling me not to call them auntie and uncle however, they were special in my childhood and deserve to still be called that.

In the research around evolutionary biology, women in kinship communities were united in supporting each other, all the babies and children, and the elderly. When I was working in western New South Wales in a remote community called Ivanhoe, we wanted to design a parenting resource for all families. We worked closely with the working party that included the Aboriginal elders of the community – such gracious and wise women. As we completed the project, the wise elder auntie who had led the team thanked me for my passion and commitment. She said the project was not just about Aboriginal children – it was about all children because her culture was inclusive regardless of gender, culture, disability or advantage.

Women had each other's backs. If someone was unwell or unable to care for their children, there were always other women to help. There was always a warm lap, a kind word and safety in the circle of women. This is the true dynamic of what 'auntie' means. I believe there is a biological hunger for little girls to be surrounded by aunties well before they begin the journey to womanhood.

PARENTS AND EDUCATORS' SURVEY

Granddaughter, aged seven, being raised by the village with young parents (26). She gardens with me, complete with a takeover by fairies, plays Lego with her uncle, science fiction watching with Granddad, dances with Auntie, and gold prospecting with Poppy and Nanny – the best life.

Even though the modern world has separated many of us from our extended families, the hunger for a village of safe women has never left us. I was very lucky when I first moved to Albany in Western Australia as a teacher to meet three fabulous girlfriends – also teachers – who helped me in the craziness of becoming a new mum. We helped each other over the years, and we still get together to laugh and cry about this crazy thing called life. I still remember clearly one night when there was a knock at the door quite late, and my girlfriend's husband handed me a sleeping toddler to take care of as they were on their way to hospital to welcome their second child into the world. That little girl never batted an eyelid in the morning to find she was at my house with her little mate, who she had regularly played with. Collectively, we had spent hours together, often taking care of each other's children.

The pandemic has been so cruel for many new mummies and daddies because that circle of caring family and friends has been kept away. Thankfully, the research suggests that women can still stay connected to their friends digitally, and many have found that extremely beneficial.

There is also plenty of research on the importance of female friendships and how they nurture, protect and sustain many women through the phases of womanhood. The findings show that safe female friendships boost overall happiness and health and contribute to resilience and coping abilities in managing adversity. If a sister relationship did not exist or is not strong, then our women friendships are often the breeding ground of the aunties for our daughters.

Dr Tracy Evans-Whipp, a research fellow with the Australian Institute of Family Studies, argues that girl connections with their friends are not only really important, they tend to be a much bigger deal than they are for boys. The tendency to be able to discuss your concerns, worries and to feel supported are incredibly valuable to wellbeing. I have a joke with my best girlfriends that if after we've had a catch-up I haven't laughed, cried, eaten cake or maybe almost wet myself, there is something seriously wrong. There is nothing left off the table and we can be totally honest and absolutely vulnerable without any embarrassment or shame. We have shared births, deaths, weddings of each other's children, perimenopause followed by menopause, and now retirement.

I'm a very proud biological auntie of many beautiful nieces, and the nonbiological auntie of even more. I take this role incredibly seriously because I know just how important it is to have someone – other than your mum – who has your back. A couple of these nonbiological nieces call me their other mother and I accept that label graciously and with gratitude. I might not be here today if it was not for some amazing auntie figures who provided guidance in my life, especially when I was a dark, moody and unpredictable teenage girl who hated herself. Every girl needs to have at least one good auntie, and the sooner she gets to have one as a little girl, the better.

I love the way that Steve Biddulph explains the benefits of aunties as our girls become tweens and teens.

> Girls need wise, cool, feisty, tough-minded aunties to do four things; confront them, comfort them, praise them and challenge them . . . As well as this, aunties can also talk tough.
>
> – Steve Biddulph, *10 Things Girls Need Most to Grow Up Strong and Free* (2017)

The role of loving, wise women in girls' lives has always mattered. Through the major transitions from birth to motherhood, having a safe circle of good women can be one of the most important protective factors we can help our girls to create. When I became a grandmother, I became even more of a warrior for all girls – not just my granddaughters. The wisdom I have gleaned and learned from being an auntie and grandmother must be passed on to the upcoming generations. This passion is what has driven me to write this book.

KEY POINTS

- Father figures are a significant influence on the development of little girls, especially in the early years of life.
- A warm connected relationship with their father can give girls a sense of security about themselves and a stronger sense of self-worth.
- Fathers need to be mindful of unintentionally continuing patriarchal norms that suggest little girls need to be princesses and that they will always need a male figure to protect them.
- Teasing may have no intention to cause harm however, due to the sensitivity of little girls' feelings and their long-term memories it can do exactly that.
- Please avoid shaming language as it can debilitate girls through adolescence and adulthood.
- The role of loving, wise women in girls' lives has always mattered from the beginning of humanity.
- The safest aunties for our little girls are the other women of our village – our friends who we have known and trusted for some time.
- Every teen needs to individuate and step back from their parents, and for girls particularly from their mum.
- Aunties can become the safe base that every girl needs during this incredibly stressful time of transformation.

20

Nurturing her spirit

A five-year-old to her daddy:

'Daddy, do you know why children are sent into the world?'

'No, tell me,' Daddy replied.

'To teach them to think in their hearts so everything goes right. Otherwise they think in their heads and life is hard,' she replied.

– Tobin Hart PhD, *The Secret Spiritual World of Children* (2003)

Our little girls are living in a very different world from the one their parents experienced as children. Putting a global pandemic to the side for a moment, statistics show that we are living in a world where we have unacceptably high rates of our tweens and teens dying by suicide, our children and teens are being damaged by early sexualisation and the damage of easily accessible porn and so many kids are struggling with anxiety. We seem to be losing the protective influence of social capital as our cultural norms are shifted from being about 'we' to 'me'; there is definitely more pressure in our 'selfie' driven world to be famous or a celebrity, or to be an influencer or a consumer of stuff.

Cyberbullying has made the already problematic issue of bullying so much worse. Technology is now so pervasive in our lives that it's influencing our children at younger and younger ages and bringing all our addictions to the fore – whether it's vaping, gaming, social media, online shopping or otherwise. And while it's difficult to compare statistics of family violence from decades gone by, we are now far more aware that it is going on. There is still an unacceptably high number of women being killed by men who are their former or current intimate partners.

We are social beings, and our deepest biological drives are about being in meaningful relationships with safe intimacy. The search to live a life of depth and meaning is as old as humanity itself. The statistics show that many of our young people are finding this world a difficult place to be in.

PARENTS AND EDUCATORS' SURVEY

When my daughter was three, I was getting all stressed and anxious about something trivial and she grabbed me, looked at me and said so wisely, 'Just breathe, Mummy'. Too cute. 😊

I have been writing about the importance of the human spirit since my very first book was published in 2003, *Saving our Children From our Chaotic World*. Maybe intuitively I was exploring a reality from my childhood that helped me overcome my own personal challenges discovering my authentic worth and value. My deep and profound connection with nature where, as a little girl, I would talk to birds, trees, clouds and rocks and feel deeply heard was perhaps more than just imagination. My attunement to the pulsing life force that I witnessed in nature has never left me. There was something deep inside me that I couldn't explain with my logical mind and I still can't totally explain today. I have serendipitous experiences occasionally that quite simply are breathtaking and inspirational. Owls have a very special place in my life, and so often they turn up and bring me an invisible gift. One evening, I heard this strange bird calling outside. I ignored it for a while, then finally went to investigate. I was standing on my deck in the dark, trying to find the source of the noise. To my surprise, when I turned my head, an owl was sitting quite close. We spent a couple of minutes just witnessing each other until the owl took off into the night sky. My heart was singing and I felt that magical transcendence that I used to discover as a little girl playing in the bush. There have been many other times when I have returned home to find an owl standing on the gate, welcoming me. Whenever I have a close encounter with a bird or animal, I intuit a message.

This connection to owls became even more meaningful when I met a Noongar elder at an art gallery. She came and spoke to me and we found that some of her people had visited our farm over the years. Then she stood in front of me and looked deeply into my eyes, and said that I was owl woman – a boobook owl woman, just like her sister. She said this meant that I could see the darkness in people's lives and not be frightened. Given that at the time I was working as a bereavement coordinator in a hospice, and completing my postgraduate diploma in counselling, I found her message validating.

Having a deep and profound connection to nature is something I have mentioned many times, and it is one of the ways that we can strengthen our little girls' spirits – a love of flowers, a love of birds, a love of clouds, a love of the moon, a love of animals – they all can strengthen the connection to herself and her world.

> Nature is one of our greatest healers. There is healing in the wind, the sun, the moon, the stars, the ocean, the stones, the songs of the birds and the flowers. It is only for us to trust this is so and allow ourselves to receive.
>
> – 'Hawai'I' by Linda Kaholokai in Renata Provenzano,
> *A Little Book of Aloha: Spirit of Healing* (2003)

Psychologist Dr Lisa Miller, author of *The Spiritual Child*, has been concerned that childhood has become increasingly competitive over the years. This means that parents feel enormous pressure to give their children that competitive edge as so much of parenting culture is now focused on accomplishment and achieving outcomes. I have been advocating for over 15 years about the potential damage we are doing to our children with this focus, especially around 'too much too soon', and endless testing and ranking. My argument is we're raising whole children, not brains on seats or sources of data. We are compromising our children's wellbeing, weakening their human spirit and damaging the depth of connectedness our children experience and later in life. I worry there will be an inevitable, disappointed sense of – is this all there is?

> The most beautiful thing we can experience is the mysterious. Recognition of the mystery of the universe is the source of all true science. He to whom emotions are a stranger, who can no longer pause to wonder and stand rapt in awe is as good as dead; his eyes are closed.
>
> – Albert Einstein, *Living Philosophies* (1931)

To be the best can come at an enormous cost if an individual's pursuit of excellence compromises their emotional and mental wellbeing. In 2021, tennis player Naomi Osaka and gymnast Simone Biles spoke publicly about their mental health problems and how they were struggling with the pressure of being elite athletes. I have read stories of young women who were exceptionally high achievers, in medicine, veterinary science and law, who ended their lives once they had attained excellence in their fields. Attaining a dream can sometimes not give our girls the authentic sense of value, worth and happiness that they were seeking.

PARENTS AND EDUCATORS' SURVEY

She was asked what she wanted to be when she grew up and my daughter said, 'Myself'.

The science of spirituality has taken off in the last 15 years. Dr Miller's definition for spirituality is:

> . . . an inner sense of relationship to a higher power that is loving and guiding. The word we give to this higher power might be God, nature, spirit, the universe, the creator or other words that represented divine presence. But the important point is that spirituality encompasses our relationship and dialogue with this higher presence.
>
> – Dr Lisa Miller, *The Spiritual Child* (2015)

Dr Miller has done research with brain imaging that shows a significant difference in the brains of highly spiritual people versus those with low spirituality – those who have less relationship or dialogue with some sort of higher power. She found the brains in more highly spiritual people were not only healthier and more robust, they were thicker and stronger in the same regions that she found to be weaker and thinner in depressed brains. Prior to this research, spirituality was considered completely insignificant to mental health, however, it can make a significant difference in the treatment of mental health challenges, particularly depression.

Dr Miller argues that science can show that this spiritual faculty is inborn – our little girls are already born spiritual. Much the same as parents can nurture their children's physical and emotional wellbeing, they can also nurture their spiritual wellbeing. Miller wrote in her book of research in medicine and psychology that shows that people with a developed spirituality get sick less, are happier, feel more connected and less isolated. For our little girls, protecting them from the things that weaken this connection is just as important as nurturing it.

The importance of connection

Raising your child in a faith can definitely be one way of nurturing this inborn spirituality. I was taught to pray at night and as a little girl, I did pray that God would help me be good, and not make Mummy angry. I also prayed he would help me stop wetting the bed and would make the scary nightmares go away. I do remember being really disappointed that he wasn't listening to my prayers, because none of those things changed. Remember, the messages that we give our little ones about God are being interpreted through the lens of children. Luckily for me, my faith gave me a 'Christ consciousness', which has helped me develop my moral compass for life, even though I no longer practise within the institution of the church.

Thankfully, my imagination allowed me to nurture my spiritual connection to the natural world. My mum was really attuned to nature, especially to anything that was wounded, and she was very caring of a pair of blue fairy wrens who used to nest on a windowsill in the farmhouse. Even though she struggled with emotional connection with me as a little girl, she modelled an emotional connection and gentleness with nature that I obviously picked up on. There are many ways that we can strengthen the spiritual world of our little girls and connection, in many different aspects, is the key.

PARENTS AND EDUCATORS' SURVEY

I have been amazed by my daughter's memory, use of imagination. She is wise beyond her years, and comprehends things a child that age generally doesn't.

Rachael Kessler was a wise woman from Boulder, Colorado, who explored the various ways we humans can be connected, and I feel her work can be a part of a call to action to reverse the tragic suicide statistics.

I had the honour and privilege of spending some time with this very wise woman in 2006. Since then, I have been sharing her key messages of how we nurture deep connectedness in our children, families, schools and communities. The more connected we feel, the healthier we are on all levels – and the stronger the human spirit will be.

Deep connection to self

Deep connection to another (family, friends)

Deep connection to community (school, sport, faith, local)

Deep connection to lineage (ancestry, cultural)

Deep connection to Nature and the environment

Deep connection to a Higher Power (the mysterious, the spiritual, the non-logical)

– Rachael Kessler, The Soul Of Education (2000)

In his book *Healing Words*, Larry Dossey discovered in his research about the power of prayer that 'love, compassion, caring and empathy catalyse healing events and that this power operates at a distance'. When I discovered this, I found it interesting because often in counselling, when I was working with little girls who were struggling with feeling disconnected and unloved, we would imagine sending love from their heart to those they love the most. So many little girls used rainbows of love to represent the love in their hearts. Maybe you could ask your daughter what colour is the love she has for you in her heart?

Dossey also discovered that prayers that were more focused on gratitude and thanksgiving rather than 'wanting things' were more effective. There are significant studies that show the power of gratitude and having a gratitude attitude to life can be a really positive thing to cultivate early. This could definitely be something you can start with your little girl as early as possible.

PARENTS AND EDUCATORS' SURVEY

My youngest daughter, who is five, constantly imitates the 'grannies' from *Bluey*; Rita and Janet. She hobbles around and puts on an old lady's voice when we are out in public. I love how she is free-spirited, has a great sense of humour and brings joy through the simplest things.

Many little girls quite simply stagger me with their spiritual understanding of themselves and their place in the world. A part of me wonders whether this spiritual awareness, combined with the struggle of growing into emotional regulation, is underneath some of the big ugly feelings that many of our little girls struggle with. They know on some level that they are born whole, wise and full of love and yet that isn't what their life experience is showing them.

An example of how children can come with spiritual wisdom was a seven-year-old girl who was brought to see me because she was sad and depressed. Angelique came into my office, sat down and said, 'I have been looking for someone like you for ages'. When I questioned how I might help she said, 'Tell me why I am with my family . . . they are so alien to me. They smoke and drink far too much, they swear, they shout awful things at each other. They have no respect or love for nature and they have no God. Why am I with them?' This little girl was struggling with being in an 'unspiritual' family. I was astounded by her maturity and her insight!

I pondered for a few moments before I responded, 'Maybe you have come to teach them another way of living and being? Maybe you have been given this family to learn how to love unconditionally and you are in the perfect place for you to discover your gifts of compassion, empathy and patience.'

Immediately, she brightened up. I gave her some reframing strategies to change her view of the world, some soul-strengthening activities, an audio CD with creative visualisations to help her connect to her beautiful heart and reassured her lots. She kept a strong spiritual practice in her life that was completely secret from her family.

Another little girl I worked with gave me even more insight into how wise children can be even when they are deeply in pain. I usually began my sessions with a child drawing me a picture, and little Millie, who was only five, drew a picture of a child with no mouth, fingers or feet; this was a symbolic representation of someone unable to speak, unable to fight and unable to flee. The child in the picture was paralysed and yet she had drawn puddles of tears on the ground beside her. Millie had been molested by her uncle and then rejected by her parents after disclosing the abuse, and this picture was her way of expressing her pain.

Another very wise little girl taught me the importance of destroying the first picture they drew when they came into my room. She usually drew highly symbolic pictures and often reached for the black crayon, or the brown with a grey. Her initial picture rarely had any colour in it, except red, and she often drew herself as a tiny figure. After we had finished the therapy session, she said, 'I need to tear up that picture now, Maggie, because it's not me anymore'. Drawing the picture was a way of externalising the problem that was causing her pain, and once she had released the emotional pain, the problem was no longer relevant. One little girl spent at least five minutes tearing her first picture into tiny little pieces before she put it into my bin!

When I was working in palliative care, I heard many stories of very ill children who started drawing pictures of bright colourful rainbows and butterflies just days before their death. These stories seem to support Dr Miller's research that children have a spirituality within them.

Dr Miller contends that we need to have opportunities to tap into our inborn capacity 'to perceive a greater reality and consciously connect to the life force that moves in, through and around us'. She believes this creates the sense of oneness that we are all hungry to feel. Finding ways that allow our little girls to feel that as often as possible builds a strong foundation for later in life. Allowing your daughter to have those long, lingering, pondering moments when she is studying a dead leaf, or a crack in the footpath is really important. These naturally transcendent moments are her in deep contemplation making sense of herself in the world around her.

> We need to return to the solitude within, to find again the dream that lies at the heart of the soul. We need to feel a dream with the wonder of a child approaching a threshold of discovery. When we rediscover our childlike nature we enter a world of gentle possibility. Consequently we will find ourselves more frequently at the place of ease, the light and celebration.
>
> – John O'Donohue, *Anam Cara: Spiritual wisdom from the Celtic world* (1996)

Nurturing the inner spirit of our little girls is possible in so many ways that parents are already doing. In other parts of the book, I have explored the importance of imagination, of awe and wonder, of the power of human connectedness, of intuition and of loving fiercely and unconditionally. Lightness and laughter are food for the human spirit – how good do you feel after a really good giggle or belly laugh? All of these can nurture your little girl's spirit.

In many shamanic societies in Africa and North America, if you came to a medicine person, commonly called the shaman, complaining of being disheartened, dispirited or depressed, they would ask one of four questions.

- When did you stop dancing?
- When did you stop singing?
- When did you stop being enchanted by stories?
- When did you stop finding comfort in the sweet territory of silence?

Some of the glimmers that certainly made a difference during the challenging years of the pandemic were TikTok dance-offs, especially when they included Dad, videos of singing from the famous and not so famous, finding healthy escapism in books and shows, and the hunger for silence. Finding ways to lift our own physical, mental and psychological wellbeing seems to have something to do with nurturing the spirit that was feeling beaten and broken.

Spiritual intelligence

Wonder
Respect and reverence
Awe
Relational spirituality
Lightness and laughter
Contemplation
Calmness, stillness and quiet
Tenderness and gratitude
Simplicity
Listening with the heart.
   – Maggie Dent, *Nurturing Kids' Hearts and Souls* (rev ed. 2010)

Listening with our heart or intuition is something we really need to prioritise with our little girls. Help them recognise their early warning signs and learn to tune in to what their bodily sensations are trying to tell them. Dr Miller argues in her book that children can not only use their intuition quite well, they are also capable of other knowing.

In her book, she shares stories of young children, many of them little girls, who have suddenly had a 'knowing' experience and tuned in to something a very long way away. This can happen to parents too, and this sudden experience of inexplicable awareness when we tune in to our children over a long distance is called *sympathetic harmonic resonance*. Essentially, this means that when we are attuned strongly with those we love, we can tap into their experiential world over distances.

Dr Miller encourages you to share your intuitive feelings with your child and encourage her to open up about hers as well. For example, she suggests you might say to your daughter:

'When you were just a baby I would always wake up just before you woke up and cried so I was already on my way.'

Or you could acknowledge that you do have a special bond, 'Even when you're away at school we always connected heart-to-heart – that's forever.' Or 'Only family bonds are so strong that we can sense each other's needs sometimes even before anybody asks!'

– Lisa Miller, *The Spiritual Child* (2015)

You can strengthen this long-distance connection when you send rainbows of love to your daughter while she is at preschool, and she sends you one as well. You might put a love heart on her hand and a matching one on your hand, which can help her feel more secure when she is away from you. Or you could put a kiss on the palm of her hand every morning. These little things are really hard to measure, however, the science now shows they matter.

Happy children have an open heart and strong spirit and know that life is full of anticipation, delight and fun, regardless of adversity. Have you seen the shiny eyes that happy children have especially after diving into a pile of leaves or a big puddle? The more of these experiences children have up to 10 years of age the better.

Richard Tichnor and Jenny Smith wrote and illustrated a wonderful picture book for children called *A Spark in the Dark*. This is a very special creation story that introduces the spiritual concept that 'all is one'. In the story, we all have a star within our hearts that came from the source of all creation. This star shines brightly when we know we are loved and special, and we feel connected to the creator. As we read this picture book to children, we combine the power of storytelling, imagery and ancient wisdom all in one amazing experience.

Another excellent resource that I believe can help to strengthen a little girl's connection to her higher self, her heart and thus her spirit is called *Little Wise One*. It is a pack of beautiful cards with positive messages and affirmations accompanied by a little book full of messages from wise little children. Here are a couple of examples of messages from the children:

I tell the butterflies to leave my tummy and fly into my heart. My heart goes warm. – Jadzia, five.

So when your heart light goes bright like when you see your mummy. That's when you can feel you're brave when it's like that then you can do tricky things. – Piper, five.

– Vicki Schaefer, *Little Wise Ones*, littlewiseone.com.au

The main reason I created creative visualisation audio tracks over the years, was so that I could take children, teens and adults out of their busy heads, away from their inner critic and deep into their heart. The one that works best for girls is 'Moonlight Magic', which is intuitively beautiful because in many traditional cultures the moon is part of the sacred feminine, while the sun is part of the sacred masculine.

I also created an audio called 'Accepting Myself', which helps children to find a new way of seeing themselves, a preferred way. I've had many reviews and messages over the years that tell me that when either of these creative visualisations was used as recommended, there was a significant shift in how much more strongly children connected to their heart and spirit. I once received an email from a teenage girl I had worked with who had travelled with her favourite visualisation right around the world. She said anytime she felt frightened or disconnected, she put the visualisation on and immediately felt safe within herself. In a way, that is what mindfulness is; it is a pathway into ourselves.

Thankfully there are many beautiful mindfulness programs now and there is even science behind the value of practising it. I am an ambassador for the not-for-profit free web and app-based program *Smiling Mind* and I highly recommend the app for its wonderful calming audios that still the mind and open the heart. Essentially, they are designed to take you into your inner world, and give yourself a break from the pressures of the outer world and the endless chatter of your ego mind.

> Human connectedness is the key to resilience, authentic happiness and a sense of wellbeing. This can only be achieved through the recognition, honouring and nurturing of the human spirit that exists within every child ever born.
>
> – Maggie Dent, *Saving Our Children from Our Chaotic World* (2003)

In my work and research over the last 45 years, I have explored the concepts of masculinity and femininity. In traditional cultures, both were recognised with respect and a sense of sacredness. The sacred feminine is often linked to the gift of life and living in harmony with all of life. As women traditionally have the womb, they are strongly linked to creation in all its forms and also with kindness and compassion. The sacred masculine is usually associated with strength and action, especially in defending and protecting the things that matter. We all have some masculine and feminine within us, and we need to work hard to correct the gender inequity and discrimination against women and girls.

Deconstructing traditional patriarchal social norms that deny the worth and value of femininity is happening, but it's happening far too slowly for our little girls. I certainly struggled in my early life with running with my masculine energy in order to cope with the demands of life – commanding, demanding and striving to the point where I burned out and became ill, several times.

When I found a much healthier balance between my masculine and feminine, I was able to create from a much more trusting and accepting place. Without a strong connection to my higher self, my creative self struggles.

Please nurture your little girl's sacred spirit from the moment of her birth.

> The body of a child will not grow if it is not fed, the mind will not flourish unless it is stimulated and guided, and the spirit will suffer if it is not nurtured.
>
> – Rachael Kessler, *The Soul of Education* (2000)

As I wrote this chapter, my granddaughter Milla asked me to play some music on my phone while she painted on some rocks in my garden. I asked what she would like and she paused and answered, 'Roar', a song by Katie Perry. She sang along, knowing all the words. She is six. The fact she knew every word of this feminist song surprised me.

I messaged my niece who has two girls aged five and seven and she responded that her girls also know the words.

My heart felt lifted with joy and hope and I think the future looks brighter for many of our girls.

Let's leave the final words with our little girls from the survey. When asked when they are the happiest these were the top five response areas:

1. With family/with Mum and/or Dad. 35 per cent
2. With her friends (playing, laughing). 16 per cent
3. Playing – imaginative/toys/dolls/games. 13 per cent

4. In nature, outside, park/with animals, pets. 12 per cent
5. Hugs, cuddles, roughhousing, tickles, touch. 9 per cent

All of these activities are nurturing their beautiful, sacred spirits.

KEY POINTS

- There is enormous pressure on parents to give their children a competitive edge and parenting has become overly focused on accomplishment and the achieving of outcomes.
- Our little girls are already born spiritual and parents can nurture that as well as their physical and emotional wellbeing.
- Having a healthy, strong imagination can nurture our little girls' spirit.
- Teaching your little girl to have a gratitude attitude to life can make a significantly positive difference to her wellbeing.
- Encourage your little girls to listen with their heart and understand their intuition, especially around the early warning signs.
- Learning mindfulness helps little girls feel safe within themselves and connects them to their heart and their spirit.
- Please nurture your little girl's sacred spirit from the moment of her birth.

Conclusion

I began this book with the aim of exploring how the early years can impact the future health and wellbeing of our girls in the hopes that we could give every little girl a stronger foundation for life. I had a sense of urgency to do this as I have four precious granddaughters and many great-nieces, and the statistics around our girls, especially in the tween and teen years, are continuing to worry me. I had a vision this would just be a short book, however, it became an unexpected journey of self-reflection and self-discovery. The research helped me to understand some of my own struggles as a girl and a woman, and for that I am grateful. I apologise for writing another big book in a world where parents are time poor!

I hope you have enjoyed the voices of little girls and the anecdotes from their parents and educators. I wish I could have included all of them. There was so much joy and so much wisdom in many of the messages. A huge thank you to everyone who took the time to respond as your messages shaped the book.

PARENTS AND EDUCATORS' SURVEY

When my mum passed away, my daughter at four spent many nights when I'd lay in bed with her, asking me how did Nanna get to heaven, would she have toys in heaven and asked why she hadn't called us to let us know she's there. I said but they don't have phones in heaven, and she replied, 'So why didn't she take her mobile?'

My message to all parents, early childhood educators and extended family is that our girls need you to be in their corner with some helpful knowledge and awareness, and a big open heart.

Some of the knowledge I have discovered for this book will help prevent you and your daughter from being conditioned to believe things that are *quite simply not true*. Unhelpful social norms and stereotypes are put under the spotlight in this book. Helping and protecting our little girls' childhoods does not have to be an onerous task; they love being little girls with spectacular imaginations, creativity, and a passion for being seen and heard. Nurture their cheeky sense of humour and encourage their inner bravery, especially through play.

Remind every little girl in your life frequently that she is enough exactly as she is, and she is not in competition with any other girl. She can be both gentle and strong, caring and assertive, cautious and fearless. Tell her to make friends with her body and to make even stronger friends with her spirit. Encourage her to have her dreams and always have a backup plan.

Teach the difference between fairness and injustice, and encourage her to be a peaceful warrior with a strong heart who is prepared to fight for the things that she believes are right and just. Teach her that by helping other girls to shine, she will automatically shine brighter.

Respect her emotional world and know how important the first few years of life are, in the creation of a healthy emotional capacity. Take time to explore the big feelings, no matter what they are; be patient as this is a very gradual process of learning emotional regulation.

PARENTS AND EDUCATORS' SURVEY

My little girl plays rugby . . . she followed her brothers into the sport. We tried dancing and gymnastics . . . she wasn't that keen on all the having to perfect, all the uniformity. She came to rugby a little uncoordinated . . . a little shy. For the first year, she was the only girl in the team. But she loved the inclusiveness of the sport. She would rock up to training in a tutu and a bright pink poncho one week and her rugby shirt and shorts the next and no-one would bat an eyelid at either. If my seven-year-old could play rugby wearing a tiara she would be the happiest little girl on the face of the earth.

Know that strong emotions can take time to subside, even for grown women, and it's not a sign we are too intense or too dramatic; it is just how our mind and heart works.

Help her to make sense of how she responds to herself, others and our world. Ensure she understands the importance of respect, again for herself, others and our world. True happiness is rarely found in the pursuit of stuff, including material possessions and fame. She is so much more than that.

Build her resilience by helping her identify her 'glimmers' – the things that nurture and protect her. Explore the difference between healthy competition and unhealthy obsessions based on competition.

Instil in her the belief that she is not defined by her grades or her academic standing, any medals she has won or any other hard-fought result. She is so much more than that. By all means she can enjoy these moments, however, they still do not define who she is.

Marinate her in the arts so she can find her own creative force and learn to express it freely and bravely. Remind her that failure is just a part of being human and that her ability to recover, and to change and adapt when hard times happen, is where true grit is found.

Your beautiful daughter has come onto our earth to make the world a better place, in some small way. She is not here just to please others, to always be good or nice or to be eye candy for boys and men. She is so much more than that.

Affirm to her that femininity has a sacredness to it that is ancient and powerful.

Finding deep meaningful relationships that are built on love, trust and respect is definitely a worthwhile ambition to have. Genuine intimacy is one of the most beautiful things in life.

Finally, please gather a healthy collective around your girls: the community that shares your passion for all children. In your neighbourhoods, your school and your communities, strive to create strong, safe networks that genuinely care for children and families and especially our young girls. Or in the words of Bella, whose voice was captured in our survey:

PARENTS AND EDUCATORS' SURVEY

Bella's friend Eleanor was saying that she was scared of falling off her bike, to which Bella replied, 'Don't worry, the world will still hold you up!'

To feel the true inspiration of women, each different and yet as one – please go to YouTube and listen to the Helen Reddy tribute, 'I Am Woman', at the ARIA Awards in 2020 – *with your daughter by your side*. Feel the message and sing loudly and dance if you are moved to and celebrate beautiful, strong women – all different, all unique and all singing with passion about women being strong and invincible despite the pain and challenges that life may bring.

Let us all step forward, lean in and surround our girls with safe big people, capable of loving fiercely and unconditionally to give them the best start in life.

Maggie Dent, 2022

– Former little girl, sister, daughter, incredibly proud mum
of four fabulous sons, grateful nanny, auntie to heaps,
'lighthouse' to more and a woman passionate about being
a voice for children of all ages

Acknowledgements

I really thought I had written my last research-based book with *From Boys to Men*, however the Publishing Director at Pan Macmillan Australia Ingrid Ohlsson was very persuasive! She convinced me that there was a window that needed to be filled about preschool-aged girls. Having four precious granddaughters, I did not need to be convinced. Thank you so much, Ingrid, for having such faith in me and for always being a total delight to work with.

Again, I need to apologise for writing yet another big book. I really thought this would be a more compact book. Hopefully, it can be used as a guide as well as a source of quality food for thought so you can give your daughter the best foundation possible for life.

My first thank you in birthing this book baby is to everyone who took the time to complete the survey. The words of little girls made me laugh and cry and they helped to shape the honest, authentic tone of the whole book. I hope I have addressed the key concerns you shared with me and I hope even more that I have truly celebrated how amazing young girls can be.

Next, my very competent editor at Pan Macmillan, Libby Turner – you did a fabulous job taming my text, and also junior editor Belinda Huang – thank you for sharing this journey with me! Also an enormous thanks to Brianne Collins as my executive editor – you were a joy to work with. Finally, I'd like to thank Publicity and Marketing Director Tracey Cheetham and campaign manager Adrik Kemp for once again helping me share this book with the world.

I wish to thank my own amazing team starting with my editor, publicist, marketing manager and my right hand – my dear friend Carmen Myler. Again, Carmen has tamed my apostrophes (I am very generous with them!), double checked all my referencing and helped me get my manuscript ready. You are an exceptionally brilliant, irreplaceable part of my life. Thank you beyond words, Carmen!

Louise Shannon again stepped up and helped with editing and proofing, often at short notice. Thanks Lou. Kelly Skinner, thank you for chasing permissions and corrections regarding references – often such a time-consuming task.

Team Maggie has also covered my back so that I could disappear and focus on writing. Even though COVID meant I was unable to run live seminars or attend conferences in 2021, my PA – my gorgeous niece Laura Browning – was taking care of the many, many enquiries and requests. To Katharine Middleton, my amazing graphic designer/web mistress/email gatekeeper and very dear friend (from when I taught her when she was 16) – thank you for keeping emails at bay so I could concentrate on writing. My behind-the-scenes team who also help me create the space to write include Caitlin Murphy, who worked hard in the social media and online community – thank you. And Will Ambrose, a huge thank you for collating and sorting through all of our enormous survey material, making it easy for me to read and understand, and for all the tech support – I am beyond grateful.

2021 was tough for me as a mum and a grandmother as we were unable to visit family in Western Australia. But my fabulous family are always supporting and encouraging me even from a distance and they are really the wind beneath my wings. Thank you for all you give me, especially the joy and the opportunities to steal your children from you so we can have special times together!

My good bloke and my husband, Steve, was again incredibly patient and supportive in the long days and weeks when I was totally absorbed in researching and writing. He is totally amazing at supporting me when I am writing very long days – by heating my wheat pack, bringing me endless cups of tea, cooking really healthy meals and allowing me to be as non-communicative as I need to be. I am so blessed and grateful that I have the unconditional love and support that my good man gives – thanks babe. Of course, Hugo Walter was a source of four-legged support with lots of cuddles and chilly walks.

I am also so grateful that I could work on the ABC *Parental As Anything* podcast while unable to travel and work face to face. Being host of the podcast has been such a positive journey and I am so thankful to Justine Kelly, Monique Bowley, Maria Tickle and Carmen Myler for all you do in creating and producing such a first-class show.

My absolute final thanks must go to you, as someone who has purchased this book. Please join me in shifting the negative and limiting social norms that hold our girls down and keep them silent. Share the messages about girls being so much more than their appearance, and that they are enough – exactly as they are. Dare them to be whoever they want to be. Show your little girl that when we help each other shine brighter, we shine brighter too.

Further resources for parents of girls

These are some of my favourite books and experts to support you in raising your girls to be happy, healthy and heard. Many of these folks share excellent content on their websites and social media accounts, so look them up!

Steve Biddulph – *10 Things Girls Need Most To Grow Up Strong and Free* and *Raising Girls in the 21st Century*. Steve has a specific Facebook page for girls' content: Steve Biddulph's Raising Girls.

Lisa Damour – *Under Pressure: Confronting the Epidemic of Stress and Anxiety in Girls* and *Untangled: Guiding Teenage Girls Through the Seven Transitions to Adulthood*

Mona Delahooke – *Beyond Behaviors. Brain-Body Parenting* is her excellent new book.

Kasey Edwards & Christopher Scanlon – *Raising Girls Who Like Themselves: In a World That Tells Them They're Flawed*

Kristy Goodwin – *Raising Your Child in a Digital World*

Katie Hurley – *No More Mean Girls*

Madonna King – *Fathers and Daughters* and also *Ten-Ager*, and her new book due out around the same time as this book looks great too: *L Platers*

Vanessa Lapointe – *Discipline Without Damage* and *Parenting Right From the Start*

Janet Lansbury – *Elevating Child Care* and *No Bad Kids*. Also check out Janet's fabulous *Unruffled* podcast.

Wendy McCarthy – *Don't Be Too Polite, Girls: A Memoir*

Dannielle Miller – *The Butterfly Effect; The Girl with the Butterfly Tattoo* and *Loveability*. Danni is CEO of Enlighten Education too and shares great content about empowering girls and women on her socials so look her up.

Michelle Mitchell – Books include *Parenting Teenage Girls in the Age of a New Normal* and *What Teenage Girls Don't Tell Their Parents* but Michelle also has books on puberty, resilience,
self-harm and more. She's worth following on social media too as she shares great content about girls (and boys).

Gisela Preuschoff – *Raising Girls: Why Girls Are Different – and How to Help Them Grow up Happy and Strong*

Michael Ray – *Who Knew? From Bouncing and Barbells to Ballet and Braids*

Bruce Robinson – *Daughters and their Dads*. Also check out The Fathering Project, of which Bruce is founder. They have a great podcast too.

Leonard Sax – *Girls on the Edge: The Four Factors Driving the New Crisis for Girls – Sexual Identity, the Cyberbubble, Obsessions, Environmental Toxins*

Rachel Simmons – *Odd Girl Out: The Hidden Culture of Aggression in Girls*

Rebecca Sparrow – Books include *Find Your Tribe; Find Your Feet* and *Ask Me Anything* (also the name of her podcast). Bec has great content for parents of tween/teen girls.

Susan Stiffelman – *Parenting with Presence* and *Parenting Without Power Struggles* (which is also the name of her fabulous podcast).

And here are a few other websites and social media accounts you might check out:
A Mighty Girl
Collective Shout – and Melinda Tankard-Reist
Girls Uniform Agenda
Fierce Girls Podcast
Best Programs 4 Kids (great content re friendships!)
Parent TV

Endnotes

xviii. Some argue that our girls' confidence drops . . .: Kay K & Shipman C (2021, 12 September). 'Girls' confidence plummets starting at age 8: Here's how to keep her confidence strong'. https://www.amightygirl.com/blog

xx. Girls think they are cleverer . . .: Gaudiano P & Hunt E (2017, 30 January). 'Gender study: Boys think they are smarter, but girls work harder and perform better'. *Forbes*.

xx. Neil Farmer, an experienced early years' educator . . .: Farmer, N (2012). *Getting It Right For Boys*. London: Bloomsbury Publishing.

Chapter 1

6. Trauma of any kind increases our chances of struggling . . .: Van der Kolk B (2015). *The Body Keeps the Score: Brain, Mind, and Body in the Healing of Trauma*. London: Penguin Publishing Group.

6. There is significant research that shows we are likely to replicate . . .: Siegel DJ & Hartzell M (2013). *Parenting from the Inside Out: How a Deeper Self-Understanding Can Help You Raise Children Who Thrive*. New York: TarcherPerigree.

Chapter 2

9. Research over the past 20 years . . .: Van der Kolk B (2015). *The Body Keeps the Score: Brain, Mind, and Body in the Healing of Trauma*. London: Penguin Publishing Group.

9. The research is quite strong that intergenerational trauma . . .: A good review of such research is: Yehuda R & Lehrner A (2018). 'Intergenerational transmission of trauma effects: putative role of epigenetic mechanisms'. *World Psychiatry*. 17(3): 243–257. doi:10.1002/wps.20568

9. At a conference I attended in Vancouver . . .: The Early Years Conference 2012: 'The development of children's mental health: How do we become who we are?' 3–4 February. Vancouver, Canada.

16. In one study, it was noted that if a baby girl . . .: Connellan J, Baron-Cohen S, Wheelwright S, Batki A & Ahluwalia J (2000). 'Sex differences in human neonatal social perception'. *Infant Behavior and Development*, 23(1), 113–118. doi: 10.1016/s0163-6383(00)00032-1

16. Given that neuroscience . . .: The Center on the Developing Child at Harvard University has excellent resources and videos explaining this concept of brain development through connection, and 'serve and return' interactions between a child and adult. developingchild.harvard.edu/

20. . . . research suggests that no-one is completely masculine . . .: Kachel S et al. (2016). 'Traditional masculinity and femininity: Validation of a new scale assessing gender roles'. *Frontiers In Psychology*, 7. doi: 10.3389/fpsyg.2016.00956.

21. Indeed, there is a fragility about little boys . . .: Kraemer S (2000). 'The fragile male'. *The British Medical Journal.* Dec 23; 321 (7276): 1609–1612.

21. Statistically, boys die in utero at a higher rate than girls . . .: Pera G (2018). 'Male entitlement and male fragility'. *ADHD Roller Coaster.* Retrieved 25 May, www.adhdrollercoaster.org/essays/male-entitlement-male-fragility/

21. We all come from the same genetic blueprint . . .: Zhao F, Franco HL, Rodriguez KF, et al. (2017). 'Elimination of the male reproductive tract in the female embryo is promoted by COUP-TFII in mice'. *Science.* 357(6352):717–720. doi:10.1126/science. aai9136

22. After birth, there can also be some gender differences . . .: Caldwell HK (2017). 'Oxytocin and Vasopressin: Powerful regulators of social behavior'. *The Neuroscientist.* 23(5):517–528. doi:10.1177/1073858417708284

22. In some studies, it has also been noted . . .: There are a range of studies that show people interact differently with babies according to whether they think they are male or female including: Seavey CA, Katz PA & Zalk SR, 'Baby X: The effect of gender labels on adult responses to infants'. *Sex Roles* (1975) 1: 103. https://doi.org/10.1007/ BF00288004.
    Also: Eliot L (2009). *Pink Brain, Blue Brain: How small differences grow into troublesome gaps – and what we can do about it.* Boston: Houghton Mifflin.
    Also: Sidorowicz L & Lunney G (1980). 'Baby X revisited'. *Sex Roles,* 6 (1), 67–73 DOI: 10.1007/BF00288362.

Chapter 3

38. The relatively new field of epigenetics . . .: Ptak C & Petronis A (2010). 'Epigenetic approaches to psychiatric disorders'. *Dialogues Clin Neurosci.* 12(1):25-35. doi:10.31887/DCNS.2010.12.1/cptak

39. Gene expression research . . .: Weizmann Institute of Science (2017, 4 May). 'Researchers identify 6,500 genes that are expressed differently in men and women: Genes that are mostly active in one sex or the other may play a crucial role in our evolution, health'. *ScienceDaily.* sciencedaily.com/releases

40. I was a little excited when I came across research . . .: Lungu O, Potvin S, Tikàsz A & Mendrek A (2015). 'Sex differences in effective fronto-limbic connectivity during negative emotion processing'. *Psychoneuroendocrinology.* Dec;62:180–8. doi: 10.1016/j.psyneuen.2015.08.012. Epub 2015 Aug 17. PMID: 26318628.

42. A study that supports this came from the Telethon Institute . . .: Whitehouse A, Mattes E, Maybery M, Sawyer M, Jacoby P, Keelan J & Hickey M (2012, January). 'Sex-specific associations between umbilical cord blood testosterone levels and language delay in early childhood', *Child and Adolescent Mental Health,* Wiley-Blackwell. DOI: 10.1111/j.1469-7610.2011.02523.x

42. In a 2019 study . . . Adani S & Cepanec M (2019). 'Sex differences in early communication development: behavioral and neurobiological indicators of more vulnerable communication system development in boys', *Croation Medical Journal.* Apr; 60(2): 141–149.

44. Stephanie Wicker, a child behaviour expert . . .: Stephanie has written about this in several blogs on growth mindset at her website simplykids.live

49. According to the social learning theory . . .: Lind J, Ghirlanda S & Enquist M (2019). 'Social learning through associative processes: A computational theory'. *R Soc Open Sci.* 6(3):181777. doi:10.1098/rsos.181777

49. Very recent research by Dr Lisa Mundy . . .: as told to Critchley C. (2019, 13 February). 'The importance of your child's middle years'. https://pursuit.unimelb. edu.au/

Chapter 4

54. One study suggests . . .: Baer A, Trumpeter N & Weathington B (2006). 'Gender differences in memory recall'. *Modern Psychological Studies.* 12(1).

54. Another study from 2013 . . .: Persson J, Herlitz A, Engman J, Morell A, Sjölie D, Wikström J & Söderlund H (2013). 'Remembering our origin: Gender differences in spatial memory are reflected in gender differences in hippocampal lateralization'. *Behavioural Brain Research*, 256, 219–228. https://doi.org/10.1016/j.bbr.2013.07.050

54. In a 2018 study . . .: Loprinzi PD & Frith E (2018). 'The role of sex in memory function: Considerations and recommendations in the context of exercise'. *J Clin Med*. 7(6):132. Published 2018 May 31. doi:10.3390/jcm7060132

69. Dr Maté argues that this pressure . . .: Caparrotta, M (2020, 2 November). 'Being nice vs kind – what's the difference? (8 Experts Explain)'. Humanwindow.com

71. Sadly, intergenerational trauma impacts many First Nationals peoples . . .: healingfoundation.org.au has some wonderful resources exploring intergenerational trauma.

Chapter 5

75. One study showed that there was a difference in interpreting . . .: Fidalgo AM, Tenenbaum HR & Aznar A (2018). 'Are there gender differences in emotion comprehension? Analysis of the test of emotion comprehension'. *J Child Fam Stud*. 27(4):1065–1074. doi: 10.1007/s10826-017-0956-5.

88. Pam Leo, in her podcast *Healing the Feeling Child* . . . information sourced with permission from Pam Leo via post on facebook.com/DanceWithMeInTheHeart (2021, 12 October).

Chapter 6

105. One of the things that can help build empathy . . .: Purewal R, Christley R, Kordas K, et al. (2017). 'Companion animals and child/adolescent development: A systematic review of the evidence'. *Int J Environ Res Public Health*. 14(3):234. Published 2017 Feb 27. doi:10.3390/ijerph14030234

114. . . . the work of BF Skinner and was called 'operant conditioning' . . .: first coined in Skinner BF (1937). 'Two types of conditioned reflex: a reply to Konorski and Miller'. *J. Gen. Psychol*. 1937;16:272–79.

115. Dr Helen Street, a social psychologist . . .: Helen has written and presented extensively on rewards and punishment, most notably at the conferences she co-convenes, Positive Schools. Also see her article 'Turning tables on Australian education' at positivetimes.com.au

120. Even though our temperament tendencies come from our DNA . . .: Bratko D, Butković A & Vukasović T (2017). 'Heritability of personality'. *Psychological Topics*, 26 (1), 1–24.

Chapter 7

122. His research suggested . . .: Boyce WT (2019, 2 January). 'Why some children are orchids and others are dandelions'. *Psychology Today*.

123. Much research has built on Boyce's work . . .: Kennedy E (2013). 'Orchids and dandelions: How some children are more susceptible to environmental influences for better or worse and the implications for child development'. *Clinical child psychology and psychiatry*. 18. 319–321. 10.1177/1359104513490338.

124. Resilience research shows . . .: Boyce (ibid).

132. While there is some research . . .: Schore A (2017). 'All our sons: The developmental neurobiology and neuroendocrinology of boys at risk'. *Infant Mental Health Journal*, 38(1), pp.15–52.

Chapter 8

146. The research suggests that up to 50 per cent . . .: Summer M (2020, 2 January). 'Introverts and leadership – World Introvert Day'. myersbriggs.com

152. Nathan Wallis argues . . .: sidsandkids.org.na (n.d.) 'Birth order & my baby'. familytimes.co.nz

152. More research research . . .: Rohrer JM, Egloff B & Schmukle SC (2015). 'Examining the effects of birth order on personality'. *Proc Natl Acad Sci U S A*. Nov 17;112(46):14224–9. doi: 10.1073/pnas.1506451112. Epub 2015 Oct 19. PMID: 26483461; PMCID: PMC4655522.

Chapter 9
158. The research is very strong about the importance of music . . .: Trimble M, Hesdorffer D (2017). 'Music and the brain: the neuroscience of music and musical appreciation'. *BJPsych Int*.14(2):28–31. doi:10.1192/s2056474000001720
161. Mother of a six-year-old girl Inbar Niv . . .: Niv (2015, 20 November). 'Are girls sexualised at dance class?' *Child*. childmags.com.au

Chapter 10
176. Significant hormonal changes . . .: Murdoch Children's Research Institute (2021). The Childhood to Adolescence Transition Study (CATS). https://cats.mcri.edu.au/
181. There is research around girls six to nine . . .: Slater A & Tiggemann M (2016). 'Little girls in a grown up world: Exposure to sexualized media, internalization of sexualization messages, and body image in 6–9 year-old girls'. *Body Image*, 18, 19–22.
184. Once girls are older, dietician and body image advocate Meg McCintock . . .: from Edwards K & Scanlon C (2021). *Raising Girls Who Like Themselves: In a World That Tells Them They're Flawed*. Sydney: Penguin Life Australia.
185. One study showed the impact of talking about disclaimer labels . . .: Paraskeva N, Lewis-Smith H & Diedrichs PC (2017). 'Consumer opinion on social policy approaches to promoting positive body image: airbrushed media images and disclaimer labels'. *Journal of Health Psychology* 22: 164–175.

Chapter 11
199. Australian children are not moving enough . . .: Australian Institute of Health and Welfare. (2020, 20 October). 'Insufficient physical activity'. Web report. aihw.gov.au
199. A recent study showed . . .: The University of Western Australia's KIDDO program is outlined in Mitchell R. (2019, 18 June). 'Researchers find Gen Z Falling behind Gen X in childhood physical skills'. *The West Australian*. thewest.com.au
203. Danish toy manufacturer Lego . . .: Razik, N (2021, 12 October). 'Lego pledges to remove "gender bias" and "harmful stereotypes" from its toys'. SBS News. sbs.com.au
204. Dannielle Miller, a former teacher and founder . . .: Miller D (2020, 26 March) 'Tell me about a time when you were brave'. enlighteneducation.com

Chapter 12
214. Many studies show that the healthy pursuit of imagination . . .: A recent example is Walker S, Fleer M, Veresov N & Duhn I (2020). 'Enhancing executive function through imaginary play: A promising new practice principle'. *Australasian Journal of Early Childhood*. 45(2):114-126. doi:10.1177/1836939120918502
215. There is an abundance of research . . .: This article by Professor Tracy Gleason offers a good summary: Gleason T (2016, 6 April). 'Why make-believe play is an important part of childhood development'. *The Conversation*. theconversation.com
216. One of the most interesting things about the human brain in childhood . . .: Medina J (2014, 2nd Edition). *Brain Rules for Baby: How to Raise a Smart and Happy Child from Zero to Five*. Seattle: Pear Press.
216. Glen Capelli, a well-respected professional . . .: Capelli B & Brealey S (2000). 'The thinking learning classroom'. Perth, Western Australia: The True Learning Centre.
217. Pretend play or dramatic play, known technically as socio-dramatic play . . .: Victorian Department of Education and Training (n.d.). 'Sociodramatic play (emergent literacy)'. Literacy Teaching Toolkit. education.vic.gov.au
219. Recent research. See Tracy Gleason reference from p.215.

222. Sometimes known as 'the Batman effect' . . .: Wiseman R (2013). *Ringleaders and Sidekicks: How to help your son cope with classroom politics, bullying, girls and growing up*. London: Piatkus.

225. In a study called *Imaginary play* . . .: Xhika M, Shehu/Dono A (2018). 'Imaginary play, strengthening the gender identity and gender role of children 3–6 years old'. *European Journal of Education and Applied Psychology*. No. 1.

Chapter 14

241. . . . the most renowned study of which was in 2009 by the National Institute of Mental Health . . .: Guyer AE, McClure-Tone EB, Shiffrin ND, Pine DS & Nelson EE (2009). 'Probing the neural correlates of anticipated peer evaluation in adolescence'. *Child Dev*. 80(4):1000-1015. doi:10.1111/j.1467-8624.2009.01313.x

247. Child psychiatrist Dr Kaylene Henderson gave the following common-sense advice at a conference . . .: Calming Today's Anxious Kids conference (2019, 18 May) hosted by Maggie Dent. Melbourne Convention Centre.

248. To find some clarity on this topic, I reached out to Michelle Mitchell . . . Personal correspondence.

252. Dana Kerford . . .: undated blog article on her urstrong.com website called, 'Think of yourself as a "Friendship Coach"'.

252. Michelle Mitchell has a modified version . . .: undated blog article at michellemitchell. org called 'How nice kids handle meanness: The art of pushing back with truth'.

255. In an episode of her podcast *Conversations with Lisa* . . .: Conversations with Lisa EP67: 'Lessons from my story – codependence' (2021, 17 August).

Chapter 15

277. Now, for some sobering statistics AND According to the National Center For Juvenile Justice . . .: Martin, H (n.d.) 'Child abuse: How education Ccan overcome Australia's hidden epidemic'. Safe4kids.com.au

278. We must remember that more than 90 per cent of perpetrators . . .: Child Sex Offenders profile at bravehearts.org.au/what-we-do/research/child-sexual-abuse-facts-stats

278. . . . disturbing increase in the number of child-to-child molestation . . .: Kozaki D (2016, 9 February). 'Internet pornography causing long-term public health crisis amongst Australian children, seminar hears'. ABC News Online.

279. Queensland Police Service victim identification specialist . . .: Australian Federal Police (2021, 11 September). AFP warn about fast-growing online child abuse trend. Media Releases. afp.gov.au

Chapter 16

285. . . . 'theory of mind' . . .: Cherry, K (2021, 4 July). 'How the theory of mind helps us understand others'. *Very Well Mind*. verywellmind.com

299. Resilience research shows that having a sense of humour . . .: Menéndez-Aller Á, Postigo Á, Montes-Álvarez P, González-Primo FJ & García-Cueto, E (2020). 'Humor as a protective factor against anxiety and depression'. *International Journal of Clinical and Health Psychology*, 20(1), 38–45.

309. Just as the research says, the shame in my late teens . . .: Dearing R (2005, August). *Addictive Behaviors*; vol 30: pp 1392–1404. News release, University of Buffalo's Research Institute on Addictions.

Chapter 17

313. In Australia, roughly one in 20 individuals have ADHD . . .: healthdirect (2020) 'Attention deficit hyperactivity disorder'. healthdirect.gov.au

313. . . . and in other parts of the world it is one in 10 . . .: Haelle T (2015). CDC: '1 in 10 Children Diagnosed with ADHD'. WebMD. webmd.com

314. In an episode of my podcast . . .: ABC (2021, 17 August). 'Parenting children with ADHD'. *Parental As Anything with Maggie Dent* podcast.
319. My friend and colleague Allison Davies . . .: allisondavies.com.au
320. I chatted to Allison for an episode of my podcast . . .: ABC (2021, 3 August). 'Parenting autistic kids'. *Parental As Anything with Maggie Dent* podcast.
321. In an episode of Grey Matter . . .: Queensland Brain Institute (2017, 17 May). 'Autism and genetics'. *Grey Matter* podcast. The University of Queensland.

Chapter 18

326. According to the Australian Early Development Census . . .: Australian Government Initiative (2018). Australian Early Development Census National Report 2018. *A Snapshot of Early Childhood Development in Australia.*
330. In an interview for my podcast with the ABC . . .: ABC (2021, 20 January). 'Tips for starting school'. *Parental As Anything with Maggie Dent* podcast.
335. Feeling brave enough to manage being away . . .: Raising Children Network (updated 2022, 28 February). 'Separation anxiety in babies and children'. raisingchildren.net.au. Australian Government Department of Social Services.
336. Student educational outcomes are influenced positively if parental involvement . . .: Erdem C & Kaya M (2020). 'A meta-analysis of the effect of parental involvement on students' academic achievement'. *Journal of Learning for Development*, 7(3), 367–383.

Chapter 19

338. However, given that more than 90 per cent . . .: Australian Bureau of Statistics 2016.
347. . . . the importance of rough-and-tumble play . . .: Freeman E (2019, 5 September). 'Kids learn valuable life skills through rough-and-tumble play with their dads'. The Conversation. theconversation.com
351. There is also plenty of research on the importance of female friendships . . . and Dr Tracy Evans-Whipp . . .: Williams S (2021, 20 February). 'For many women, the pain of the pandemic led to stronger friendships'. *The Sydney Morning Herald*. smh.com.au

Reference list

Adani S & Cepanec M (2019). 'Sex differences in early communication development: Behavioral and neurobiological indicators of more vulnerable communication system development in boys'. *Croatian Medical Journal*, 60(2), pp. 141–149. DOI.org/10.3325/cmj.2019.60.141.

Aitken L (2021). *Let's Talk About Emotions*. Melbourne: Hinkler Books.

Aron E (2012). *The Highly Sensitive Child: Helping Our Children Thrive When the World Overwhelms Them*. London: Harper Collins Publishing.

Aron E (2022). *The Highly Sensitive Person*. 'Is this you?' https://hsperson.com/

Australian Federal Police (2021, 11 September). 'AFP warn about fast growing online child abuse trend'. https://www.afp.gov.au/news-media/media-releases/afp-warn-about-fast-growing-online-child-abuse-trend

Australian Government Initiative (2018). Australian Early Development Census National Report 2018. *A Snapshot of Early Childhood Development in Australia.*

Australian Institute of Health and Welfare. (2020). *Insufficient Physical Activity*. https://www.aihw.gov.au/reports/risk-factors/insufficient-physical-activity

Axness M (2012). *Parenting for Peace: Raising the Next Generation of Peacemakers*. Boulder, CO: Sentient Publications.

Barrett LF (2018). *How Emotions Are Made: The Secret Life of the Brain*. London: Pan Macmillan.

Benard B (1991). *Fostering Resiliency in Kids: Protective factors in the family, school and community*. Portland, USA: North West Education Library.

Biddulph S (2017). *10 Things Girls Need Most To Grow Up Strong and Free*. Sydney: HarperCollins Australia.

Biddulph S (2018). *Raising Boys in the 21st Century*. Sydney: Simon & Schuster Australia.

Biddulph S (2019). *Raising Girls in the 21st Century*. Sydney: Simon & Schuster Australia.

Bisdee A (2020). *Some Days*. Perth, AU: Little House of Books.

Blythe SG (2008). *What Babies and Children Really Need*. Stroud: Hawthorne Press.

Borba M (2021). *Thrivers: The Surprising Reasons Why Some Kids Struggle and Others Shine*. New York: Bantam Press.

Boyce WT (2019). *Orchids and Dandelions: Why Some Children Struggle and How All Can Thrive*. London: Pan Macmillan.

Boyce WT (2019, 2 January). 'Why some children are orchids and others are dandelions'. *Psychology Today*. https://www.psychologytoday.com/au/articles/201901/why-some-children-are-orchids-and-others-are-dandelions

Branden N (2013). *Our Urgent Need for Self Esteem*. https://nathanielbranden.com/our-urgent-need-for-selfesteem/

Brizendine, L (2006). *The Female Brain*. New York: Bantam Press.

Brooks K (2008). *Consuming Innocence: Popular Culture and our Children*. Brisbane: University of Queensland Press.

Brown B (2013). *The Gifts of Imperfect Parenting: Raising Children with Courage, Compassion and Connection*. Audio CD. Boulder, CO: Sounds True.

Brown S (2010). *Play: How it Shapes the Brain, Opens the Imagination, and Invigorates the Soul*. Melbourne: Scribe Publishing.

Bryson T (2019, 20 January). 'Understanding the importance of play with the developing mind'. https://www.tinabryson.com/publications-articles/mattelcom-understanding-the-importance-of-play-with-the-developing-mind

Cachia R (2021). *Parenting Freedom: Transform Stress and Depletion to Connectedness & Meaning*. Austin, TX: Lioncrest Publishing.

Cain J (2005). *The Way I feel*. Seattle, WA: Parenting Press.

Caldwell HK (2017, October). 'Oxytocin and Vasopressin: Powerful regulators of social behavior'. *Neuroscientist*, 23(5), pp. 517–528. DOI: 10.1177/1073858417708284.

Caparrotta M (2020, 2 November). 'Being nice vs kind – what's the difference? (8 Experts Explain)'. *Human Window*. https://humanwindow.com/nice-vs-kind/

Chapman G & Campbell R (2016, 2nd Edition). *The 5 Love Languages of Children: The Secret to Loving Children Effectively*. Chicago: Moody Publishers.

Cherry K (2021, 28 July). 'Gardner's Theory of Multiple Intelligences'. *Very Well Mind*. https://www.verywellmind.com/gardners-theory-of-multiple-intelligences-2795161

Choleris E, Galea L, Sohrabji F & Frick K (2018). 'Sex Differences in the brain: Implications for behavioral and biomedical research'. *Neuroscience & Biobehavioral Reviews*, 85, pp. 126–145. DOI.org/10.1016/j.neubiorev.2017.07.005.

Clews G (2015). *Wired to Play: The metacognitive athelete*. Canberra, ACT: Wired to Play Consulting.

Collins A (2020). *The Music Advantage: How Learning Music Helps Your Child's Brain and Well-Being*. Sydney: Allen & Unwin.

Commissioner for Children and Young People WA (2021). 'Exploring the decline in wellbeing for Australian girls'. Commissioner for Children and Young People WA. https://www.ccyp.wa.gov.au/media/4678/exploring-the-decline-in-wellbralian-girls-report-web-file.pdf

Damour L (2019). *Under Pressure: Confronting the Epidemic of Stress and Anxiety in Girls*. London: Atlantic Books.

Dana D (2018). *The Polyvagal Theory in Therapy: Engaging the Rhythm of Regulation*. New York: Norton Agency Titles.

Davidson H & Orange C (2017). *Friends, Fitting in & All That Stuff*. 'What To Do About Series'. Perth, AU: Best Programs 4 Kids.

Delahooke M (2020). *Beyond Behaviours: Using Brain Science and Compassion to Understand and Solve Children's Behavioural Challenges*. London: Hodder & Stoughton.

Delahooke M (2022). *Brain-Body Parenting: How to Stop Managing Behavior and Start Raising Joyful, Resilient Kids*. New York: Harper Wave.

Dent M (2014). *9 Things: A Back-to-Basics Guide to Calm, Common-Sense, Connected Parenting Birth–8*. Gerringong, AU: Pennington Publications.

Dent M (2016). *Building Children's Resilience: One Building Block at a Time*. Murwillumbah, AU: Pennington Publications.

Dent M (2020). *From Boys to Men: Guiding our Teen Boys to Grow into Happy, Healthy Men*. Sydney, Pan Macmillan Australia.

Dent M (2018). *Mothering Our Boys: A Guide for Mums of Sons*. Gerringong, AU: Pennington Publications.

Dent M (2005). *Nurturing Kids' Hearts and Souls: Building Emotional Social and Spiritual Competency*. Murwillumbah, AU: Pennington Publications.

Dent M (2021). *Parental As Anything: A common-sense guide to raising happy, healthy kids – from toddlers to tweens*. Sydney: ABC Books/HarperCollins*Publishers*

Dent M (2016, Rev Edition). *Real Kids in an Unreal World: How to Build Resilience and Self-Esteem in Today's Children*. Murwillumbah, AU: Pennington Publications.

Dent M (2003). *Saving Our Children from Our Chaotic World: Teaching Children the Magic of Silence and Stillness*. Murwillumbah, AU: Pennington Publications.

Doidge N (2007). *The Brain that Changes Itself: Stories of Personal Triumph from the Frontiers of Brain Science*. New York: Viking Press.

Dossey L (1995). *Healing Words*. New York: HarperOne.

Duckworth A (2017). *Grit: Why Passion and Resilience are the Secrets to Success*. London: Ebury Publishing.

Dunbar R (2022). *Friends: Understanding the Power of Our Most Important Relationships*. London: Little Brown Book Group.

Dweck, CS (2012). *Mindset: The new psychology of success – How you can fulfil your potential*, London: Robinson.

Dye LK (2016, 1 November). 'Dear strangers, please stop telling me my active daughter might get hurt'. *The Washington Post*.

Edwards K and Scanlon C (2021). *Raising Girls Who Like Themselves: In a World That Tells Them They're Flawed*. Sydney: Penguin Life Australia.

Einstein A (1931). *Living Philosophies*. New York: Simon and Schuster. https://sciphilos.info/docs_pages/docs_Einstein_fulltext_css.html

Eliot L, Ahmed A, Khan H & Patel J (2021). 'Dump the "dimorphism": Comprehensive synthesis of human brain studies reveals few male-female differences beyond size'. *Neuroscience & Biobehavioral Reviews*, 125: 667. DOI: 10.1016/j.neubiorev.2021.02.026.

Enlighten Education (2019, 5 June). 'Our girls are being killed with kindness'. https://www.enlighteneducation.com/our-girls-are-being-killed-with-kindness/

Fidalgo A, Tenenbaum H & Aznar A (2017, 11 December). 'Are there gender differences in emotion comprehension? Analysis of the test of emotion comprehension'. *J Child Fam Stud*. 27(4):1065–1074. doi: 10.1007/s10826-017-0956-5.

Galea L, Frick K, Hampson E, Sohrabji F & Choleris E (2017). 'Why estrogens matter for behavior and brain health'. *Neuroscience and biobehavioral reviews*, 76(Pt B), pp. 363–379. DOI.org/10.1016/j.neubiorev.2016.03.024.

Gardner H (1993). *Frames of Mind: The Theory of Multiple Intelligences*. London: Harper Collins Publishing.

Garey J (n.d.) 'Raising girls with healthy self-esteem'. Child Mind Institute. childmind.org

Gill T (2007). *No Fear: Growing Up in a Risk Averse Society*. Lisbon: Calouste Gulbenkian Foundation.

Gleason T (2016, 6 April). 'Why make-believe play is an important part of childhood development'. *The Conversation*. https://theconversation.com/why-make-believe-play-is-an-important-part-of-childhood-development-49693

Goleman D (2021, 25th Anniversary edition). *Emotional Intelligence: Why it can Matter More than IQ*. London: Bloomsbury.

Goleman D (2006). *Social Intelligence: The New Science of Human Relationships*. London: Cornerstone Publishing.

Goodwin K (2016). *Raising Your Child in a Digital World*. Sydney: Finch Publishing.

Gray P (2013). *Free to Learn: Why unleashing the instinct to play will make our children happier, more self-reliant, and better students for life*. New York: Basic Books.

Gray P (2013, September). 'The play deficit'. *Aeon*. Retrieved 3 October 2013. www.aeonmagazine.com/being-human/children-today-are-suffering-a-severe-deficit-of-play

Greenfield S (2011). *ID – The Quest for Meaning in the 21st Century*. London: Hodder & Stoughton.

Gregory L (2020, 6 October). 'Taming the after-school meltdown: "Show up with your heart first and the rest will follow"'. *Global News Canada*. globalnews.ca

Grille R (2008). *Heart to Heart Parenting*. Asheville: Vox Cordis Press.

Gurian M (2017). *Saving our Sons: A New Path to Raising Healthy and Resilient Boys*. Spokane, WA: Gurian Institute Press.

Han S (2021, 20 May). 'You can only maintain so many close friendships'. *The Atlantic Daily*.

Hart T (2003). *The Secret Spiritual World of Children*. California: New World Library.

Hart B & Risley TR (1995). *Meaningful Differences in the Everyday Experience of Young American Children*. Baltimore, MD: Paul H. Brookes Publishing Company.

Harter S & Chao C (1992). 'The role of competence in children's creation of imaginary friends'. *Merrill-Palmer Quarterly*, 38(3), 350–363.

Healing Foundation (2022). National Aboriginal and Torres Strait Islander Organisation. https://healingfoundation.org.au/heal-together/

Heywood L (2011, 7 April). 'Mean girls'. *Catalyst* television program. ABC Broadcasting. https://www.abc.net.au/catalyst/mean-girls/11012748

Hough L (Winter 2019). 'Girlhood', *Harvard Ed Magazine*. gse.harvard.edu

Howes C & Wishard A (2004). 'Revisiting shared meaning: Looking through the lens of culture and linking shared pretend play through proto-narrative development to emergent literacy'. In *Children's play: The Roots of reading*, ed. Zigler E, Singer D and Bishop-Josef S, pp. 143–158.

Hurley K (2018). *No More Mean Girls: The Secret to Raising Strong, Confident and Compassionate Girls*. New York: Tarcher Putnam.

Jacobson R (n.d.). 'Why girls apologize too much'. Child Mind Institute. childmind.org

Jensen E (2008). *Enriching the Brain: How to Maximize Every Learner's Potential*. Hoboken, NJ: Jossey-Bass.

Joseph J (2006). *Learning in the Emotional Rooms*. Sydney: Focus Education Australia.

Kachel S, Steffens MC & Niedlich C (2016). 'Traditional masculinity and femininity: Validation of a new scale assessing gender roles'. *Front. Psychol.* 7:956. DOI: 10.3389/fpsyg.2016.00956.

Kay K & Shipman C (2021, 12 September). 'Girls' confidence plummets starting at age 8: Here's how to keep her confidence strong'. A Mighty Girl website: https://www.amightygirl.com/blog

Kendall Dye L (2016, 1 November). 'Dear strangers, please stop telling me my active daughter might get hurt'. *The Washington Post*. washingtonpost.com

Kennedy (2013, 7 January). 'Orchids and dandelions: How some children are more susceptible to environmental influences for better or worse and the implications for child development'. *Clinical Child Psychology and Psychiatry*, 18. DOI: 10.1177/1359104513490338.

Kessler R (2000). *The Soul of Education: Helping Students Find Connection, Compassion and Character at School*. Philadelphia, PA: ASCD Publishing.

King JJ (2010). *Raising the Best Possible Child: How to Parent Happy and Successful Kids from Birth to Seven*. Sydney: Harper Collins Australia.

King M (2018). *Fathers and Daughters: Helping teen girls and their dads build unbreakable bonds*. Sydney: Hachette Australia

King M (2021). *Ten-Ager: What Your Daughter Needs You to Know About the Transition from Child to Teen*. London: Headline Publishing.

Kohn A (2006). *Unconditional Parenting: Moving from Rewards and Punishments to Love and Reason*. New York: Atria Books.

Koutsoukis D (2005). *366 Fun Quotes and Observations of Life*. Shelley, WA: Funstar Publishing.

Laney MO (2005). *The Hidden Gifts of the Introverted Child*. New York: Workman Publishing Company.

Lapointe V (2016). *Discipline Without Damage: How to Get Kids to Behave Without Messing Them Up*. Vancouver: Life Tree Media.

Lapointe V (2019). *Parenting Right from the Start: Laying a Healthy Foundation in the Baby and Toddler Years*. Vancouver: Life Tree Media.

Lee R (2021, 15 July). 'I'm teaching my daughter to take up space in the world'. SBS Voices. sbs.com.au

Leo P (2014, 16 January). *Healing the Feeling Child*. YouTube. https://www.youtube.com/watch?v=Pi2dEqoPjMU

Leo P (2020, 13 June). *Teaching Children Respect*. https://connectionparenting.com/articles/f/teaching-children-respect

Lieberman M PhD. & Eisenberger N PhD. (2008). 'The pains and pleasures of social life: A social cognitive neuroscience approach'. *Neuroleadership Journal*.

Lind J, Ghirlanda S & Enquist M (2019). 'Social learning through associative processes: A computational theory'. *R Soc Open Sci*, 6(3). DOI:10.1098/rsos.181777.

Little Wise One (2022). Education of the Heart Guidance and Affirmation Cards. https://littlewiseone.com.au/

Loprinzi P & Frith E (2018). 'The role of sex in memory function: Considerations and recommendations in the context of exercise'. *Journal of Clinical Medicine*, 7(6), p. 132. DOI.org/10.3390/jcm7060132.

Louv R (2010). *Last Child in the Woods: Saving our Children from Nature-Deficit Disorder*. London: Atlantic Books.

Mackay H (2020). *The Inner Self: The Joy of Discovering Who We Really Are*. Sydney: Pan Macmillan Australia.

Marano HE (2008). *A Nation of Wimps: The High Cost of Invasive Parenting*. New York: Crown Archetype.

Maté G (2021). *The Wisdom of Trauma Film*. Science & Nonduality. Maurizio and Benazzo. https://thewisdomoftrauma.com/

Medina J (2014, 2nd Edition). *Brain Rules for Baby: How to Raise a Smart and Happy Child from Zero to Five*. Seattle: Pear Press.

Mergler A (2020, 3 June). *Where We Have Come from And Where We Are Going*. http://girlsuniformagenda.org/2020/06/30/where-we-have-come-from-and-where-we-are-going/

Miller L (2015). *The Spiritual Child: The New Science on Parenting for Health and Lifelong Thriving*. Pan Macmillan.

Milne AA (1926). *Winnie-the-Pooh*. E. P Dutton & Company.

Murdoch Children's Research Institute (2021). The Childhood to Adolescence Transition Study (CATS). https://cats.mcri.edu.au/

Neufeld G & Maté G (2006). *Hold on to Your Kids: Why Parents Need to Matter More Than Peers*. New York: Ballantine Books.

Niv I (2015, 20 November). 'Are girls sexualised at dance class?' *ChildMag*. https://www.childmags.com.au/are-girls-sexualised-at-dance-class/

O'Donoghue J (1998). *Anam Cara: Spiritual Wisdom from the Celtic World*. New York: Harper Collins Publishing.

Ólafsdóttir MP (2018, 23 February). 'Margrét Pála Ólafsdóttir: Getting girls out of the "Pink Haze"'. *Euronews*.

Osteopathy for All (2022). *Trauma Release Exercises*. https://osteopathyforall.co.uk/toolkits/mindbody-toolkit/trauma-release-exercises/

Paraskeva N, Lewis-Smith H & Diedrichs P (2015). 'Consumer opinion on social policy approaches to promoting positive body image: Airbrushed media images and disclaimer labels'. *Journal of Health Psychology*. Vol 22.

Pascale R & Primavera L (2019). 'Male and female brains: Are they wired differently?' *Psychology Today*. https://www.psychologytoday.com/au/

Paul C (2016). 'To raise brave girls, encourage adventure'. *TedTalks*. https://www.ted.com/talks/

Perry B (2021). *What Happened to You: Conversations on Trauma, Resilience and Healing*. New York: Flatiron Books: An Oprah Book.

Persson J, Herlitz A, Engman, J, Morell A, Sjölie D, Wikström J & Söderlund H (2013). 'Remembering our origin: Gender differences in spatial memory are reflected in gender differences in hippocampal lateralization'. *Behavioural Brain Research*. 256, pp. 219–228. DOI.org/10.1016/j.bbr.2013.07.050.

Preuschoff G (2006). *Raising Girls: Why Girls Are Different—and How to Help Them Grow up Happy and Strong*. Toronto: Celestial Arts Publishing.

Provenzano R (2003). *A Little Book of Aloha: Spirit of Healing*. Hawaii: Mutual Publishing.

Queensland Brain Institute (2017, 17 May). *Podcast: Autism and Genetics*. https://qbi.uq.edu.au/news/podcasts/podcast-autism-and-genetics

Razik N (2021, 12 October). 'Lego pledges to remove "gender bias" and "harmful stereotypes" from its toys'. *SBS News*. https://www.sbs.com.au/news/article/lego-pledges-to-remove-gender-bias-and-harmful-stereotypes-from-its-toys/jvxbsow2p

Reber D (2020). *Differently Wired: A Parent's Guide to Raising an Atypical Child with Confidence and Hope*. New York: Workman publishing.

Reist MT (2016, 6 July). 'Early sexualisation and pornography exposure: the detrimental impacts on children'. *Australian Childhood Foundation*. https://professionals.childhood.org.au/prosody/2016/07/melinda-tankard-reist/

Reist MT (2013, 4 February). 'Stop selling-out our daughter's potential: Steve Biddulph on Raising Girls'. *Collective Shout*. https://www.collectiveshout.org/stop_selling_out_our_daughter_s_potential_steve_biddulph_on_raising_girls

Rippon G, Eliot L, Genon S, Joel D (2021). 'How hype and hyperbole distort the neuroscience of sex differences'. *PLoS Biol*, 19(5). DOI.org/10.1371/journal.pbio.3001253.

Robinson B (2008). *Daughters and their Dads: Tips for fathers, women, husbands and father-figures*. WA: Bruce Robinson.

Rodgers R, Damiano S, Wertheim E, and Paxton S (2017). 'Media exposure in very young girls: Prospective and cross-sectional relationships with BMIs, self-esteem and body size stereotypes'. *Developmental Psychology*, 53(12), 2356–2363. https://doi.org/10.1037/dev0000407

Rohrer J, Egloff B and Schmukle S (2015, 19 October). 'Examining the effects of birth order on personality'. *PNAS Articles*, 112 (46). DOI.org/10.1073/pnas.1506451112.

Ruiz DM (2011). *The Four Agreements: Practical Guide to Personal Freedom*. San Rafael, CA: Amber Allen Publishing.

Sanders J (2017). *How Big Are Your Worries Little Bear?* Macclesfield, VIC: Educate2Empower Publishing.

Sanders J (2021). *Little BIG Chats*. Macclesfield, VIC: Educate2Empower Publishing.

Sax L (2010). *Girls on the Edge: The Four Factors Driving the New Crisis for Girls – Sexual Identity, the Cyberbubble, Obsessions, Environmental Toxins.* New York: Basic Books.

Schaefer V (2021). *Little Wise Ones*. littlewiseone.com.au

Schore A (2017). 'All our sons: The developmental neurobiology and neuroendocrinology of boys at risk'. *Infant Mental Health Journal*, 38(1), pp.15–52.

Seligman M (2011). *The Optimistic Child: A Revolutionary Approach to Raising Resilient Children*. North Sydney, NSW: Random House Australia.

Seymour S (2011). *Sometimes I Feel... How to Help your Child Manage Difficult Feelings*. Sydney: Finch Publishing.

Shadyac N (2010). '*I Am*' Documentary. United States. https://mubi.com/films/i-am-2010

Shanker S & Barker T (2016). *Self-reg: How to Help Your Child (and you) Break the Stress Cycle and Successfully Engage with Life*. Toronto: Penguin Random House.

Shumaker H (2016). *It's OK to Go Up the Slide: Renegade Rules for Raising Confident and Creative Kids*. New York: TarcherPerigree.

Siegel D (2012). *Mindsight: Change Your Brain and Your Life*. Melbourne: Scribe Publications.

Siegel D & Bryson TP (2011). *The Whole-Brain Child: 12 Revolutionary Strategies to Nurture Your Child's Developing Mind*. New York: Bantam Press.

Siegel D & Hartzell M (2013). *Parenting from the Inside Out; How a Deeper Self-Understanding Can Help You Raise Children Who Thrive*. New York: TarcherPerigree.

Sigler E (2005). 'ADHD looks different in women. Here's how – and why'. *ADDitude Magazine*. https://www.additudemag.com/add-in-women/

Simmons R (2018, 8 March). 'How to teach your 3-year-old daughter she is "enough"'. *Romper*. https://www.romper.com/p/how-to-raise-a-confident-daughter-in-a-toxic-culture-8425163

Simmons R (2011). *Odd Girl Out: The Hidden Culture of Aggression in Girls*. Boston: Houghton & Mifflin Publishing.

Slater A & Tiggemann M (2016). 'Little girls in a grown up world: Exposure to sexualized media, internalization of sexualization messages, and body image in 6–9 year-old girls'. *Body Image* Vol 18, pp.19–22. DOI.org/10.1016/j.bodyim.2016.04.004.

Stace S (2018). *My Feelings Matter*. Burleigh Heads, QLD: TeePee Learning.

Stafford RM (2022). 'How I changed from a toxic mom-manager to an encouraging soul builder'. https://www.positiveparentingsolutions.com/parenting/changed-toxic-mom-manager-encouraging-soul-builder

Stiffelman S (2012). *Parenting Without Power Struggles*. New York: Simon & Schuster.

Street H (2015, 21 June). Mythbusting Education. *The Positive Times.* https://
positivetimes.com.au/mythbusting-education-by-dr-helen-street/

Stroud G (2018). *Teacher: One Woman's Struggle to Keep the Heart in Teaching.*
Sydney: Allen & Unwin.

Sunderland M (2016 2nd Edition). *The Science of Parenting.* London: DK
Publishing.

Taylor M (2001). *Imaginary Companions and the Children Who Create Them.*
Oxford: Oxford University Press.

Tichnor R & Smith J (1997). *A Spark in the Dark.* Nevada City, CA: Dawn
Publications.

Tiller E, Fildes J, Hall S, Hicking V, Greenland N, Liyanarachchi D & Di Nicola K
(2020). *Youth Survey Report 2020,* Sydney, NSW: Mission Australia.

Trioli V (2022, 12 February). 'The reaction to Grace Tame leads to a question:
Why are so many of us uncomfortable with the face of an angry woman?'.
abc.net.au/news

University of South Australia (2018). 'Aussie kids – a hop, skip and jump away from
better health and fitness'. https://www.unisa.edu.au/Media-Centre/Releases/2018/
aussie-kids---a-hop-skip-and-jump-away-from-better-health-and-fitness/

Van der Kolk B (2015). *The Body Keeps the Score: Brain, Mind, and Body in the
Healing of Trauma.* London: Penguin Publishing Group.

Walker S, Fleer M, Veresov N & Duhn I (2020). 'Enhancing executive function
through imaginary play: A promising new practice principle'. *Australasian
Journal of Early Childhood,* 45(2), pp. 114–126. DOI.org/10.1177/
1836939120918502.

Walker S (2018). *School Ready: A Practical and Supportive Guide for Parents with
Sensitive Kids.* Surrey Hills, VIC: Michael Hanrahan Publishing.

Williams S (2021, 20 February). 'For many women, the pain of the pandemic led
to stronger friendships'. *Sydney Morning Herald.*

Williams Z (2021, 20 September). 'Psychiatrist Bessel van der Kolk on how to
recover from our deepest pain'. *The Guardian Newspaper.*

Wolynn M (2017) *How Inherited Family Trauma Shapes Who We Are and How
to End the Cycle.* USA: Penguin.

Worsely L (2015). *The Resilience Doughnut: The Secret of Strong Kids.* NSW:
The Resilience Doughnut.

Xhika M, Shehu A & Dono (2018). 'Imaginary play, strengthening the gender
identity and gender role of children 3–6 years old'. *European Journal of
Education and Applied Psychology.*

Young K (2017). *Hey Warrior: A Book for Kids About Anxiety.* Brisbane, QLD:
Hey Sigmund Publishing.

Zsembery A (2019). *Real Kids, Real Play: The Ultimate Play Guide 0–5.* Melbourne:
Jack & Lu's.

Index

Froebel, Friedrich 210
frustration *see* meltdowns

games 108, 200–201, 295–296
gaming 150, 296, 355
gardens 169, 208–209
Gardner, Howard 154, 156, 164
gender differences
    brain development 22, 36–43
    emotions 22, 40–41, 75
    expectations 264–265
    friendships 241, 351
    gender bias in toys 203
    inequality 367–368
    memory 53–55
    robustness 20–24
    traditional communities 43–44
    workforce 280–281
gender identity 20–21, 261–262 *see also* authentic identity
    development of 21–23, 38–39
    play and 224–230
Gerber, Magda 151
gifts 79, 154–171
Gill, Tim 205
goal setting 294
Goleman, Daniel 75, 206
gratitude 361
Gray, Peter 227
Greene, Ross 71
Greenfield, Susan 111
grit, the gift of 294–297 *see also* disappointment; resilience
grown-ups *see* adult allies
growth and development *see* brain development; child development
guilt 345–346
Gurian, Michael 41

habits 59–60
handheld devices *see* screens and technology
happiness 75, 193–194, 196, 211, 214, 216
Hart, Tobin 171, 354
Harter, Susan 220–221
hearing *see* listening
Heather Shumaker, 243–244
'hedging' 271–273
Henderson, Kaylene 247, 330

Higgins, Brittany 262
Hinshaw, Stephen 272
hitting *see* aggression
hormones 35, 42, 50, 176, 291
'hot' emotions 68, 90–99 *see also* meltdowns
humour 137–139, 273–274, 299–300
Hurley, Katie 242
hyperactivity *see* ADHD
hypervigilance 71, 127

identity *see* authentic identity; gender identity
images, fake 184–185
imaginary friends and protectors 219–222, 334
imagination 56, 213–230, 333–334
    see also creative visualisations; pretend play
imitation *see* modelling (imitation)
implicit memories 59
impulsiveness 41, 147, 149–150, 317
independence *see* autonomy
infants, first 1,000 days 9–27
inner locus of control 115
inner voices 274–275
instincts 38, 251
intelligence *see* multiple intelligences
intergenerational trauma 9, 70–71
    see also epigenetics
interoception 31–33, 127, 315
introverts 146–148, 239–240 *see also* shyness
intuitive feelings 364–365
iPads *see* screens and technology

Jacobson, Rae 272
jealousy 131
Jensen, Eric 56
jokes *see* humour
Joseph, John 198
joy and delight 193–194

Kaholokai, Linda 356
Kay, Katty 291
Keeble, Christina 314, 317
Kelly, Rebecca 50
Kerford, Dana 252
Kerr, Sam 307
Kessler, Rachael 360, 368

swimming 166, 181, 185, 207
symbolic play *see* pretend play

Tame, Grace 23, 262
tantrums *see* meltdowns
tapping, on acupressure points 67, 93–94, 97, 133
taste, gift of 162–163
Taylor, Marjorie 214
teachers 15, 17, 206, 327–328, 332, 335 *see also* learning; school
teasing 342–346
technology *see* digital world; screens and technology
teenagers 20, 345 *see also* puberty
television 185–186, 229, 233–234, 245, 344 *see also* screens and technology
temperament 101–121
'tend and befriend' behaviour 43–44, 245–246
tension *see* stress
testosterone 21–22, 42
'theory of mind' 112, 285
therapy 17–20, 67–69, 361–362 *see also* emotional release techniques
for mothers 5–8, 64–65
thoughtfulness 80–81 *see also* kindness
threats 107
Thunberg, Greta 263
time with parents *see* quality time
toddlers, first 1,000 days 9–27
touch 79
toughness 21, 23, 285 *see also* dandelion girls
toys 197–198, 202–203, 218, 226
trauma 21–22, 53, 65–72 *see also* adverse childhood experiences; bullying; epigenetics; family violence; mental health; sexual behaviour and abuse
trauma responses 65, 68, 71
triggers 2–5, 81–82, 88–89

unconditional love 25–26, 46, 109, 135, 188
understanding 91 *see also* emotional intelligence
uniforms 178–179
unmet needs 33, 89–90, 152

validation 93, 346
van der Kolk, Bessel 66
violence *see* aggression; family violence
visualisation *see* creative visualisations
voice *see* communication
vulnerability 21

Wallis, Nathan 152
warning systems 278, 303–304 *see also* anxiety
wellbeing, girls' rating of 284–285
Whitehouse, Andrew 42
Wicker, Stephanie 44
Winfrey, Oprah 65
wishful thinking 251
Wolynn, Mark 70
workforce, male norms in 280–281
working parents 15–16
worry *see* anxiety
Worsley, Lyn 286
worthlessness *see* self-esteem and self-worth; shame

Young, Karent 303
Yousafzai, Malala 263

Zsembery, Alice 198